Henry A. Virkler is
assistant professor of
psychology and direc-
tor of curriculum
plan...
...

HERMENEUTICS

HERMENEUTICS

Principles and Processes of Biblical Interpretation

Henry A. Virkler

BAKER BOOK HOUSE
GRAND RAPIDS, MICHIGAN 49506

Unless otherwise noted all Scripture quotations are from the *New International Version*, copyright 1978 by New International Bible Society, and used with permission of The Zondervan Corporation.

To Mary

*Whose interpretation of God's Word
through her life is a constant
source of encouragement to me*

Acknowledgments

I would like to thank Dr. Gordon Lewis and Randy Russell, whose encouragement when the text was in mimeographed form was instrumental in my decision to consider publication to a wider audience. I would also like to thank Grey Temple, Glenn Wagner, Max Lopez-Cepero, Buddy Westbrook and Doug McIntosh, each of whom have read the manuscript through in its entirety and made valuable criticisms. I would especially like to acknowledge Betty DeVries and Diane Zimmerman of Baker Book House and Pam Spearman for their fine editorial assistance.

I would also like to thank the following publishing houses for permission to quote from the following books:

InterVarsity Press: *Christ and the Bible,* by John W. Wenham, 1972. *Jesus and the Old Testament* by R. T. France, 1971.

Wm. B. Eerdmans Publishing Company: *The Epistle of Paul to the Galatians,* by Alan Cole, 1965.

Baker Book House: *Protestant Biblical Interpretation: Third Revised Edition,* by Bernard Ramm, 1970.

7

Cambridge University Press: *The Targums and Rabbinic Literature*, by J. Bowker, 1969.

Zondervan Publishing House: *Biblical Hermeneutics*, by Milton S. Terry, reprinted 1974.

Preface

In the study of any subject area there are four identifiable but overlapping developmental stages. The first stage involves the recognition of an area of existence that is important and relevant, yet unexplored. Initial exploration takes the form of naming what is there.

In the second stage attempts are made to articulate certain broad principles that characterize the area of investigation. One set of conceptual categories is offered, then others, as investigators try to develop conceptual systems that organize or explain the data cogently and coherently. For example, is it most valid to view Scripture from an orthodox, neo-orthodox, or liberal perspective?

During the third stage the focus shifts from elucidation of broad principles to the investigation of more specific principles. Investigators within various theoretical camps pursue the study of specific principles despite the fact that they may start with different presuppositions and may disagree about which set of broad principles yields the most accurate conceptual system.

In the fourth stage the principles discovered in stages two and three are translated into specific skills that can be easily taught and applied to the field being studied.

The majority of hermeneutics texts available today appear to have as their primary goal the elucidation of proper principles of biblical interpretation (stage three). It is in the fourth stage—the translation of hermeneutical theory into the practical steps needed to interpret a biblical passage—that I hope to make a contribution.

The goal of this text is to give the reader not only an understanding of the principles of proper biblical interpretation, but also the ability to apply those principles in sermon preparation or personal Bible study. Past experience in teaching hermeneutics has suggested to me that if students are given seven rules for interpreting parables, five for interpreting allegories, and eight for interpreting prophecy, they may be able to memorize these for a final examination but may not be able to retain them for longer periods. For this reason I have attempted to develop a common conceptual system that can be applied to all biblical literature with memorization restricted to specific differentiating characteristics. In order to give practice in applying hermeneutical principles, I have included exegetical exercises (called "brain teasers" and labeled *BTs*) drawn primarily from public sermons or counseling situations. The answers to the BTs should be written out, for they will be a better learning aid that way.

This textbook is intended for those who accept historical, orthodox presuppositions concerning the nature of revelation and inspiration. There are thoughtful Christians who study Scripture from other perspectives. These other views are presented briefly for comparison and contrast. Interested readers will find a brief bibliography of works in hermeneutics written from other perspectives in Appendix A.

We only see as far as we do because we build on the work of those who have gone before us. I acknowledge my debt to many careful scholars in the field—Terry, Trench, Ramm, Kaiser, Mickelsen, and Berkhof—to name just a few. The work of these men will be referred to repeatedly in the text, and there are undoubtedly instances when they should be cited and are not.

It is perhaps the height of audacity (or foolhardiness) to attempt to write a book outside one's major area of competence, which in my case is the integration of theology and psychology. This book was written because I could find no text written by a theologian who translated hermeneutical principles into practical exegetical steps.[1] It was originally intended for limited distribution in the Christian counselor-training program where I presently teach, and is offered to the broader field of theological students only after strong encouragement from a number of people. Various controversial issues in theology have been presented, with every intention of fairly and accurately presenting alternative evangelical positions. I would welcome correspondence, sent in care of the publisher, from my more theologically informed colleagues on areas where revision is needed.

Henry A. Virkler
Psychological Studies Institute
Atlanta, Georgia
August, 1980

---

1. A. B. Mickelsen's *Interpreting the Bible* (Grand Rapids: Eerdmans, 1963) is a notable exception to this statement. However, his translation from theory to practical exegesis is done only for certain literary forms.

Contents

1. Introduction to Biblical Hermeneutics   15
2. The History of Biblical Interpretation   47
3. Historical-Cultural and Contextual Analysis   75
4. Lexical-Syntactical Analysis   93
5. Theological Analysis 117
6. Special Literary Methods: *Similes, Metaphors, Proverbs, Parables, and Allegories* 157
7. Special Literary Methods: *Types, Prophecy, and Apocalyptic Literature* 183
8. Applying the Biblical Message: *A Proposal for the Transcultural Problem* 211

   Epilogue: *The Task of the Minister* 233

   Summary 239

   Appendixes:

   A. *A Sample Bibliography of Works Relating to Hermeneutics from Various Theological Viewpoints* 245
   B. *Readings on Revelation, Inspiration, and Inerrancy from a Variety of Theological Perspectives* 247
   C. *A Bibliography on* Sensus Plenior 249

   Bibliography 251

chapter one

Introduction to Biblical Hermeneutics

After completing this chapter, you should be able to:

1. Define the terms *hermeneutics, general hermeneutics,* and *special hermeneutics.*
2. Describe the various fields of biblical study (study of the canon, textual criticism, historical criticism, exegesis, biblical theology, systematic theology) and their relationship to hermeneutics.
3. Explain the theoretical and biblical basis for the need for hermeneutics.
4. Identify three basic views of the doctrine of inspiration and explain the implications of these views for hermeneutics.
5. Identify five of the controversial issues in contemporary hermeneutics and explain each issue in a few sentences.

Some Basic Definitions

The word *hermeneutics* is said to have had its origin in the name Hermes, the Greek god who served as messenger for the gods, transmitting and interpreting their communications to their fortunate, or often unfortunate, recipients.

In its technical meaning, hermeneutics is often defined as *the science and art of biblical interpretation.* Hermeneutics is considered a science because it has rules and these rules can be classified into an orderly system. It is considered an art because communication is flexible, and therefore a mechanical and rigid application of rules will sometimes distort the true meaning of a communication.[1] To be a good interpreter one must learn the rules of hermeneutics as well as the art of applying those rules.

Hermeneutical theory is sometimes divided into two subcategories—general and special hermeneutics. General hermeneutics is the study of those rules that govern interpretation of the entire biblical text. It includes the topics of historical-cultural, contextual, lexical-syntactical, and theological analyses. Special hermeneutics is the study of those rules that apply to specific genres, such as parables, allegories, types, and prophecy. General hermeneutics is the focus of chapters 3 through 5; chapters 6 and 7 are devoted to special hermeneutics.

Relation of Hermeneutics to Other Fields of Biblical Study

Hermeneutics is not isolated from other fields of biblical study. It is related to study of the canon, textual criticism, historical criticism, exegesis, and biblical and systematic theology.[2]

Among these various fields of biblical study, the area which conceptually precedes all others is the study of canonicity; that is, the differentiation between those books that bear the stamp of divine inspiration and those that do not. The historical process by which certain books came to be placed in the canon

1. Bernard Ramm, *Protestant Biblical Interpretation,* 3rd rev. ed. (Grand Rapids: Baker, 1970), p. 1.
2. Ibid., pp. 7-10.

and others excluded is a long but interesting one, and can be found elsewhere.[3] Essentially the process of canonization was a historical one in which the Holy Spirit guided the church to recognize that certain books bear the impress of divine authority.

The field of biblical study that conceptually follows the development of the canon is textual criticism, sometimes referred to as lower criticism. Textual criticism is the attempt to ascertain the original wording of a text. Textual criticism is needed because we have no original manuscripts, only many copies of the originals, and these copies have variations among them. By carefully comparing one manuscript with another, textual critics perform an invaluable service by providing us with a biblical text that closely approximates the original writings given to the Old and New Testament believers. One of the world's most renowned New Testament scholars, F. F. Bruce, has said in this regard, "The variant readings about which any doubt remains among textual critics of the New Testament affect no material question of historic fact or of Christian faith and practice."[4]

A third field of biblical study is known as historical or higher criticism. Scholars in this field study the authorship of a book, the date of its composition, the historical circumstances surrounding its composition, the authenticity of its contents, and its literary unity.[5]

Many of those who have engaged in higher criticism have begun with liberal presuppositions, and for this reason conservative Christians have often equated historical criticism with liberalism. This need not be the case. It is possible to engage

3. N. H. Ridderbos, "Canon of the Old Testament" and J. N. Birdsall, "Canon of the New Testament," in *The New Bible Dictionary*, ed. J. D. Douglas (Grand Rapids: Eerdmans, 1962), pp. 186-199; Clark Pinnock, *Biblical Revelation* (Chicago: Moody, 1971), pp. 104-106.

4. F. F. Bruce, *The New Testament Documents: Are They Reliable?* 5th rev. ed. (Chicago: Inter-Varsity, 1960), pp. 19-20.

5. Ramm, *Protestant Biblical Interpretation*, p. 9.

in historical criticism starting with conservative presuppositions. The introductions to each book of the Bible found in
the Harper Study Bible, in the Scofield Reference Bible, and
in conservative commentaries are examples. Knowledge of the
historical circumstances surrounding the composition of a book
is crucial to a proper understanding of its meaning. Chapter
3 is devoted to this topic.

Only after a study of canonicity, textual criticism, and historical criticism is the scholar ready to do exegesis. Exegesis
is the application of the principles of hermeneutics to arrive
at a correct understanding of the text. The prefix *ex* ("out
of," or "from") refers to the idea that the interpreter is attempting to derive his understanding *from* the text, rather
than reading his meaning *into* the text (eisegesis).

Following exegesis are the twin fields of biblical theology
and systematic theology. Biblical theology is the study of divine
revelation as it was given throughout the Old and New Testament. It asks the question, "How did this specific revelation
add to the knowledge that believers already possessed at that
time?" It attempts to show the development of theological
knowledge throughout the Old and New Testament era.

In contrast to biblical theology, systematic theology organizes the biblical data in a logical rather than historical manner. It attempts to place together all the information on a
given topic (e.g., the nature of God, the nature of the afterlife,
the ministry of angels) so that we may understand the totality
of God's revelation to us on that topic. Biblical and systematic
theology are complementary fields: together they give us
greater understanding than either one would alone.

The diagram below summarizes the previous discussion and
shows the crucial and central role that hermeneutics plays in
the development of a proper theology.

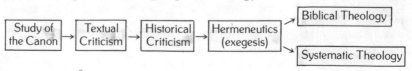

The Need for Hermeneutics

Our understanding of what we hear or read is usually spontaneous. . . the rules by which we interpret meaning occur automatically and unconsciously. When something blocks that spontaneous understanding of the meaning, we become more aware of the processes we use to understand (for example, when translating from one language to another). Hermeneutics is essentially a codification of the processes we normally use at an unconscious level to understand the meaning of a communication. The more blocks to spontaneous understanding, the greater the need for hermeneutics.

When we interpret Scripture, there are several blocks to a spontaneous understanding of the original meaning of the message.[6] There is an historical gap caused by the fact that we are widely separated in time from the original writers and readers. Jonah's antipathy for the Ninevites, for example, takes on added meaning when we understand the extreme cruelty and sinfulness of the people of Nineveh.

Secondly, a cultural gap exists, resulting from the fact that there are significant differences between the culture of the ancient Hebrews and our contemporary one. Harold Garfinkel, the controversial UCLA sociologist and founder of ethnomethodology, suggests that it is impossible for an observer to be objective and dispassionate when studying a phenomenon (which in our case would be the study of Scripture). Each of us sees reality through eyes conditioned by our culture and a variety of other experiences. To use a favorite analogy of Garfinkel, it is impossible to study people or phenomena as if we were looking at fish in a goldfish bowl from a detached position outside the bowl: each of us is inside a bowl ourselves.

Applied to hermeneutics, the analogy suggests that we are goldfish in one bowl (our own time and culture) looking at goldfish in another bowl (biblical times and culture). Failure

6. Ibid., pp. 4-7.

to recognize either that cultural environment or our own, or
the differences between the two, can result in serious misunderstanding of the meaning of biblical words and actions.[7]
More will be said about this in chapters 3 and 8.

A third block to spontaneous understanding of the biblical
message is the linguistic gap. The Bible was written in Hebrew,
Aramaic, and Greek—three languages that have very different structures and idioms from our own. Consider the distortion in meaning that would result, for example, if one were
to translate the phrases "I love to see Old Glory paint the
breeze" into another language without recognizing the presence of the idioms "Old Glory" and "paint the breeze." The
same can happen in translating from other languages if the
reader is not aware that phrases such as "God hardened Pharaoh's heart" may contain Hebrew idioms that make the original meaning of this phrase something different from that
conveyed by the literal English translation.

A fourth significant block is the philosophical gap. Views
of life, of circumstances, of the nature of the universe differ
among various cultures. To transmit a message validly from
one culture to another, a translator or reader must be aware
of both the similarities and the contrasts in world views.

Hermeneutics is needed, then, because of the historical,
cultural, linguistic, and philosophical gaps that block a spontaneous, accurate understanding of God's Word.

Alternative Views of Inspiration

The view of inspiration that a biblical scholar holds has
direct implications for hermeneutics. In this section I am offering only a very simplified introduction to the three main

7. In Tim Tyler, "The Ethnomethodologist," *Human Behavior* (April, 1974):
pp. 56-61.

views of inspiration. There are several excellent discussions of the topic available elsewhere.[8]

The typical liberal position on inspiration is that the biblical writers were inspired in somewhat the same sense as Shakespeare and other great writers. What they transcribed were primitive Hebrew religious conceptions about God and His workings. Much of the emphasis of this position is on developing theories of how redactors pieced the ancient manuscripts together from previous writings, and what these compilations reveal about the growing spiritual awareness of the compilers.

Within the neoorthodox school there is so much variation on the topic of inspiration that no generalization can accurately include all views. However, the majority believe that God revealed Himself only in mighty acts, not in words. The words of Scripture attributed to God are human understandings of the significance of God's actions. The Bible *becomes* the Word of God when individuals read it and the words acquire personal, existential significance for them. The emphasis of this view is on the process of demythologizing, i.e., removing the mythological event that has been used to convey the existential truth, so that the reader may have a personal encounter with that truth.

The orthodox view of inspiration is that God worked through the personalities of the biblical writers in such a way that, without suspending their personal styles of expression or freedom, what they produced was literally "God-breathed" (2 Tim. 3:16; Greek: *theopneustos*). The emphasis of the text is that Scripture itself, not the writers only, was inspired ("All Scripture is inspired by God," NASB). Had only the writers been inspired, it would be possible to argue that their writings were contaminated by the interaction of the message with

8. Carl F. H. Henry, *Revelation and the Bible* (Grand Rapids: Baker, 1958); J. I. Packer, *"Fundamentalism" and the Word of God* (London: InterVarsity, 1958); J. I. Packer, "Revelation," in *The New Bible Dictionary;* B. B. Warfield, *The Inspiration and Authority of the Bible* (Philadelphia: Presbyterian and Reformed, 1948).

their own primitive and idiosyncratic conceptions. The teaching of 2 Timothy 3:16, however, is that God guided the scriptural authors in such a way that their *writings* bear the impress of divine "in-spiration."

Based on such verses as 2 Timothy 3:16 and 2 Peter 1:21, the orthodox Christian view is that the Bible is an objective truth deposit. Unlike the neoorthodox position that conceives Scripture as becoming the Word of God when it acquires personal existential significance, the orthodox position is that Scripture is and always will remain a repository of truth, whether or not we read and appropriate it personally. For orthodox Christians, then, hermeneutical skills possess great importance because they give us a means for discovering more accurately the truths we believe Scripture possesses.

Controversial Issues in Contemporary Hermeneutics

Before moving on to look at the history and then principles of biblical hermeneutics, we should become acquainted with some of the pivotal yet controversial issues in hermeneutics. Just as the view of inspiration affects the reader's approach to exegesis, so these five issues affect hermeneutics.

Validity in Interpretation

Perhaps the most basic question in hermeneutics is, "Is it possible to say what constitutes *the* valid meaning of a text?" Or are there multiple valid meanings? If there are more than one, are some more valid than others? In that case, what criteria can be used to distinguish the more valid from less valid interpretations? To experience the important issues raised by these questions, consider the Naphtunkian's problem.

BT1: The Naphtunkian's Dilemma

Situation: You once wrote a letter to a close friend. Enroute to its destination the postal service lost your message, and it remained lost for the next two thousand years, amidst nuclear wars and other historical transitions. One day it is discovered and reclaimed. Three poets from the contemporary Naphtunkian society translate your letter separately, but unfortunately arrive at three different meanings. "What this means to me," says Tunky I, "is . . ." "I disagree," says Tunky II. "What this means to me is . . ." "You're both wrong," claims Tunky III. "My interpretation is the correct one."

Resolution: As a dispassionate observer viewing the controversy from your celestial (we hope) perspective, what advice would you like to give the Tunkies to resolve their differences? We will assume that you had been a fairly articulate writer.

   a. Is it possible that your letter actually has more than one valid meaning? If your answer is "Yes," go to (b). If "No," go to (c).

   b. If your letter can have a variety of meanings, is there any limit on the number of its valid meanings? If there is a limit, what criteria would you propose to differentiate between valid and invalid meanings?

   c. If there is only one valid meaning of your letter, what criteria will you use to discern whether Tunky I, II, or III has the best interpretation?

If you conclude that Tunky II's interpretation is superior, how would you justify this to Tunkies I and III?

If you haven't spent at least fifteen minutes trying to help the Tunkies resolve their problem, go back and see what you can do to help them. The problem they are wrestling with is probably the most crucial issue in all of hermeneutics.

E. D. Hirsch, in his volume *Validity in Interpretation*, discusses the philosophy that has been gaining acceptance since the 1920s—that "the meaning of a text is what it means to me." Whereas previously the prevailing belief had been that a text means what its author meant, T. S. Eliot and others contended that "the best poetry is impersonal, objective and autonomous;

that it leads an afterlife of its own, totally cut off from the life of its author."[9]

Such a belief, fostered by the relativism of our contemporary culture, soon influenced literary criticism in areas other than poetry. The study of "what a text says" became the study of "what it says to an individual critic."[10] Such a belief was not without its difficulties, as Hirsch cogently points out:

> When critics deliberately banished the original author, they themselves usurped his place [*as the determiner of meaning*], and this led unerringly to some of our present-day theoretical confusions. Where before there had been but one author [*one determiner of meaning*], there now arose a multiplicity of them, each carrying as much authority as the next. To banish the original author as the determiner of meaning was to reject the only compelling normative principle that could lend validity to an interpretation. . . . For if the meaning of a text is not the author's, then no interpretation can possibly correspond to *the* meaning of the text, since the text can have no determinate or determinable meaning.[11]

In the study of Scripture, the task of the exegete is to determine as closely as possible what *God* meant in a particular passage, rather than what it means to me. If we accept the view that the meaning of a text is what it means to me, then God's Word can have as many meanings as it does readers. We also have no reason for saying that an orthodox interpretation of a passage is more valid than a heretical one: indeed, the distinction between orthodox and heretical interpretations is no longer meaningful.

9. T. S. Eliot, "Tradition and the Individual Talent," *Selected Essays* (New York, 1932), cited in E. D. Hirsch, *Validity in Interpretation* (New Haven: Yale University, 1967), p. 1. The Hirsch volume is an excellent source for further discussion of this and other related topics.

10. Hirsch, *Validity in Interpretation*, p. 3.

11. Ibid., pp. 5-6.

At this juncture it may be helpful to distinguish between interpretation and application. To say that a text has one valid interpretation (the *author's* intended meaning) is not to say that his writing has only one possible application. For example, the command in Ephesians 4:27 ("Never go to bed angry—don't give the devil that sort of foothold," *Phillips*), has one meaning, but can have multiple applications depending on whether the reader is angry with his employer, his wife, or his child. Likewise the promise in Romans 8 that nothing can "separate us from the love of God" has one meaning, but will have different applications (in this case, emotional significances), depending on the particular life situation a person is facing.

The position scholars take on this issue of the validity of interpretation influences their exegesis. It is thus a crucial issue for the study of hermeneutics.

Double Authorship and *Sensus Plenior*

A second controversy in hermeneutics is the double author issue. The orthodox view of Scripture is one of confluent authorship; that is, the human and divine authors worked together (flowed together) to produce the inspired text. This issue raises these important questions: "What meaning did the human author intend?" "What meaning did the divine author intend?" "Did the intended meaning of the divine author exceed that of the human author?"

The question of whether or not Scripture does have a fuller sense (referred to as *sensus plenior*) than that intended by the human author has been debated for centuries. Donald A. Hagner discusses this issue in the following way:

> To be aware of *sensus plenior* is to realize that there is the possibility of more significance to an Old Testament passage than was consciously apparent to the original author, and more than can be gained by strict grammatico-

historical exegesis. Such is the nature of divine inspiration that the authors of Scripture were themselves often not conscious of the fullest significance and final application of what they wrote. This fuller sense of the Old Testament can be seen only in retrospect and in the light of the New Testament fulfillment.[12]

Several arguments are used to support a *sensus plenior* position, including these: (1) 1 Peter 1:10-12 seems to suggest that the Old Testament prophets did at times speak things they did not understand; (2) Daniel 12:8 seems to indicate that Daniel did not understand the meaning of all the prophetic visions that had been given to him; and (3) a number of prophecies seem unlikely to have had contemporaneous comprehension (e.g., Dan. 8:27, John 11:49-52).

Those who argue against a *sensus plenior* position make the following points: (1) Accepting the idea of double meanings in Scripture may open the way for all sorts of eisegetical interpretations; (2) the 1 Peter 1:10-12 passage can be understood to mean that the Old Testament prophets were ignorant only of the *time* of the fulfillment of their predictions but not of the *meaning* of their predictions; (3) in some instances prophets understood the meaning of their predictions but not the full implications of them (e.g., in John 11:50 Caiaphas *did* understand that it was better that one man die for the people than that the whole nation perish, but did not understand the full implications of his prophecy); and (4) in some instances the prophets may have understood the meaning of their prophecy but not its historical referent.

The *sensus plenior* controversy is one of those issues not likely to be settled before we enter eternity. The interpretation of prophecy will be discussed more fully in chapter 7. Perhaps a guiding canon that can be agreed on by the majority of

12. Donald A. Hagner, "The Old Testament in the New Testament," in *Interpreting The Word of God,* ed. Samuel J. Schultz and Morris Inch (Chicago: Moody, 1976), p. 92.

those on both sides of the issue at this time is this: any passage that seems to have a fuller meaning than is likely to have been comprehended by the human author should be so interpreted only when God has expressly declared the nature of His fuller meaning through later revelation.[13] A bibliography that introduces many of the important writings on this subject is found in Appendix C.

Literal, Figurative, and Symbolic Interpretations of Scripture

A third controversial issue in contemporary hermeneutics involves the literalness with which we interpret the words of Scripture. As Ramm points out, conservative Christians are sometimes accused of being "wooden-headed literalists" in their interpretations.[14] Their more theologically liberal brethren claim that incidents such as the fall, the flood, and the story of Jonah's submarine voyage should be understood as metaphors, symbols, and allegories rather than as actual historical events. Since all words are symbols representing ideas, say these liberals, we should not seek to apply these words in a strictly literal sense.

Conservative theologians agree that words can be used in literal, figurative, or symbolic senses. The following three sentences exemplify this:

1. *Literal:* A crown, sparkling with jewels, was placed on the king's head.
2. *Figurative:* (Angry father to son) "If you do that once more, I'll crown you!"
3. *Symbolic:* "A great and wondrous sign appeared in heaven: a woman clothed with the sun, with the moon under her feet and a crown of twelve stars on her head" (Rev. 12:1).

13. J. Barton Payne, *Encyclopedia of Biblical Prophecy* (New York: Harper & Row, 1973), p. 5.
14. Ramm, *Protestant Biblical Interpretation*, pp. 122, 146.

The difference between the three uses of the word *crown* is
not that one sense refers to actual historical events while the
others do not. Literal and figurative expressions usually do
refer to actual historical events, as little Johnny (sentence 2)
could testify when he did "that" once more. The relationship
between the ideas expressed by the words and reality is direct,
rather than symbolic. However, ideas conveyed in symbolic
language (e.g., allegorical and apocalyptic literature) also frequently have historical referents. Thus the woman in Revelation 12:1 may signify the nation of Israel, with the twelve
stars representing the twelve tribes, the moon the Old Testament revelation, and the sun the light of New Testament
revelation.[15]

Problems result when readers interpret statements in a mode
other than the one intended by the author. As much distortion
of the author's meaning results from interpreting a literal
statement figuratively as from interpreting a figurative statement literally. If Johnny believes he will receive a gold-plated
headpiece the next time he misbehaves, he has an unexpected
surprise awaiting him. And the onlookers at the king's coro-
nation (sentence 1) would be equally surprised to see the gem-
studded crown applied to his seat of learning.

If all words are in some sense symbols, how can we determine when they are to be understood literally, or figuratively,
or symbolically? The conservative theologian would reply that
the same criterion for determining the valid interpretation of
all other types of literature applies here, namely, that the words
are to be interpreted according to the author's intention. If
the author meant them to be interpreted literally, we err if we
interpret them symbolically. If the author meant them to be
interpreted symbolically, we err equally if we interpret them
literally. The principle is easier to state than to apply; however,

15. Leon Morris, *The Revelation of St. John* (Grand Rapids: Eerdmans, 1969),
p. 156.

as shown in later chapters, the context and syntax provide important clues to intent and thus to meaning.

Spiritual Factors in the Perceptual Process

A fourth controversial issue in contemporary hermeneutics has to do with whether or not spiritual factors affect ability to perceive accurately the truths contained in Scripture. One school of thought maintains that if two people are equally prepared intellectually to do hermeneutics (educated in the original languages, history, culture, etc.), they will be equally good interpreters.

A second school of thought holds that Scripture itself teaches that spiritual commitment, or lack of it, influences ability to perceive spiritual truth. Romans 1:18-22 describes the end result of a continuous suppression of the truth as a darkened understanding. First Corinthians 2:6-14 speaks of wisdom and gifts which are the potential possession of the believer, but which the unregenerate person does not possess. Ephesians 4:17-24 describes the blindness to spiritual realities of a person living in the old nature, and the new realities open to the believer. First John 2:11 declares that the man who harbors hatred experiences a blindness resulting from that hatred. Based on such passages as these, this view believes that spiritual blindness and darkened understanding hinder a person's ability to discern the truth regardless of one's knowledge and application of hermeneutical principles.

This issue is more important to hermeneutics than it might initially seem. On one hand if, as asserted earlier, the meaning of Scripture is to be found in a careful study of words and of the culture and history of its writers, then where do we look to find this added dimension of spiritual insight? If we rely on the spiritual intuitions of fellow believers for added insights we soon end in a hopeless babble of confusion because we no longer have any normative principles for comparing the validity of one intuition with another. On the other hand, the alternative idea that the meaning of Scripture can be found by mastering the prerequisite exegetical knowledge and skills without regard to spiritual condition seems to contradict the verses cited above.

A hypothesis that attempts to resolve this dilemma is based on a definition of the term *know*. According to Scripture, persons do not truly possess knowledge unless they are living in the light of that knowledge. True faith is not only knowledge about God (which even the demons possess) but knowledge acted on. The unbeliever can *know* (intellectually comprehend) many of the truths of Scripture using the same means of interpretation he would use with nonbiblical texts, but he cannot truly *know* (act on and appropriate) these truths as long as he remains in rebellion against God.

This hypothesis needs, however, a slight corrective. A common experience illustrates the point: We set our minds on a certain course of action, and then use selective attention to focus on those data that support our decision and minimize those data that would argue against it. The same principle can apply to sin in a person's life. Scripture teaches that yielding to sin causes an individual to become enslaved to it and blind to righteousness (John 8:34; Rom. 1:18-22; 6:15-19; 1 Tim. 6:9; 2 Peter 2:19). Thus the truth principles in Scripture, available through application of the same skills of textual interpretation used with nonbiblical texts, become less and less clear to one who continually rejects those truths. Thus unbelievers do not *know* the full meaning of scriptural teaching, not because that meaning is unavailable to them in the words of the text, but because they refuse to act on and appropriate spiritual truths for their own lives. Furthermore, the psychological results of such refusal make them less and less able (and willing) to comprehend these truths.

In conclusion, this moderate viewpoint suggests that the meaning of God's Word is contained in the words He authored, and that it is unnecessary to make recourse to spiritual intuitions not supported by an understanding of those words.

One of the ministries of the Holy Spirit is the work of illumination, of helping believers understand the full meaning of the words of Scripture. The concept of illumination need not extend beyond the Holy Spirit's work of explicating the full meaning of the text; indeed, if we once extend our definition of illumination beyond this point, we have no logically coherent rationale for discriminating the divinely intended meaning from the intuitions and additions of a thousand different interpreters.

The Question of Inerrancy

Of all the controversial issues with implications for hermeneutics, probably one of the most important being debated by evangelicals today is the issue of biblical inerrancy. This issue has divided evangelicals (those who stress the importance of personal salvation through Jesus Christ) into two groups, whom Donald Masters has called conservative and liberal evangelicals. *Conservative evangelicals* are those who believe that Scripture is totally without error; *liberal evangelicals* are those who believe that Scripture is without error whenever it speaks on matters of salvation and the Christian faith, but that it may possess errors in historical facts and other details.[16]

There are a number of reasons why the inerrancy issue is important for evangelicals. First, if the Bible errs when it speaks on matters not essential to salvation, then it may be in error whenever it speaks about the nature of man, interpersonal and family relationships, sexual lifestyles, the will and emotions, and a host of other issues related to Christian living. An errant Scripture may be only a reflection of ancient Hebrew philosophy and psychology, with little to offer us. Second, as church history has repeatedly shown,[17] groups who begin by

16. Donald C. Masters, *The Rise of Evangelicalism* (Toronto: Evangelical Publishers, 1961), p. 15.

17. Harold Lindsell, *Battle for the Bible* (Grand Rapids: Zondervan, 1976), pp. 141-160.

questioning the validity of small details of Scripture eventually question larger doctrines as well. Many observers of contemporary American seminaries have seen this pattern repeated: acceptance of an errant Scripture in peripheral matters has soon been followed by the allegation that Scripture is errant in more central teachings.

The issue of inerrancy is also important in the field of hermeneutics. If we begin with the presupposition that Scripture does contain errors, and then find an apparent discrepancy between two or more texts, we may decide that one or both of them contains errors. If we begin with the presupposition that Scripture does not contain errors, we are motivated to find an exegetically justifiable way of resolving any seeming discrepancy. The different results of these presuppositional bases becomes most apparent in that part of hermeneutics called "theological analysis" (see chapter 5), which consists essentially of comparing a given text with all other texts on the same subject. Our approach to theological analysis will differ according to whether we assume that the teaching of the various texts, properly interpreted, represents a unity of thought, or that the texts may represent a diversity of thought occasioned by the inclusion of errors. Because this issue has such importance for hermeneutics, the final section of this chapter will look at the arguments in the inerrancy debate.

Jesus and the Bible

If Jesus Christ is, as we believe, the Son of God, then His attitude toward Scripture will provide the best answer to the question of inerrancy. A full discussion can be found in John W. Wenham's *Christ and the Bible*. Several points are here summarized.

First, Jesus consistently treated the historical narratives of the Old Testament as straightforward records of fact. Wenham notes:

> We have references [by Christ] to: Abel (Lk. 11:51), Noah (Mt. 24:37-39; Lk. 17:26, 27), Abraham (Jn. 8:56),

the institution of circumcision (Jn. 7:22; cf. Gn. 17:10-12; Lv. 12:3), Sodom and Gomorrah (Mt. 10:15; 11:23, 24; Lk. 10:12), Lot (Lk. 17:28-32), Isaac and Jacob (Mt. 8:11; Lk. 13:28), the manna (Jn. 6:31, 49, 58), the wilderness serpent (Jn. 3:14), David eating the shewbread (Mt. 12:3, 4; Mk. 2:25, 26; Lk. 6:3, 4) and as a psalm-writer (Mt. 22:43; Mk. 12:36; Lk. 20:42), Solomon (Mt. 6:29; 12:42; Lk. 11:31; 12:27), Elijah (Lk. 4:25, 26), Elisha (Lk. 4:27), Jonah (Mt. 12:39-41; Lk. 11:29, 30, 32), Zechariah (Lk. 11:51). This last passage brings out his sense of the unity of history and his grasp of its wide sweep. His eye surveys the whole course of history from "the foundation of the world" to "this generation." There are repeated references to Moses as the giver of the law (Mt. 8:4; 19:8; Mk. 1:44; 7:10; 10:5; 12:26; Lk. 5:14; 20:37; Jn. 5:46, 7:19); the sufferings of the prophets are also mentioned frequently (Mt. 5:12; 13:57; 21:34-36; 23:29-37; Mk. 6:4 [cf. Lk. 4:24; Jn. 4:44]; 12:2-5; Lk. 6:23; 11:47-51; 13:34; 20:10-12); and there is a reference to the popularity of the false prophets (Lk. 6:26). He sets the stamp of his approval on passages in Genesis 1 and 2 (Mt. 19:4, 5; Mk. 10:6-8).

Although these quotations are taken by our Lord more or less at random from different parts of the Old Testament and some periods of the history are covered more fully than others, it is evident that he was familiar with most of our Old Testament and that he treated it all equally as history.[18].

Second, Jesus often chose as the basis of His teaching those very stories that most modern critics find unacceptable (e.g., the Noahic flood—Matt. 24:37-39; Luke 17:26, 27; Sodom and Gomorrah—Matt. 10:15; 11:23, 24; the story of Jonah— Matt. 12:39-41; Luke 11:29-32).

18. John W. Wenham, *Christ and the Bible* (Downers Grove, Ill.: InterVarsity, 1972), pp. 12-13. Several of the ideas in the following pages are also borrowed or adapted from his book.

Third, Jesus consistently used the Old Testament Scriptures as the authoritative court of appeal in His controversies with the scribes and Pharisees. His complaint with them was not that they gave too much credence to Scripture, but that they had, by their rabbinic casuistry, managed to circumvent the clear and authoritative teachings to be found in it.

Fourth, Jesus taught that nothing could pass from the law until all had been fulfilled (Matt. 5:17-20) and that Scripture could not be broken (John 10:35).

Finally, Jesus used Scripture in His rebuttal to each of Satan's temptations. It is noteworthy that *both Jesus and Satan* accepted the scriptural statements as arguments against which there was no further argument (Matt. 4:4-11; Luke 4:4-13).

Jesus does not seem to have made any distinction between the validity and accuracy of revelatory versus nonrevelatory (historical, incidental) matters. His attitude, as recorded in the Gospels, seems to be an unquestioning acceptance. Lindsell points out that even liberal and neoorthodox scholars, who themselves deny biblical inerrancy, agree that Jesus viewed the Scriptures as infallible.[19] Kenneth Kantzer, former dean of Trinity Evangelical Divinity School and current editor of *Christianity Today,* discusses the testimony of these liberal scholars:

> H. J. Cadbury, Harvard professor and one of the more extreme New Testament critics of the last generation, once declared that he was far more sure as a mere historical fact that Jesus held to the common Jewish view of an infallible Bible than that Jesus believed in His own messiahship. Adolph Harnack, greatest church historian of modern times, insists that Christ was one with His apostles, the Jews, and the entire early Church, in complete commitment to the infallible authority of the Bible. John Knox, author of what is perhaps the most highly

19. Harold Lindsell, *The Battle for the Bible* (Grand Rapids: Zondervan, 1976) pp. 43-44.

regarded recent life of Christ states that there can be no
question that this view of the Bible was taught by our
Lord himself.

Rudolph Bultmann, a radical antisupernaturalist but
acknowledged by many to be the greatest New Testament
scholar of modern times, asserts that Jesus accepted the
common notion of His day regarding the infallibility of
Scripture.[20]

Bultmann wrote:

> Jesus agreed always with the scribes of his time in ac-
> cepting without question the authority of the [Old Tes-
> tament] Law. When he was asked by the rich man, "What
> must I do to inherit eternal life," he answered, "You know
> the commandments," and he repeated the well-known
> Old Testament Decalogue. . . . Jesus did not attack the
> Law but assumed its authority and interpreted it.[21]

The words of J. I. Packer summarize much of what has
been said and place it in perspective:

> The fact we have to face is that Jesus Christ, the Son of
> God incarnate, who claimed divine authority for all that
> He did and taught, both confirmed the absolute authority
> of the Old Testament for others and submitted to it un-
> reservedly Himself. . . . If we accept Christ's claims, there-
> fore, we commit ourselves to believe all that He taught—
> on His authority. If we refuse to believe some part of
> what He taught, we are in effect denying Him to be the
> divine Messiah—on our own authority.[22]

Objections and Answers

Even if the Gospel records portray Jesus as having unquestioning faith in the validity and authority of Scripture,

20. Kenneth Kantzer, *Christ and Scripture* (Deerfield, Ill.: Trinity Evangelical
Divinity School, n.d.), p. 2, cited in Lindsell, *Battle for the Bible,* p. 43.
21. Rudolph Bultmann, *Jesus and the Word* (New York: Scribners, 1934), pp. 61-62.
22. J. I. Packer, *"Fundamentalism" and the Word of God,* pp. 55-59.

there are a number of writers and theologians who maintain that Christians need no longer accept this stance. Literature on this subject usually cites about nine major objections offered by those who hold an errantist view of Scripture. These objections are discussed briefly below. Fuller discussions can be found in the references noted and in the suggested readings at the end of this chapter.

Objection one: It is possible that Jesus understood and used the Old Testament stories in a nonliteral fashion, meaning them to be understood as nonhistorical events used for illustrative purposes only.

Jesus certainly made use of stories to illustrate points as He spoke. However, in the majority of incidents He cites, the illustrations make more sense if understood as actual historical events. For example, in Matthew 12:41 Jesus is quoted as saying, "The men of Nineveh will arise at the judgment with this generation and condemn it; for they repented at the preaching of Jonah, and behold, something greater than Jonah is here." T. T. Perowne comments: "Is it possible to understand a reference like this on the non-historic theory of the book of Jonah? . . . [Are we] to suppose him [Christ] to say that imaginary persons who at the imaginary preaching of an imaginary prophet repented in imagination, shall rise up in that day and condemn the actual impenitence of those his actual hearers[?]"[23]

The argument that Jesus used in His dispute with the Sadducees concerning the resurrection (Mark 12:18-27), for example, would carry no strength unless both He and His opponents understood that Abraham, Isaac, and Jacob were literal, historical figures. Jesus' claim to deity, for which He was nearly stoned (John 8:56-59), contains an allusion to Abraham that could have meaning only if He and His opponents recognized Abraham as a historical figure. Wenham remarks that "as the matter is pursued the impression gains

23. T. T. Perowne, *Obadiah and Jonah* (Cambridge: University Press, 1894), p. 51.

in strength that our Lord understood the Bible stories in a natural way and that his teaching should be taken quite straightforwardly."[24]

Objection two: It is possible that Jesus knew there was error in Scripture, but accommodated His teaching to the prescientific views of His time.

Jesus was not hesitant to refute other aspects of the Jewish religious tradition that were in error. He clearly repudiated nationalistic misconceptions about the Messiah, even to the point of the cross. He was not slow to reject Pharisaic traditionalism. If the Scriptures are a combination of divine truth and human error, it is hardly like Him not to repudiate the human error.[25]

In addition, if Jesus knew that Scripture contained human error yet never made this fact known to His followers, misleading them rather by His insistently positive attitude toward it, He can hardly qualify as a great moral teacher and as the incarnate God of truth.

Objection three: As part of His self-emptying, it is possible that Jesus also emptied Himself of the knowledge that Scripture contains errors, and became a product of His conditioning.

Christ's *kenosis* is undoubtedly the most beautiful love story of all time and eternity. Scripture tells us that when Christ left heaven to become a man He gave up His riches and glory (2 Cor. 8:9; Phil 2:7), His immunity from temptation and trials (Heb. 4:15; 5:7, 8), His divine powers and prerogatives (Luke 2:40-52; John 17:4), and His perfect unbroken relationship with the Father when He took our sins on Himself (Matt. 27:46). However, although Christ did empty Himself of His glory, His riches, and many of His divine prerogatives, His own words make it clear that this self-limitation did not include a concession to error. Jesus claimed complete truth and authority for His teachings (Matt. 7:24-26; Mark 8:38),

24. Wenham, *Christ and the Bible*, p. 14.
25. Ibid., p. 21.

including His teachings on Scripture (Matt. 5:17-20; John 10:35). He said, "Heaven and earth will pass away, but my words will not pass away" (Matt. 24:35; Mark 13:31; Luke 21:33).

Objection four: The views expressed by Jesus, including His view of Scripture, really belong to the Gospel writers more than to Jesus Himself.

Clark Pinnock answers this important objection in a concise statement documented with several important and careful studies. (His footnotes are included within brackets in this quotation.)

A convenient way to dodge this evidence is to attempt to attribute to the *writers* of the Gospels the view of Scripture Jesus is represented as having held. T. F. Torrence in his review of Warfield's book on inspiration stated that biblical studies have advanced since his day, making an appeal to Jesus' actual views impossible [Torrence, *Scottish Journal of Theology*, VII (1954), p. 105]. This statement, accompanied by no exegetical or critical evidence of any kind, reflects a negative view of the historicity of the Gospels widely held today [J. W. Wenham gives ample reasons for not subjecting the Gospels to radical criticism (*Christ and the Bible*, 1972, pp. 38-42). It is more reasonable to suppose that Jesus created the community than that the community created Jesus.] In reply, let two points be made. The logical consequence of denying the authenticity of Jesus' doctrine of Scripture which pervades all our channels of information about him leads a person to total pessimism regarding any historical knowledge about Jesus of Nazareth, a view completely unacceptable on critical grounds [Jeremias is now prepared to say, on the basis of his investigations, that "in the synoptic tradition it is the inauthenticity, and not the authenticity, of the sayings of Jesus that must be demonstrated" (*New Testament Theology. The Proclamation of Jesus.* 1971, p. 37)]. And furthermore, it is far more likely that Jesus' understanding and use of the Scriptures conditioned the writers' understanding and use rather than the reverse. The originality with which the Old Testament is interpreted with respect to the person and work of Jesus is too coherent and impressive to be secondary. Certainly this question deserves a fuller treatment than can be attempted here. Nevertheless, there can be little doubt as to what the results of such a study would be [Cf. the impressive work of R. T. France, *Jesus and the Old Testament*, 1971].[26]

Jesus' teaching on the authority of Scripture so pervades His entire ministry that if we were to develop a critical theory that would successfully remove Jesus' teaching on Scripture from the Gospels, application of this theory to the Synoptics would leave us unable to make *any* historical statements about the person Jesus Christ.

Objection five: Since inerrancy is claimed only for the autographs (original manuscripts) and none of these are extant, inerrancy is a moot question.

The careful work of the Jewish scribes in transmitting the text and the present work of textual critics combine to give us a text that reflects with a very high degree of accuracy the wordings of the original.[27] The vast majority of variant readings concern grammatical details that do not significantly affect the meaning of the text. The words of F. F. Bruce are worth repeating in this regard: "The variant readings about which any doubt remains among textual critics of the New Testament affect no material question of historic fact or of Christian faith and practice."[28] The question of the authority and veracity of the biblical texts as we have them today should be decided on bases other than the fact that we do not possess the autographs.

26. Clark Pinnock, "The Inspiration of Scripture and the Authority of Jesus Christ," in *God's Inerrant Word,* ed. John Warwick Montgomery (Minneapolis: Bethany, 1974), p. 207.

27. R. K. Harrison, *Introduction to the Old Testament* (Grand Rapids: Eerdmans, 1969), p. 249.

28. Bruce, *The New Testament Documents,* pp. 19-20.

Objection six: Inerrancy should be claimed for the gospel but not for all of Scripture; that is, Scripture is infallible with regard to matters of faith and practice in spite of incidental errors of historical and other facts.

Daniel Fuller, dean of Fuller Theological Seminary, is one of the most noted contemporary proponents of this view. He believes that Scripture can be divided into two categories— the revelational (matters which make men wise unto salvation), and the nonrevelational (those matters of science, history, and culture that "facilitate the transmission of the revelational").[29] Fuller argues that the scriptural author's intent was to convey truth about spiritual matters (2 Tim. 3:15-16) and therefore we should not claim freedom from errors in those areas that were only incidental to the author's primary interest.

Although 2 Timothy 3:15 does teach that the primary purpose of Scripture is to teach men spiritual truth, this verse was certainly not intended to be used as a critical scalpel to divide between that which is inerrant and that which is not.[30] Verse 16 asserts that "All Scripture is God-breathed." No Old Testament prophet, nor Jesus Christ, nor any New Testament writer gives any support for the idea that the portions of Scripture having to do with space-time events contain errors. Had Scripture originated with man, then cultural conditioning and human error would certainly be a factor to be reckoned with; however, Scripture affirms that "prophecy never had its origin in the will of man, but men spoke from God as they were carried along by the Holy Spirit" (2 Peter 1:21). Adding to this the teaching of Numbers 23:19 ("God is not a man, that he should lie"), the conclusion seems inescapable that neither Christ nor Scripture makes a distinction between revelatory and nonrevelatory data. Francis Schaeffer argues that the

29. Daniel Fuller, "Benjamin B. Warfield's View of Faith and History," *Bulletin of the Evangelical Theological Society*, XI (1968), pp. 80-82.

30. Clark Pinnock, "Limited Inerrancy: A Critical Appraisal and Constructive Alternative," in *God's Inerrant Word*, p. 149.

medieval dichotomy between "upper and lower storey knowledge" is unbiblical.[31] John Warwick Montgomery's epistemological arguments on the unity of knowledge[32] are also appropriate to this issue for those who wish to study it from a philosophical perspective.

Objection seven: The important issue is to have a saving Christ, not to hold to an inerrant Scripture.

A number of people prefer not to become involved in doctrinal and theological issues. For them the important issue is a saving relationship with Jesus Christ, and they neither see nor wish to be concerned with the relationship between Christology and other issues. Harold Lindsell points out the close relationship between Christology and inerrancy: "If Jesus taught biblical inerrancy, either He knew inerrancy to be true, or He knew it to be false but catered to the ignorance of his hearers, or He was limited and held to something that was not true but He did not know it."[33]

Accepting either of the last two alternatives leads to a strange Christology. If Jesus knew inerrancy was false but taught otherwise, He was guilty of deception and could not have been a sinless being; therefore, He was unable to provide a sinless atonement for our sins. If Jesus' understanding of truth was limited to the point that He was teaching untruth, then we have no assurance that His teaching on other matters such as salvation is also not untrue. The only alternative that leaves us with our Christology intact is that Jesus knew the Scripture to be inerrant and that His knowledge was correct.[34]

Objection eight: Some biblical passages seem to contradict each other or to be contradicted by modern science.

Probably every believer has been confronted with texts that seem difficult to reconcile either with other texts or with sci-

---

31. Francis Schaeffer, *Escape from Reason* (Downers Grove: InterVarsity, 1968).
32. John Warwick Montgomery, "Biblical Inerrancy: What Is at Stake?" in *God's Inerrant Word,* pp. 23-28.
33. Lindsell, *Battle for the Bible* p. 45.
34. Ibid.

entific discoveries. Those who hold to an errant Scripture are fond of searching out such texts and holding them up to prove their position. As our knowledge of proper principles of interpretation, of archeology, and of ancient languages and cultures has grown, however, one after another of these seeming discrepancies has been resolved. One of the experiences that can most build one's faith in the accuracy of Scripture is to read several examples of how difficult texts have, with the aid of continuing scientific investigation, been shown to be correct.

Several helpful books in this regard are:

J. W. Haley. *Alleged Discrepancies of the Bible.*

K. A. Kitchen. *Ancient Orient and the Old Testament.*

Harold Lindsell. *The Battle for the Bible.* (Chapter 9 explores the resolution of several difficult scriptural passages.)

Bernard Ramm. *Protestant Biblical Interpretation,* 3rd rev. ed. (Chapter 8: "The Problem of Inerrancy and Secular Science in Relation to Hermeneutics.")

Raymond Surburg. *How Dependable Is the Bible?*

Edwin Thiele. *The Mysterious Numbers of the Hebrew Kings.* (This book discusses the ancient Hebrew manner of dating kingship reigns, reconciling the chronologies of 2 Samuel, 1 and 2 Kings and 1 and 2 Chronicles, a feat once considered impossible by those who hold an errant Scripture position.)

Objection nine: Inerrancy is proved by a circular argument. Inerrantists start with the assumption that Scripture is infallible, proceed to show (based on its own testimony) that both Jesus and the writers considered it to be infallible, and then conclude that it is infallible.

Although some have used an argument very similar to the above objection to support their belief in infallibility, R. C. Sproul has suggested that a more rigorous logical rationale for belief in scriptural infallibility can be made. An adaptation of Sproul's reasoning is given below:

Premise A: The Bible is a basically reliable and trustworthy document [cf. C. K. Barrett, *Luke the Historian in Recent Study;* James Martin, *The Reliability of the Gospels;* F. F. Bruce, *The New Testament Documents: Are They Reliable?*]

Premise B: On the basis of this reliable document we have sufficient evidence to believe confidently that (1) Jesus Christ claimed to be the Son of God (John 1:14, 29, 36, 41, 49; 4:42; 20:28) and (2) that He provided adequate proof to substantiate that claim (John 2:1-11; 4:46-54; 5:1-18; 6:5-13, 16-21; 9:1-7; 11:1-45; 20:30-31).

Premise C: Jesus Christ, being the Son of God, is a completely trustworthy (i.e., infallible) authority.

Premise D: Jesus Christ teaches that the Bible is the very Word of God.

Premise E: The Word of God is completely trustworthy because God is completely trustworthy.

Conclusion: On the basis of the authority of Jesus Christ, the church believes the Bible to be utterly trustworthy.[35]

A Conclusion to the Matter

When we affirm that God's Word is without error, we should understand this statement in the same way that we would the statement that a particular report or analysis is accurate and without error. It is important to distinguish levels of intended precision. For example, most of us would agree with the statement that the population of the United States is 220 million, even though this figure may actually be incorrect by several million people. However, both the speaker and the hearer recognize that this figure is intended to be an approximation, and that when understood within its intended level of precision it is a true statement.

35. R. C. Sproul, "The Case for Infallibility: A Methodological Analysis," in *God's Inerrant Word,* pp. 242-261. An alternative way of avoiding circular reasoning is to start with the hypothesis of the truth of the Bible as revelation from God, and test this hypothesis in terms of the coherence criterion of truth: its internal consistency and fitting of all the facts, including the historicity of the Bible, the person of Jesus, His works, His teachings, His claims, His resurrection, personal conversion experiences of believers, etc. For development of this approach see Gordon Lewis, *Testing Christianity's Truth Claims* (Chicago: Moody, 1976) chapters 7-11.

The same principle must be applied when understanding the affirmations of Scripture: they should be understood within the parameters of precision intended by their authors. Specific principles for interpretation include these:

1. Numbers are often given approximately, a frequent practice in popular communication.
2. Speeches and quotations may be paraphrased rather than reproduced verbatim, a usual practice when summarizing someone else's words.
3. The world may be described in phenomenological terms (how events appear to human viewers).
4. Speeches made by men or Satan are recorded or paraphrased accurately without implying that what these persons affirmed was correct.
5. Sources were sometimes used by a writer to make a point without implying divine affirmation of everything else which that source said.

These qualifications are so universal that we apply them to all natural communication usually without even being aware that we are doing so. A statement is considered accurate when it meets the level of precision intended by the writer and expected by his audience. A technical scientific article may be much more detailed and precise than an article written for the general public, yet both are accurate when understood within the context of their intended purpose. Thus, the affirmation that God is accurate and truthful in all that He says in Scripture should be understood within the context of the level of precision which He intended to communicate.

The hermeneutical principles discussed in the following chapters are relevant whether one takes a conservative evangelical or liberal evangelical view of Scripture. The process of determining the author's intended meaning is similar for both groups. Differences, when they emerge, are likely to concern the *validity* of the author's teaching, rather than the *content* of his teaching. For example, conservative and liberal evangelicals may have a high level of agreement regarding what Paul intended to teach; where they disagree may be over the validity of what he taught. Thus, while my position on inerrancy is a conservative evangelical one, the hermeneutical principles found in the following chapters are also relevant for those who adopt a liberal evangelical view of Scripture.

Chapter Summary

Hermeneutics is the science and art of biblical interpretation. General hermeneutics is the study of those rules that govern interpretation of the entire biblical text. Special hermeneutics is the study of those rules which govern the interpretation of specific literary forms, such as parables, types, and prophecy.

Hermeneutics (applied exegesis) plays an integral role in the process of theological study. The study of canonicity attempts to determine which books bear the stamp of divine inspiration and which do not. Textual criticism attempts to ascertain the original wording of a text. Historical criticism studies the contemporaneous circumstances surrounding the composition of a particular book.

Exegesis is an application of the principles of hermeneutics to understand the author's intended meaning. Biblical theology organizes those meanings in a historical manner while systematic theology arranges those meanings in a logical fashion.

Hermeneutics is essentially a codification of those processes we normally use at an unconscious level to understand the intended meaning of another person. It is only when something blocks our spontaneous understanding of another person's message that we recognize the need for some method of understanding what they intended. Blocks to spontaneous understanding of another person's communication arise when there are differences in history, culture, language, or philosophy between ourselves and the speaker.

There are several issues that affect how one will "do" hermeneutics. We must decide whether Scripture represents the religious theorizing of the ancient Hebrews, divinely-guided but not infallible writings of men, or divinely-guided and infallible writings written by men but initiated and superintended by God.

We must also decide whether there is a single valid meaning of a text, or whether any individual application of a text represents a valid meaning. As you have probably experienced in BT 1, once we leave the premise that the meaning of a text is the author's intended meaning, we have no normatively-compelling criterion for determining that an orthodox interpretation of a passage is more valid than any number of heretical ones.

Other issues that affect how we will do hermeneutics include: (1) whether or not we believe that God's intended meaning includes a fuller sense than the human author's, (2) how to determine when a passage is to be interpreted literally, when figuratively, and when symbolically, and (3) how one's spiritual commitment affects one's ability to understand spiritual truth.

Some of the ways Jewish and Christian believers have answered these questions throughout history are discussed in the following chapter.

A bibliography including books cited in this volume and others relating to hermeneutics from a variety of theological viewpoints may be found in Appendix A. Those interested in further study on the topic of revelation, inspiration, and inerrancy will find a number of resources in Appendix B. Those interested in further reading on the *sensus plenior* issue will find material in Appendix C.

chapter **two**

The History of Biblical Interpretation

After completing this chapter, you should be able to identify the most important exegetical presuppositions and principles found in each of the following periods of biblical interpretation.

1. Ancient Jewish Exegesis
2. New Testament Use of the Old Testament
3. Patristic Exegesis
4. Medieval Exegesis
5. Reformation Exegesis
6. Post-Reformation Exegesis
7. Modern Hermeneutics

Why a Historical Overview?

Throughout the centuries since God revealed the Scriptures, there have been a number of approaches to the study of God's Word. More orthodox interpreters have emphasized the importance of a literal interpretation, by which they meant interpreting God's Word the way one interprets normal human communication. Others have practiced an allegorical approach, and still others have looked at individual letters and words as having secret significance which needed to be deciphered.

A historical overview of these practices will enable us to overcome the temptation to believe that our system of interpretation is the *only* system that has ever existed. An understanding of the presuppositions of other methods provides a more balanced perspective and a capacity for more meaningful dialogue with those who believe differently.

By observing the mistakes of those who have preceded us, we can be more aware of possible dangers when we are similarly tempted. Santayana's adage that "he who doesn't learn from history is bound to repeat it" is as applicable to the field of interpretation as it is to any other field.

Furthermore, as we study the history of interpretation we will see that many great Christians (e.g., Origen, Augustine, Luther) understood and prescribed better hermeneutical principles than they practiced. We may thus be reminded that knowing a principle needs also to be accompanied by applying it to our own study of the Word.

This historical survey makes use of material found in classic works on hermeneutics, to which the reader is referred for more extensive coverage. Bernard Ramm's *Protestant Biblical Interpretation* (3rd rev. ed.) has an excellent chapter on history. Other sources are listed at the end of this chapter.

Ancient Jewish Exegesis

A discussion of the history of biblical interpretation usually begins with the work of Ezra. On their return from the Babylonian exile, the people of Israel requested that Ezra read to them from the Pentateuch. Nehemiah 8:8 recalls: "They [Ezra and the Levites] read from the Book of the Law of God, making it clear and giving the meaning so that the people could understand what was being read."

Since the Israelites had probably lost their understanding of Hebrew during the exilic period, most biblical scholars assume that Ezra and his helpers translated the Hebrew text and read it aloud in Aramaic, adding explanations to make the meaning clear. Thus began the science and art of biblical interpretation.[1]

The scribes that followed took great care in copying the Scriptures, believing every letter of the text to be the inspired Word of God. This profound reverence for the scriptural text had both its advantages and disadvantages. A chief advantage was that the texts were carefully preserved in their transmission across the centuries. A major disadvantage was that the rabbis soon began interpreting Scripture by methods other than the ways in which communication is normally interpreted. The rabbis presupposed that since God is the author of Scripture, (1) the interpreter could expect numerous meanings in a given text, and (2) every incidental detail of the text possessed significance. Rabbie Akiba, in the first century A.D., eventually extended this to maintain that every repetition, figure of speech, parallelism, synonym, word, letter, and even the shapes of letters had hidden meanings.[2] This letterism (undue focus on the *letters* from which the words of Scripture were composed) was often carried to such an extent that the author's intended meaning was overlooked and fantastic speculation introduced in its place.

At the time of Christ, Jewish exegesis could be classified into four main types: literal, midrashic, pesher, and allegorical.[3] The *literal method* of interpretation, referred to as *peshat*,

---

1. Adherents of redaction criticism suggest that the interpretation of Scripture began considerably before Ezra.

2. Milton S. Terry, *Biblical Hermeneutics* (reprint ed., Grand Rapids: Zondervan, 1974), p. 609.

3. Richard Longenecker, *Biblical Exegesis in the Apostolic Period* (Grand Rapids: Eerdmans, 1975), pp. 28-50.

apparently served as the basis for other types of interpretations. Richard Longenecker, citing Lowy, suggests that the reason for the relative infrequency of literalistic interpretations in Talmudic literature is "that this type of commentary was expected to be known by everyone; and since there were no disputations about it, it was not recorded."[4]

Midrashic interpretation included a variety of hermeneutical devices which had developed considerably by the time of Christ and which continued to develop for several centuries thereafter.

Rabbi Hillel, whose life antedates the rise of Christianity by a generation or so, is credited with developing the basic rules of rabbinic exegesis that emphasized the comparison of ideas, words, or phrases found in more than one text, the relationship of general principles to particular instances, and the importance of context in interpretation.[5]

The trend toward more fanciful rather than conservative exposition continued, however. The result of this was an exegesis that (1) gave meaning to texts, phrases, and words without regard to the context in which they were meant to apply; (2) combined texts that contained similar words or phrases whether or not such texts were referring to the same idea; and (3) took incidental aspects of grammar and gave them interpretive significance.[6] Two examples of such exegesis are given below:

> By the superfluous use of three [Hebrew] particles, the
> Scriptures indicate . . . that something more is included
> in the text than the apparent declaration would seem to
> imply. This rule is illustrated by Genesis 21:1, where it is
> said "Jehovah visited Sarah," and the particle is supposed

4. Ibid., p. 29.
5. For a fuller discussion of Rabbi Hillel's rules, see J. Bowker, *Targums and Rabbinic Literature* (Cambridge: University Press, 1969), p. 315; and Longenecker, *Biblical Exegesis in the Apostolic Period,* pp. 34-35.
6. Longenecker, *Biblical Exegesis in the Apostolic Period,* p. 35.

to show that the Lord also visited other women besides Sarah.

. . . .

Explanations are obtained by reducing the letters of a word to their numerical value, and substituting for it another word or phrase of the same value, or by transposing the letters. Thus, for example, the sum of the letters in the name of Eliezer, Abraham's servant, is equivalent to 318, the number of his trained men (Gen. 14:14), and, accordingly, shows that Eliezer alone was worth a host of servants.[7]

Thus by focusing on the identification of hidden meanings from incidental grammatical details and contrived numerical speculations, midrashic exegesis often lost sight of the actual meaning of the text.

Pesher Interpretation existed particularly among the Qumran communities. This form borrowed extensively from midrashic practices, but included a significant eschatological focus. The community believed that everything the ancient prophets wrote had a veiled prophetic meaning which was to be imminently fulfilled through their covenant community.[8] Apocalyptic interpretation (see chapter 7) was common, together with the idea that through the Teacher of Righteousness, God had revealed the meaning of the prophecies that had formerly been shrouded in mystery. Pesher interpretation was often denoted by the phrase "this is that," indicating that "*this* present phenomenon is a fulfillment of *that* ancient prophecy."

Allegorical exegesis was based on the idea that beneath the literal meaning of Scripture lay the true meaning.[9] Histori-

7. Adapted from Terry, *Biblical Hermeneutics*, p. 608. Hebrew words have been omitted.

8. W. H. Brownlee, "Biblical Interpretation among the Sectaries of the Dead Sea Scrolls," *The Biblical Archeologist* 14 (1951): 60-62, in Longenecker, *Biblical Exegesis in the Apostolic Period*, p. 39.

9. Bernard Ramm, *Protestant Biblical Interpretation*, 3rd rev. ed. (Grand Rapids: Baker, 1970), p. 24.

cally, allegorism had been developed by the Greeks to resolve the tension between their religious myth tradition and their philosophical heritage.[10] Because the religious myths contained much that was immoral or otherwise unacceptable, the Greek philosophers allegorized these stories; i.e., the myths were not to be understood literally, but as stories whose real truth lay at a deeper level. At the time of Christ, Jews who wished to remain faithful to the Mosaic tradition yet adopt Greek philosophy, were faced with a similar tension. Some Jews resolved this by allegorizing the Mosaic tradition. Philo (c. 20 B.C.–A.D. c. 50) is well known in this regard.

Philo believed that the literal meaning of Scripture represented an immature level of understanding; the allegorical meaning was for the mature. The allegorical interpretation should be used in the following cases: (1) if the literal meaning says something unworthy of God, (2) if the statement seems to be contradictory to some other statement in Scripture, (3) if the record claims to be an allegory, (4) if expressions are doubled or superfluous words are used, (5) if there is a repetition of something already known, (6) if an expression is varied, (7) if synonyms are employed, (8) if a play on words is possible, (9) if there is anything abnormal in number or tense, or (10) if symbols are present.[11]

As can be seen, criteria (3) and (10) are valid indications that the author intended his writing to be understood allegorically. However, the allegorizing of Philo and his contemporaries went far beyond this, often reaching fantastic proportions. Ramm cites this example: "Abraham's trek to Palestine is *really* the story of a Stoic philosopher who leaves Chaldea (sensual understanding) and stops at Haran, which means 'holes,' and signifies the emptiness of knowing things by the

10. Ibid., p. 26.
11. Ibid., pp. 27-28; F. W. Farrar, *History of Interpretation*, pp. 149-151, in A. Berkeley Mickelsen, *Interpreting the Bible* (Grand Rapids: Eerdmans, 1963), p. 29.

holes, that is the senses. When he becomes Abraham he becomes a truly enlightened philosopher. To marry Sarah is to
marry abstract wisdom."[12]

To sum up, during the first century A.D. Jewish interpreters
agreed that Scripture represents the words of God, and that
these words are full of meaning for believers. Literal interpretation was employed in the areas of judicial and practical
concerns. Most interpreters employed midrashic practices,
particularly the rules developed by Hillel, and most used allegorical exegesis mildly. Within the Jewish community, however, some groups went in separate directions. The Pharisees
continued to develop midrashic exegesis in order to tie their
oral tradition more closely to Scripture. The Qumran community, believing themselves to be the faithful remnant and
recipients of the prophetic mysteries, continued to use midrashic and pesher methods to interpret Scripture. And Philo
and those who desired to reconcile Jewish Scripture with Greek
philosophy continued to develop allegorical exegetical
methods.[13]

New Testament Use of the Old Testament

Approximately ten percent of the New Testament is direct
quotations, paraphrases, or allusions to the Old Testament. Of
the thirty-nine books of the Old Testament, only nine are not
expressly referred to in the New Testament.[14] Consequently,
there is a significant body of literature illustrating the interpretive methods of Jesus and the New Testament writers.

12. Ramm, *Protestant Biblical Interpretation,* p. 28.
13. Longenecker, *Biblical Exegesis in the Apostolic Period,* pp. 48-50.
14. Roger Nicole, "Old Testament Quotations in the New Testament," in *Hermeneutics,* ed. Bernard Ramm (Grand Rapids: Baker, 1971), pp. 41-42.

Jesus' Use of the Old Testament

Several general conclusions can be drawn from an examination of Jesus' use of the Old Testament. First, as noted in
chapter 1, He consistently treated the historical narratives as
straightforward records of fact.[15] The allusions to Abel, Noah,
Abraham, Isaac, Jacob, and David, for example, all seem to be
intended and were understood as references to actual people
and historical events.

Second, when Jesus made an application of the historical
record, He drew it from the normal, as opposed to the allegorical, meaning of the text. He showed no tendency to divide
scriptural truth into levels—a superficial level based on the
literal meaning of the text and a deeper truth based on some
derived mystical level.

Third, Jesus denounced the way the religious leaders had
developed casuistic methods that set aside the very Word of
God they claimed to be interpreting, and replaced it with their
own traditions (Mark 7:6-13; Matt. 15:1-9).

Fourth, the Scribes and Pharisees, much as they would have
liked to accuse Christ of wrongdoing, never accused Him of
using any Scripture unnaturally or illegitimately. Even when
Jesus was directly repudiating the Pharisaic accretions and
misinterpretations of the Old Testament (Matt. 5:21-48), the
scriptural record tells us that "the crowds were amazed at his
teaching, because he taught as one who had authority, and
not as their teachers of the law" (Matt. 7:28-29).

Fifth, when Jesus occasionally used a text in a way that
seems unnatural to us, it was usually a legitimate Hebraic or
Aramaic idiom or thought pattern that does not directly translate into our culture and time. An example of this is found in
Matthew 27:9-10. Though the passage is not a direct quotation from Jesus, it illustrates the point that what would be

15. John Wenham, *Christ and the Bible* (Downers Grove, Ill.: InterVarsity, 1972),
p. 12.

considered inaccurate by our set of cultural norms was a legitimate and accepted hermeneutical practice in that day. The passage reads: "Then what was spoken by Jeremiah the prophet was fulfilled: 'They took the thirty silver coins, the price set on him by the people of Israel, and they used them to buy the potter's field, as the Lord commanded me.' " The quotation is actually a compilation from Jeremiah 32:6-9 and Zechariah 11:12-13. To our way of thinking, combining quotations from two different men with reference made only to one is an error of reference. However, in the Jewish culture of Jesus' day, this was an accepted hermeneutical practice, understood by author and audience alike. Common procedure was to group two or more prophecies and ascribe them together to the most prominent prophet of the group (in this case Jeremiah). Thus what appears to be an interpretive error is actually a legitimate hermeneutical application when viewed within its proper context.

The New Testament usages of the Old Testament that probably raise the most question with regard to their hermeneutical legitimacy are the fulfillment passages. To the English reader it may seem that the New Testament writer is giving an interpretation to these verses different from the original intention of the Old Testament author. The issue is a complex one. Chapter 7 includes a detailed discussion of the Hebrew conceptions of historical, prophetic, and typological fulfillment.

The Apostles' Use of the Old Testament

The apostles followed their Lord in regarding the Old Testament as the inspired Word of God (2 Tim. 3:16; 2 Peter 1:21). In at least fifty-six instances God is explicitly referred to as the author of the biblical text.[16] Like Christ, they accepted the historical accuracy of the Old Testament (e.g., Acts 7:9-50; 13:16-22; Heb. 11). As Nicole observes:

16. Nicole, "Old Testament Quotauons," p. 44.

> They appeal to Scripture when in debate; they appeal
> to it when requested to answer questions, whether serious
> or captious; they appeal to it in connection with their
> teaching even to those who would not be inclined to press
> them for other authorities than their own word; they
> appeal to it to indicate the purpose of some of their own
> actions or their insight into God's purpose in relation to
> contemporary developments; and they appeal to it in their
> prayers.[17]

The high esteem with which the New Testament writers regarded the Old Testament strongly suggests that they would
not consciously or intentionally have misinterpreted the words
that they believed God Himself had spoken.

Having said that, however, there are several questions that
commonly arise about the New Testament writers' use of the
Old Testament. One of the most frequently asked is: *When
quoting the Old Testament, the New Testament frequently modifies the
original wording. How can that practice be justified hermeneutically?*

Three considerations are relevant here. *First,* there were
several Hebrew, Aramaic, and Greek versions of the biblical
text circulating in Palestine at the time of Christ, some of
which had different wording than others.[18] An exact quotation from one of these versions might not have the same wording as the texts from which our present English translations
are made, yet still represent a faithful interpretation of the
biblical text available to the New Testament writer.

Second, as Wenham notes, it was not necessary for the writers to quote Old Testament passages word for word unless
they claimed to be quoting verbatim, particularly since they
were writing in a language different from the original Old
Testament texts.[19]

17. Ibid., pp. 46-47.
18. Longenecker, *Biblical Exegesis in the Apostolic Period,* p. 64. See also Donald A.
Hagner, "The Old Testament in the New Testament," in *Interpreting the Word of God,*
ed. Samuel Schultz and Morris Inch (Chicago: Moody, 1976), pp. 78-104.
19. Wenham, *Christ and the Bible,* p. 92.

Third, in ordinary life, freedom from quotation is usually a sign of mastery of one's material; the more sure a speaker is that he understands an author's meaning, the less afraid he is to expound those ideas in words that are not exactly those of the author.[20] For these reasons, then, the fact that the New Testament writers sometimes paraphrased or quoted indirectly from the Old Testament in no way indicates that they were using inaccurate or illegitimate interpretive methods.

A second question sometimes raised is: *The New Testament seems to use some of the Old Testament in unnatural ways. How is this practice justifiable hermeneutically?*

Paul's discussion of the word *seed* in Galatians 3:16 is often used as an example of the New Testament's unnatural, and thus illegitimate, handling of an Old Testament passage. The promise had been given to Abraham that through him all the nations of the world would be blessed (Gal. 3:8). Verse 16 says, "The promises were spoken to Abraham and to his seed. The Scripture does not say 'and to seeds,' meaning many people, but 'and to your seed,' meaning one person, who is Christ." Some scholars have assumed in this instance that Paul borrowed from illegitimate rabbinic methods to try to make his point, since it seems impossible that a word could have a singular and a plural referent simultaneously.

However, even in English, *seed* (or offspring, RSV) can have a collective sense in the singular. Paul is saying that the promises were given to Abraham and to his offspring, but their ultimate fulfillment is found only in Christ.[21] In the Hebrew culture of that time, the idea of corporate identify (a "complex of thought in which there is a constant oscillation between the individual and the group—family, tribe or nation—to which he belongs"[22]) was even stronger than in the collective sense expressed by the idea of offspring. There was frequent oscil-

---

20. Ibid., p. 93.
21. Alan Cole, *The Epistle of Paul to the Galatians* (Grand Rapids: Eerdmans, 1965), pp. 102-103.
22. Longenecker, *Biblical Exegesis in the Apostolic Period*, pp. 93-94.

lation between the king or some representative figure within the nation, on the one hand, and the elect remnant or the Messiah, on the other. The nature of the relationship is not exactly translatable into modern categories, but was one that was readily understood by Paul and his audience.

In conclusion, the vast majority of the New Testament references to the Old Testament interpret it literally; that is, they interpret according to the commonly accepted norms for interpreting all types of communication—history as history, poetry as poetry, and symbols as symbols. There is no attempt to separate the message into literal and allegorical levels.[23] The few cases where the New Testament writers seem to interpret the Old Testament unnaturally can usually be resolved as we understand more fully the interpretive methods of biblical times. Thus the New Testament itself lays the basis for the grammatical-historical method of modern evangelical hermeneutics.

BT2: A number of New Testament scholars claim that Jesus and the New Testament writers borrowed both legitimate and illegitimate hermeneutical methods from their contemporaries.
  a. How would you define an illegitimate hermeneutical method?
  b. Do you agree that Jesus and the New Testament writers borrowed illegitimate hermeneutical methods from their contemporaries? Why or why not?
  c. What are the implications of the doctrine of inspiration for this question?
  d. What are the implications of your Christology for this question?

Patristic Exegesis (A.D. 100–600)

Despite the practice of the apostles, an allegorical school of interpretation dominated the church in the succeeding cen-

23. See chapter 6 for a discussion of Paul's allegory in Galatians 4.

turies. This allegorization sprang from a proper motive—the desire to understand the Old Testament as a Christian document. However, the allegorical method as practiced by the church fathers often neglected completely the author's intended meaning and the literal understanding of a text to develop speculations the author himself would never have recognized. When once the author's intended meaning, as expressed through his words and syntax, was abandoned, there remained no regulative principle to govern exegesis.[24]

Clement of Alexandria (c. 150–c. 215)

A well-known patristic exegete, Clement believed that Scriptures hide their true meaning so that we might be inquisitive, and because it is not suitable for everyone to understand. He theorized that there are five senses to Scripture (historical, doctrinal, prophetic, philosophical, and mystical), with the deepest riches available only to those who understand the deeper senses. His exegesis of Genesis 22:1-4 (Abraham's journey to Moriah to sacrifice Isaac) gives the flavor of his writings:

> Abraham, when he came to the place which God told him of on the third day, looking up, saw the place afar off. For the first day is that which is constituted by the sight of good things; and the second is the soul's best desire; on the third the mind perceives spiritual things, the eyes of the understanding being opened by the Teacher who rose on the third day. The three days may be the mystery of the seal (baptism) in which God is really believed. It is, consequently, afar off that he perceives the place. For the reign of God is hard to attain, which Plato calls the reign of ideas, having learned from Moses that it was a place that contained all things universally. But it is seen by

24. K. Fullerton, *Prophecy and Authority*, p. 81, cited in Ramm, *Protestant Biblical Interpretation*, p. 31.

Abraham afar off, rightly, because of his being in the realms of generation, and he is forthwith initiated by the angel. Thence says the apostle, "Now we see through a glass, but then face to face," by those sole pure and incorporeal applications of the intellect.[25]

Origen (185?–254?)

Origen was the noted successor of Clement. He believed that Scripture is one vast allegory in which every detail is symbolic,[26] and made much of 1 Corinthians 2:6-7 ("We speak the wisdom of God in a mystery," KJV).

Origen believed that even as man consists of three parts—body, soul, and spirit—so too Scripture possesses three senses. The body is the literal sense, the soul the moral sense, and the spirit the allegorical or mystical sense. In practice Origen typically disparaged the literal sense, rarely referred to the moral sense, and constantly employed allegory, since only allegory yielded true knowledge.[27]

Augustine (354–430)

In terms of originality and genius, Augustine was by far the greatest man of his age. In his book on Christian doctrine, he laid down a number of rules for exposition of Scripture, some of which remain in use today. His rules include the following, summarized from Ramm:

1. The interpreter must possess a genuine Christian faith.
2. The literal and historical meaning of Scripture should be held in high regard.

25. Cited in Terry, *Biblical Hermeneutics,* p. 639.
26. Daniélou, *Origen,* p. 184, cited in Ramm, *Protestant Biblical Interpretation,* p. 32.
27. Louis Berkhof, *Principles of Biblical Interpretation* (Grand Rapids: Baker, 1950), p. 20.

3. Scripture has more than one meaning and therefore the allegorical method is a proper one.

4. There is a significance in biblical numbers.

5. The Old Testament is a Christian document because Christ is pictured throughout it.

6. The task of the expositor is to understand the meaning of the author, not to bring his own meaning to the text.

7. The interpreter must consult the true orthodox creed.

8. A verse should be studied in its context, not in isolation from the verses around it.

9. If the meaning of a text is unclear, nothing in the passage can be made a matter of orthodox faith.

10. The Holy Spirit is not a substitute for the necessary learning to understand Scripture. The interpreter should know Hebrew, Greek, geography, and other subjects.

11. The obscure passage must yield to the clear passage.

12. The expositor should take into account that revelation is progressive.[28]

In practice Augustine forsook most of his own principles and tended toward excessive allegorizing; this practice makes his exegetical commentaries some of the least valuable of his writings. He justified his allegorical interpretations from 2 Corinthians 3:6 ("For the written code kills, but the Spirit gives life," RSV), which he interpreted to mean that a literal interpretation of the Bible kills, but an allegorical or spiritual interpretation gives life.[29]

Augustine believed that Scripture had a fourfold sense—historical, aetiological, analogical, allegorical. His view became the predominant view of the Middle Ages.[30] Thus Augustine's influence on the development of a scientific exegesis was mixed: in theory he articulated many of the principles of sound exegesis, but in practice he failed to apply those principles in his own biblical study.

28. Ramm, *Protestant Biblical Interpretation*, pp. 36-37.
29. Ibid., p. 35.
30. Berkhof, *Principles of Biblical Interpretations*, p. 22.

The Syrian School of Antioch

A group of scholars at Antioch in Syria attempted to avoid both the letterism of the Jews and the allegorism of the Alexandrians.[31] They, and particularly one of their number, Theodore of Mopsuestia (c. 350–428), staunchly defended the principle of grammatical-historical interpretation, i.e., that a text should be interpreted according to the rules of grammar and the facts of history. They avoided dogmatic exegesis, asserting that an interpretation must be justified by a study of its grammatical and historical context, and not by an appeal to authority. They criticized the allegorists for casting into doubt the historicity of much of the Old Testament.

The Antiochian view of history differed from that of the Alexandrians. According to the allegorists, floating above the historical meaning of the Old Testament events was another, more spiritual, meaning. The Antiochians, in contrast, believed that the spiritual meaning of an historical event was implicit within the event itself.[32] For example, according to the allegorists, Abraham's departure from Haran signified his rejection of knowing things by means of the senses; to the Antiochians, Abraham's departure from Haran represented an act of faith and trust as he followed God's call to go from the historical city of Haran to the land of Canaan.

The exegetical principles of the Antiochian school laid the groundwork for modern evangelical hermeneutics. Unfortunately, one of Theodore's students, Nestorius, became involved in a major heresy concerning the person of Christ, and his association with the school, together with other historical circumstances, led to the eventual demise of this promising school of thought.

31. Ramm, *Protestant Biblical Interpretation*, p. 48.
32. Ibid., pp. 49-50.

Medieval Exegesis (600–1500)

Little original scholarship was done during the Middle Ages; most students of Scripture devoted themselves to studying and compiling the works of the earlier Fathers. Interpretation was bound by tradition, and the allegorical method was prominent.

The fourfold sense of Scripture articulated by Augustine was the norm for biblical interpretation. These four levels of meaning, expressed in the following verse that circulated during this period, were believed to exist in every biblical passage:

> The *letter* shows us what God and our fathers did;
>
> The *allegory* shows us where our faith is hid;
>
> The *moral* meaning gives us rules of daily life;
>
> The *anagogy* shows us where we end our strife.[33]
>
> [eschatologically]

The city of Jerusalem can be used to illustrate this idea. Literally, Jerusalem refers to the historical city itself; allegorically, it refers to the church of Christ; morally, it indicates the human soul; and anagogically, (eschatologically) it points to the heavenly Jerusalem.[34]

During this period the principle was generally accepted that any interpretation of a biblical text must adapt itself to the tradition and doctrine of the church. The source of dogmatic theology was not the Bible alone, but the Bible as interpreted by church tradition.[35]

---

33. Robert Grant, *A Short History of the Interpretation of the Bible* (New York: Macmillan, 1963), p. 119.

34. Ibid., pp. 119-120.

35. George Eldon Ladd, *A Theology of the New Testament* (Grand Rapids: Eerdmans, 1974), p. 13.

Although the fourfold method of interpretation was predominant, other strains of exegesis were still being developed. Throughout the late medieval period, the Cabbalists in Europe and Palestine continued in the tradition of earlier Jewish mysticism. They carried the practice of letterism to the point of absurdity. They believed that every letter, and even every possible transposition or substitution of letters, had supernatural significance. Attempting to unlock divine mysteries, they resorted to the following methods: substituting one biblical word for another that had the same numerical value; adding to the text by regarding each individual letter of a word as the initial letter of other words; substituting new words into a text by an interchange of some of the letters of the original words.[36]

Among some groups, however, a more scientific method of interpretation was in use. The Spanish Jews of the twelveth to fifteenth centuries sparked a return to a grammatical-historical method of interpretation. The Victorines at the Abbey of Saint Victor in Paris advocated that the meaning of Scripture is to be found in its literal rather than allegorical exposition. They suggested that exegesis should give rise to doctrine rather than making the meaning of a text coincide with previous ecclesiastical teaching.

One individual who had a significant impact on the return to literal interpretation was Nicolas of Lyra (1270?–1340?). Although he agreed that there are four senses to Scripture, he gave decided preference to the literal and urged that the other senses be founded firmly on the literal. He complained that other senses were often used to choke the literal, and asserted that only the literal should be used as a basis for doctrine.[37] Nicolas of Lyra's work affected Luther profoundly, and there are many who believe that without his influence, Luther would not have sparked the Reformation.

36. Berkhof, *Principles of Biblical Interpretation*, p. 17.
37. Ibid., p. 25.

Reformation Exegesis (1500s)

In the fourteenth and fifteenth centuries, dense ignorance prevailed concerning the content of Scripture: there were some doctors of divinity who had never read the Bible through in its entirety.[38] The Renaissance called attention to the necessity of knowing the original languages in order to understand the Bible. Erasmus facilitated this study by publishing the first critical edition of the Greek New Testament, and Reuchlin by translating a Hebrew grammar and lexicon. The fourfold sense of Scripture was gradually abandoned and replaced with the principle that Scripture has but a single sense.[39]

Luther (1483–1546)

Luther believed that faith and the Spirit's illumination were prerequisites for an interpreter of the Bible. He asserted that the Bible should be viewed with wholly different eyes from those with which we view other literary productions.[40]

Luther also maintained that the church should not determine what the Scriptures teach, but rather that Scripture should determine what the church teaches. He rejected the allegorical method of interpreting Scripture, calling it "dirt," "scum," and "obsolete loose rags."

According to Luther, a proper interpretation of Scripture must come from a literal understanding of the text. The interpreter should consider historical conditions, grammar, and context in his exegesis. He also believed that the Bible is a clear book (the perspicuity of Scripture), in opposition to the Roman Catholic dogma that the Scriptures are so obscure that only the church can uncover their true meaning.

38. Ibid.
39. Ibid., pp. 25-26.
40. The materials on Luther and Calvin have been summarized from Ramm, *Protestant Biblical Interpretation*, pp. 53-59.

By abandoning the allegorical method which had so long served as a means of making the Old Testament a Christian book, Luther was forced to find another way of explaining its relevance to New Testament believers. He did this by maintaining that all of the Old and New Testament points to Christ. This organizing principle, which in reality became a hermeneutical principle, caused Luther to see Christ in many places (such as some of the Psalms which he designated as messianic) where later interpreters failed to find christological· references. Whether or not we agree with all of Luther's designations, his christological principle did enable him to show the unity of Scripture without recourse to mystical interpretations of the Old Testament text.

One of Luther's major hermeneutical principles was that one must carefully distinguish between Law and Gospel. For Luther, Law refers to God in His wrath, His judgment, and His hatred of sin; Gospel refers to God in His grace, His love, and His salvation. Repudiation of the Law was wrong, according to Luther, for that leads to lawlessness. Fusion of Law and Gospel was also wrong, for that leads to the heresy of adding works to faith. Thus Luther believed that recognition and careful maintenance of the Law-Gospel distinction was crucial to proper biblical understanding. (See chapter 5 for a further discussion of Law and Gospel.)

Melanchthon, Luther's companion in exegesis, continued the application of Luther's hermeneutical principles in his own expositions of the biblical text, sustaining and augmenting the impetus of Luther's work.

Calvin (1509–1564)

Probably the greatest exegete of the Reformation was Calvin, who agreed in general with the principles articulated by Luther. He, too, believed that spiritual illumination is necessary, and regarded allegorical interpretation as a contrivance of Satan to obscure the sense of Scripture.

"Scripture interprets Scripture" was a favorite phrase of Calvin, which alluded to the importance Calvin placed on studying the context, grammar, words, and parallel passages rather than importing one's own meaning onto the text. In a famous sentence he stated that "it is the first business of an interpreter to let the author say what he does say, instead of attributing to him what we think he ought to say."[41]

Calvin probably surpassed Luther in aligning his exegetical practices with his theory. He did not share the opinion of Luther that Christ is to be found everywhere in Scripture (e.g., he differed from Luther on the number of Psalms that are legitimately messianic). In spite of some differences, the hermeneutical principles articulated by these Reformers were to become the major guiding principles for modern orthodox Protestant interpretation.

Post-Reformation Exegesis (1550–1800)

Confessionalism

The Council of Trent met at various times from 1545 through 1563 and drew up a list of decrees setting forth the dogmas of the Roman Catholic church and criticizing Protestantism. In response, Protestants began developing creeds to define their own position. At one point nearly every important city had its own favorite creed, with bitter theological controversies prevailing. Hermeneutical methods were often poor during this time, for exegesis became the handmaid of dogmatics, and often degenerated into mere proof-texting.[42] Farrar describes theologians of that day as reading "the Bible by the unnatural glare of theological hatred."[43]

---

41. Cited in F. W. Farrar, *History of Interpretation* (1885; reprint ed., Grand Rapids: Baker, 1961), p. 347.
42. Berkhof, *Principles of Biblical Interpretation*, p. 29.
43. Farrar, *History of Interpretation*, pp. 363-64, cited in Ramm, *Protestant Biblical Interpretation*, p. 60.

Pietism

Pietism rose as a reaction to the dogmatic and often bitter exegesis of the confessional period. Philipp Jakob Spener (1635-1705) is considered the leader of the Pietist revival. In a tract titled *Pious Longings,* he called for an end to needless controversy, a return to mutual Christian concern and good works, better Bible knowledge on the part of all Christians, and better spiritual training for ministers.

A. H. Francke exemplified many of the qualities which Spener's tract had called for. In addition to being a scholar, linguist, and exegete, he was active in forming many institutions for the care of the destitute and the sick. He was also involved in forming mission work to India.

Pietism made significant contributions to the study of Scripture, but was not immune from criticism as well. At its highest moments the Pietists combined a deep desire to understand the Word of God and appropriate it for their lives with a fine appreciation of grammatical-historical interpretation. However, many later Pietists discarded the grammatical-historical basis of interpretation, and depended instead on an "inward light" or "an unction from the Holy One." These expositions, based on subjective impressions and pious reflections, often resulted in interpretations which contradicted one another and had little relationship to the author's intended meaning.

Rationalism

Rationalism, the philosophical position of accepting reason as the only authority for determining one's opinions or course of action, emerged as an important position during this period and was soon to have a profound effect on theology and hermeneutics.

For several centuries before this time the church had emphasized the reasonableness of faith. Revelation was considered superior to reason as a means of understanding truth, but revelational truth was considered to be inherently reasonable.

Luther made a distinction between the magisterial and ministerial use of reason. By ministerial use of reason he referred to the use of human reason to help us understand and obey God's Word more fully. By magisterial use of reason he referred to the use of human reason to stand in judgment *over* God's Word. Luther clearly affirmed the former and disapproved of the latter.

During the period following the Reformation the magisterial use of reason began to emerge more fully than it had ever done before. Empiricism, the belief that the only valid knowledge we can possess is that which can be obtained through the five senses, emerged and joined hands with rationalism. The combination of rationalism with empiricism meant that: (1) many noted thinkers were claiming that reason rather than revelation was to guide our thinking and actions, and (2) that reason would be used to judge which parts of revelation were considered acceptable (which came to include only those parts subject to natural physical laws and empirical verification).

Modern Hermeneutics (1800 to the Present)

Liberalism

Rationalism in philosophy laid the basis for liberalism in theology. Whereas in previous centuries revelation had determined what reason ought to think, by the late 1800s reason determined what parts of revelation (if any) were to be accepted as true. Where in previous centuries the divine authorship of Scripture had been emphasized, during this period its human authorship was the focus. Some authors suggested that various parts of Scripture possessed various *degrees* of inspiration, with the lower degrees (such as historical details) being capable of error. Other writers, such as Schleiermacher, went further by totally denying the supernatural character of inspiration. For many *inspiration* no longer referred to the process whereby God guided the human authors to produce a Scriptural product that was His truth. Rather, *inspiration* referred to the (humanly-produced) Bible's ability to inspire religious experience.

A thorough-going naturalism was also applied to the Bible. The rationalists claimed that whatever was not in conformity with "educated mentality" was to be rejected. This included such doctrines as human depravity, hell, the virgin birth, and frequently even Christ's vicarious atonement. Miracles and other examples of divine interventions were regularly explained away as examples of pre-critical thinking.[44] Influenced by both the thinking of Darwin and of Hegel, the Bible came to be viewed as a record of the evolutionary development of Israel's religious consciousness (and later the church's), rather than God's revelation of Himself to man. Each of these presuppositions had profound influence on the credibility that interpreters gave to the biblical text, and thus had important implications for interpretive methods. Frequently the interpretive focus itself changed: The scholars' question no longer was "What is God saying in the text?" but rather "What does the text tell me about the developing religious consciousness of this primitive Hebrew cult?"

Neoorthodoxy

Neoorthodoxy is a twentieth-century phenomenon. It occupies, in some respects, a position midway between the liberal and orthodox views of Scripture. It breaks with the liberal view that Scripture is only a product of man's deepening re-

44. Ramm, *Protestant Biblical Interpretation*, pp. 63-69.

ligious awareness, but stops short of the orthodox view of revelation.

Those within neoorthodox circles generally believe that Scripture is man's witness to God's revelation of Himself. They maintain that God does not reveal Himself in words, but only by His presence. When a person reads the words of Scripture and responds to God's presence in faith, revelation occurs. Revelation is not considered to be something that happened at a historical point in time which is now transmitted to us in the biblical texts, but is a present experience that must be accompanied by a personal existential response.

Neoorthodox positions on several issues differ from traditional orthodox ones. Infallibility or inerrancy has no place in the neoorthodox vocabulary. Scripture is seen as a compendium of sometimes conflicting theological systems accompanied by a number of factual errors. Bible stories about the interaction between the supernatural and the natural are considered to be myths—not in the same sense as pagan myths, but in the sense that they do not teach literal history. Biblical "myths" (such as the creation, the fall, the resurrection) seek to introduce theological truths as historical incidents. In neoorthodox interpretation, the fall, for example, "informs us that man inevitably corrupts his moral nature." The incarnation and the cross show us that man cannot achieve his own salvation, but that it "must come from beyond as an act of God's grace."[45] The major task of the interpreter, then, is to divest the myth of its historical wrappings in order to discover the existential truth contained within.

The "New Hermeneutic"

The "new hermeneutic" has been primarily a European development since World War II. It emerged basically from the work of Bultmann and was carried further by Ernst Fuchs

45. Ibid., pp. 70-79.

and Gerhard Ebeling. Much of what has been said regarding the neoorthodox position applies to this category of interpretation as well. Building on the work of the philosopher Martin Heidegger, Fuchs and Ebeling assert that Bultmann did not go far enough. Language, they maintain, is not reality, but only a personal interpretation of reality. One's use of language, then, is a hermeneutic—an interpretation. Hermeneutics for them is no longer the science of stating principles whereby texts can be understood, but is rather an investigation of the hermeneutical function of speech as such, and thus has a much wider and more profound scope.[46]

Hermeneutics Within Orthodox Christianity

During the last 200 years there have continued to be interpreters who believed that Scripture represents God's revelation of Himself—His words and His actions—to humanity. The task of the interpreter, according to this group, has been to try to understand more fully the intended meaning of the original author. Studies of the surrounding history, culture, language, and theological understanding of the original recipients are undertaken in order to understand what the Scriptural revelation meant to its original recipients. Important scholars within this general tradition (and this list is by no means exhaustive) include E. W. Hengstenberg, Carl F. Keil, Franz Delitzsch, H. A. W. Meyer, J. P. Lange, F. Godet, Henry Alford, Charles Ellicott, J. B. Lightfoot, B. F. Westcott, F. J. A. Hort, Charles Hodge, John A. Broadus, Theodore B. Zahn, and others.[47] Hermeneutical manuals within this tradition have included those by C. A. G. Keil, Davidson, Patrick Fairbairn,

---

46. Ernst Fuchs, "The New Testament and the Hermeneutical Problem," in *The New Hermeneutic*, ed. James M. Robinson and John B. Cobb (New York: Harper & Row, 1964), p. 125. Cited in Ramm, pp. 83-92.

47. This list is from A. Berkeley Mickelsen, *Interpreting the Bible*, pp. 47-48.

A. Immer, Milton S. Terry, Louis Berkhof, A. Berkeley Mickelsen, and Bernard Ramm.

Chapter Summary

This chapter has attempted to provide a very brief overview of some of the major trends in the historical development of hermeneutics. More complete discussions may be found in the books listed below, and the reader with access to them is strongly encouraged to develop further historical understanding than this brief discussion provides.

Throughout history we can see the gradual emergence of the presuppositions and practices now known as the grammatical-historical method of interpretation. This method suggests that the meaning of a text is the author's intended meaning and that the author's intention can be derived most accurately by observing the facts of history and the rules of grammar as they apply to the text being studied. Major contributions to the development of the grammatical-historical method include: (1) the predominant use of literal exegesis by Christ and the New Testament writers, (2) the theoretical principles (but not the practice) of Augustine, (3) the Syrian school of Antioch, (4) the Spanish Jews of the twelveth to fifteenth centuries, (5) the work of Nicolas of Lyra, Erasmus, and Reuchlin, (6) the work of Luther and Calvin, and (7) those persons named in the last section.

Throughout history there has been a second set of presuppositions and methods that have been manifested in a variety of ways. The basic premise has been that the meaning of a text is discoverable, not by the methods usually used to understand communication between persons, but by the use of some special interpretive key. The net result of the use of most of these interpretive keys has been to impart the reader's meaning into the text (*eisegesis*), rather than to read the author's meaning from the text (*exegesis*). Examples of such interpretive keys have included: (1) Jewish and Christian allegorism, (2) the fourfold medieval exegesis, and (3) the letterism and numerology of the Cabbalists. Post-Reformation liberalism and neoorthodoxy have supplied interpretive keys growing out of their presuppositions about the origin and nature of Scripture.

Resources for Further Reading

Louis Berkhof. *Principles of Biblical Interpretation,* chapters 2 and 3.

F. W. Farrar. *History of Interpretation.*

K. Fullerton. *Prophecy and Authority: A Study in the History of the Doctrine of the Interpretation of Scripture.*

Robert M. Grant. *A Short History of the Interpretation of the Bible* (rev. ed.).

Richard Longenecker. *Biblical Exegesis in the Apostolic Period.*

A. Berkeley Mickelsen. *Interpreting the Bible,* chapter 2.

Bernard Ramm. *Hermeneutics,* chapters 3, 6, and 9.

Bernard Ramm. *Protestant Biblical Interpretation* (3rd rev. ed.), chapter 2.

Milton S. Terry. *Biblical Hermeneutics,* part 3.

chapter three

Historical-Cultural and Contextual Analysis

When you have completed this chapter, you should be able to:

1. Define the following terms:
   a. Historical-cultural analysis
   b. Contextual analysis
   c. Lexical-syntactical analysis
   d. Theological analysis
   e. Literary analysis
2. Describe a six-step model that can be used to interpret any biblical text.
3. List and describe three basic steps involved in historical-cultural and contextual analysis.
4. Identify three ways of discerning an author's intention for writing a specific book.
5. List six important secondary steps involved in contextual analysis.
6. Apply the above principles in identifying misinterpretations of selected biblical texts and advancing more accurate interpretations of them.

Introductory Comments

Chapter 1 discussed the principle that, based on the assumption that an author is an articulate communicator (as we believe God to be), the primary presupposition of hermeneutical theory must be that *the meaning of a text is the author's intended meaning,* rather than the meanings we may wish to ascribe to his words. If we abandon this principle, there remains no normative, compelling criterion for discriminating between valid and invalid interpretations.

Chapter 2 surveyed historical trends in interpretation, observing that some interpreters have followed normal principles of communication while others have fallen into vagaries of interpretation through development of unusual hermeneutical principles.

Chapters 3 through 8 present the principles of hermeneutics and show how to apply them to the interpretation of scriptural texts. The complex skill of biblical interpretation and application is divided into six steps. These are:

1. *Historical-cultural analysis* considers the historical-cultural milieu in which an author wrote, in order to understand his allusions, references, and purpose. *Contextual analysis* considers the relationship of a given passage to the whole body of an author's writing, for better understanding results from a knowledge of the overall thought.

2. *Lexical-syntactical analysis* develops an understanding of the definitions of words (lexicology) and their relationship to one another (syntax) in order to understand more accurately the meaning the author intended to convey.

3. *Theological analysis* studies the level of theological understanding at the time a revelation was given in order to ascertain the meaning of the text for its original recipients. Thus it takes into account related Scriptures, whether given before or after the passage being studied.

4. *Literary analysis* identifies the literary form or method used in a given passage for various forms such as historical

narrative, letters, doctrinal exposition, poetry, and apocalyptic. Each have their unique methods of expression and interpretation.

5. *Comparison with other interpreters* compares the tentative interpretation derived from the four steps above with the work of other interpreters.

6. *Application* is the important step of translating the meaning a biblical text had for its original hearers into the meaning it has for believers in a different time and culture. In some instances the transmission is accomplished fairly easily; in other instances such as biblical commands that were obviously influenced by cultural factors (e.g., greeting with the holy kiss), the translation across cultures becomes more complex.

In this six-step procedure steps one through three belong to general hermeneutics. Step four constitutes special hermeneutics. Step six—transmission and application of the biblical message from one time and culture to another—is not usually considered an integral part of hermeneutics per se, but is included in this text because of its obvious relevance for the twentieth-century believer so widely separated by both time and culture from the original recipients of Scripture.

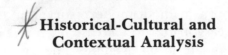

Historical-Cultural and Contextual Analysis

The meaning of a text cannot be interpreted with any degree of certainty without historical-cultural and contextual analysis. The following two examples show the importance of such analysis:

BT3: Proverbs 22:28 commands "Remove not the ancient landmark which your fathers have set," (RSV). Does this verse mean:
  a. Do not make changes from the way we have always done things.
  b. Do not steal.

c. Do not remove the guideposts that direct travelers from town to town.
d. None of the above.
e. All of the above.

BT4: Hebrews 4:12 affirms: "The word of God is living and active. Sharper than any double-edged sword, it penetrates even to dividing soul and spirit, joints and marrow; it judges the thoughts and attitudes of the heart." Does this verse:

a. Teach that man is trichotomous, since it speaks of a division of soul and spirit?
b. Teach that the truth contained in God's Word is dynamic and changing rather than dead and static?
c. Give a warning to professing believers?
d. Encourage Christians to use the Word of God aggressively in their witnessing and counseling?
e. None of the above?

The answer to BT3 is (b). If you answered either (a) or (c) it is likely that you came to the text subconsciously asking, "What does this text mean to me?" The important question, however, is "What did this text mean to the original writer and his audience?" In this instance the ancient landmark refers to the boundary marker that separated one man's land from his neighbor's. Without modern surveying techniques it was a relatively easy matter to increase one's acreage by moving such markers late in an evening. The prohibition is directed against a specific type of stealing.

The solution to BT4 will become clearer by the end of the chapter and should be answered then. The point of these exercises is to demonstrate that unless we have a knowledge of the writer's background, supplied through historical-cultural and contextual analysis, our tendency is to interpret his writings by asking, "What does this mean to me?" rather than "What did this mean to the original author?" Until we can answer the latter question with some degree of certainty, we have no basis for claiming validity for our interpretation.

Historical-cultural and contextual analysis can be done by asking three basic questions, each of which is more specific than the previous one. The three questions are:

1. What is the general historical milieu in which the writer speaks?
2. What is the specific historical-cultural context and purpose of this book?
3. What is the immediate context of the passage under consideration?

Each of these general questions or steps is further subdivided in the following discussion.

Determining the General Historical-Cultural Context

Three secondary questions are important in determining the historical-cultural context. *First, what is the general historical situation facing the author and his audience?* What were the political, economic, and social situations? What was the main source of livelihood? What were the major threats and concerns? Knowledge of the historical-cultural context is crucial for answering basic questions about a text, such as "What is happening to the author of Lamentations? Is he suffering from a 'nervous breakdown' or from a normal grief reaction?" Or, "What are the implications of the Song of Solomon for a theology of Christian sexual expression?"

Second, knowledge of what customs will clarify the meaning of given actions? In Mark 7, for example, Jesus upbraids the Pharisees soundly for their concept of corban. In the practice of corban a man could declare that all his money would go to the temple treasury when he died, and that, since his money belonged to God, he was therefore no longer responsible for maintaining his aging parents. Jesus argues that men were using this Pharisaic tradition to render God's command (the fifth commandment) of no account. Without a knowledge of the cultural practice of corban, we would be unable to understand this passage.

Other examples of the added meaning that an understanding of cultural customs brings may be easily found. The familiar parable of the ten virgins (Matt. 25:1-13) was designed to impress on its hearers the importance of careful, as opposed to careless, preparation for the coming of the Lord. The carelessness of the ten foolish virgins is even more pointed when we become aware that the bridegroom watches generally took several hours, and that the lamps often used in these watches were tiny (several could be held in the palm of one's hand simultaneously). The foolishness of coming to a bridegroom watch with such a small lamp and no extra oil (v. 3) made Christ's point effectively.

Similarly, when Christ sent two of His disciples to find a room in which they could eat the Passover the night before His crucifixion, He sent them with unmistakable instructions, a fact which often escapes our untrained attention. The hostility of the Pharisees was so great that secrecy was of the utmost importance if He wished to finish this meal with His disciples uninterrupted. Christ's command (Mark 14:12-14) was to meet a man carrying a jug of water on his head and follow this man to the place where they would eat the Passover. In ancient Palestine carrying water was considered woman's work; no man normally would be seen carrying a water jar. Such a designation would leave no doubt about whom they were to follow. This may have been a secret, prearranged sign, giving us a glimpse of the tension and danger of those last days before His crucifixion.[1] Again, an awareness of cultural details alerts us to the significance of actions that could escape our understanding otherwise.

Third, what was the level of spiritual commitment of the audience? Many of the biblical books were written at times when the believers' level of commitment was low because of carnality, discouragement, or temptation from unbelievers or apostates.

---

1. G. Ernest Wright, ed., *Great People of the Bible and How They Lived* (Pleasantville: Reader's Digest, 1974), p. 11.

The meaning of the text cannot be understood properly if divorced from a knowledge of these factors. How, for example, should we understand a person who intentionally marries a prostitute, has three children by her to whom he gives bizarre names, mourns for her when she continues her prostitution and unfaithfulness, finds her after she has left him and become a slave prostitute, buys her back, then talks to her as if in a mentally dissociated state? Is this person suffering from an overly active "rescuer complex," or is he blatantly psychotic? Neither, of course, as we find when we examine the context of the life of Hosea, within which these actions take on powerful meaning and significance.

In summary, then, an important first step in properly understanding any biblical passage is to determine the historical-cultural milieu in which the author wrote. Good exegetical commentaries often supply such information as part of their introductions; study Bibles provide such information in highly condensed form. Several resource books are listed at the end of this chapter.

Determining the Specific Historical-Cultural Context and Purpose of a Book

A second, more specific step is determining the specific purpose(s) of a book. Several secondary questions are helpful guides:

1. Who was the writer? What was his spiritual background and experience?
2. To whom was he writing (e.g., believers, unbelievers, apostates, believers who were in danger of becoming apostates)?
3. What was the writer's purpose (intention) in writing this particular book?

The author and his recipients can usually be discovered from internal (textual) data or external (historical) data. In some instances the evidence seems fairly conclusive; in other instances the best that can be gathered is an educated hypothesis. An example is the Book of Hebrews. The book itself contains no direct evidence regarding its recipients or its author. It was given its name, *To the Hebrews,* on the basis of deductive evidence. The epistle contains numerous allusions to the Old Testament that would not be meaningful to the average pagan. It constantly contrasts the Mosaic covenant to the Christian, showing the superiority of the new to the old, a line of reasoning that would not be meaningful to those who had no loyalty to the Hebrew faith. For these and a number of other reasons we can be certain that the book was written primarily to Jews rather than Gentiles, and that the name *To the Hebrews* is therefore appropriate.

The authorship of Hebrews is entirely another matter. We can say with considerable certainty that it was probably not Paul because the literary expression, thought forms, and attitudes toward the Mosaic law found in this book differ significantly from those found in books of known Pauline authorship. However, beyond this we have little solid evidence of its exact author. Most hypotheses offered are conjectures unsupported by hard evidence. For practical purposes the question of the book's exact authorship is not as important as the fact that the early church recognized its divine inspiration and authority and thus included it in the canon.[2]

2. At this point we should consider the relationship between historical criticism and historical-cultural analysis. Some evangelical Christians may be concerned with the procedural similarity between the two. As mentioned in chapter 1, historical criticism studies the authorship of a book, the date and historical circumstances surrounding its composition, the authenticity of its contents, and its literary unity. Historical-cultural analysis also engages in these tasks in an attempt to understand the author's meanings. Thus the two terms significantly overlap.

Historical criticism, however, starts with positivistic presuppositions and concludes with statements contrary to the orthodox Christian faith. (Positivism is the philosophical position that men can have knowledge of nothing but observable phenomena, and therefore should reject all speculation about ultimate origins or causes.) Historical-cultural analysis begins with orthodox biblical presuppositions, a radically different point from historical criticism. To affirm the value of historical-cultural analysis is not to affirm the validity of historical criticism.

After study has revealed the specific historical-cultural context within which a book was written, the author's purpose should be determined. There are three basic ways[3] to determine this:

First, note the author's explicit statement or his repetition of certain phrases. For example, Luke 1:1-4 and Acts 1:1 tell us that Luke's purpose in writing was to present an orderly account of the beginning of the Christian era. John tells us in John 20:31 that his purpose was to present an account of Christ's ministry so that men might believe. The Book of 1 Peter is an exhortation to stand fast amid persecution (5:12). The tenfold repetition of the phrase "these are the generations of" in the Book of Genesis suggests that the purpose of this book is to record the earliest development of humankind and God's initial interventions in human history.

Second, observe the parenetical (hortatory) part of his writing. Since the exhortations flow from the purpose, they often give an important clue regarding the author's intentions. The Book of Hebrews, for example, is interspersed with exhortations and warnings, so there is little doubt that the author's purpose was to persuade Jewish believers who were undergoing persecution (10:32-35) not to return to Judaism but to stay true to their new profession of faith (10:19-23; 12:1-3). The Pauline books likewise are filled with theological facts immediately followed by a "therefore" and an exhortation. If the meaning of the theological fact is uncertain, the nature of the exhortation will often be valuable in understanding its meaning.

Third, observe points that are omitted or issues that are focused on. The writer of 1 and 2 Chronicles, for example, does not give us a complete history of all national events during Solomon's reign and the divided kingdom. He selects events which illustrate that Israel can endure only as she remains faithful to God's commandments and His covenant. In support of this,

3. W. C. Kaiser, Jr., Classnotes given at Trinity Evangelical Divinity School, Spring, 1974.

we see that he frequently uses the phrase "_____ did what was evil [or right] in the sight of the Lord."

A good check on whether or not you understand the author's purpose(s) is to summarize his purpose(s) in a single sentence. Beware of interpreting any passage without first understanding the author's intention in writing the book which contains it.

Developing an Understanding of the Immediate Context

Prooftexting is generally disparaged as a method of Bible study because it misses this important step: it interprets verses without paying proper attention to their context. Several secondary questions help to understand a text in its immediate context.

First, what are the major blocks of material and how do they fit together into a whole? Alternatively, what is the outline of the book? (Outlines should take into account the fact that some biblical writers were more organized than others.)

Second, how does the passage under consideration contribute to the flow of the author's argument? Alternatively, what is the connection between the passage under study and the blocks of material immediately preceding and following it? There is usually a logical and/or theological connection between any two adjacent passages. Parts of the Book of Proverbs might be considered an exception to this, but even there, logical groupings of ideas are frequently evident.

Third, what was the perspective of the author? The authors sometimes write as if looking through the eyes of God (as spokesmen for God), particularly in moral matters, but in narrative sections they frequently describe things the way they appear from a human perspective (as reporters speaking phenomenologically). We speak of the sun's setting, a phenomenological metaphor for the more cumbersome description of a section of the earth rotating out of the path of the sun's direct rays. Distinguishing the author's intention to be understood as a direct spokesman for God from his intention to speak as a human reporter describing an event phenomenologically is important for an accurate understanding of his meaning.

As an example of the importance of this principle, consider the question of whether the flood was universal or local. It is difficult to determine from the context whether the language in Genesis 6-9 was intended to be understood noumenologically (from God's perspective) or phenomenologically (from man's perspective). If the phrases "all flesh died" and "all the high hills were covered" are understood noumenologically, a universal flood is implied. If these same phrases are understood phenomenologically, they could mean "all the animals that I could observe died," and "all the high hills that I could observe were covered." A phenomenological description could then imply either a universal or a local flood.

The traditional interpretation of these verses has been noumenological. Milton Terry believes that the flood description should be understood phenomenologically. He states:

> The narrative of the flood is probably the account of an eyewitness. Its vividness of description and minuteness of details contain the strongest evidence that it is such. It was probably a tradition handed down from Shem to his descendants until it was finally incorporated in the Books of Moses. The terms "all flesh," "all the high hills," and "all the heavens," denote simply all those known to the observer.[4]

From the standpoint of hermeneutics, the important principle is that scriptural writers sometimes intended to write from a noumenological perspective and sometimes from a

4. Milton Terry, *Biblical Hermeneutics* (reprint ed., Grand Rapids: Zondervan, 1974), p. 543.

phenomenological one. Our interpretation of their meaning may err if we fail to make this distinction.

Fourth, is the passage stating descriptive or prescriptive truth? *Descriptive* passages relate what was said or what happened at a particular time. What God says, is true; what man says, may or may not be true; what Satan says, usually mixes truth and error. When Scripture describes human actions without comment, it should not necessarily be assumed that those actions are approved.

When Scripture describes an action of God with respect to human beings in a narrative passage, it should not be assumed that this is the way He will always work in believers' lives at every point in history. The methods God used in the Gospels or the Book of Acts are often wrongly asserted to be His methods in all believers' lives. However, God has responded in various ways to different men. Which of these can be considered the norm for today? How should one choose one instance above another as the normative incident?

Prescriptive passages of Scripture claim to be articulating normative principles. The Epistles are primarily prescriptive; but occasionally they contain instances of individual rather than universal prescriptions (e.g., the variety of church governments that seem to have prevailed in the early church communities). Differences between various prescriptive passages suggest that one should not universalize any of them, but apply each one as appropriate. When there is only one prescriptive passage on an issue, or when the various prescriptive passages concur with one another, the teaching of the passage is generally considered to be normative. Contextual analysis is the most valid way of differentiating descriptive from prescriptive passages.

Fifth, what constitutes the teaching focus of the passage and what represents incidental detail only? Some of the major heresies of church history have been supported by exegesis that failed to maintain the above distinction. For example, a major teaching of the allegory of Christ as the vine (John 15) is that we derive the power to live spiritual lives from Christ, not from ourselves. Using an incidental detail as a teaching focus, one group of early theologians (later branded heretics) declared that since Christ is the vine, and vines are part of the created order, it follows that Christ is part of the created order! The Pelagians of the early fifth century did a similar thing with the story of the prodigal son. They argued that since the prodigal son repented and returned to his father without the aid of a mediator, it follows that we do not need a mediator.

A contemporary example of the failure to make a distinction between incidental details and the teaching focus of a passage was given by a Christian educator in a classroom lecture a few years ago. The discussion centered around the 1 Corinthians 3:16 passage: "You are God's temple." Paul's central point in this verse is the sacredness of Christ's body, the church. Focusing on an incidental detail (the structure of the Old Testament temple), this educator concluded that since the temple had three parts (an outer court, an inner court, and a holy of holies) and since Christians are called temples, it therefore follows that man has three parts—body, soul, and spirit!

Finally, who is being addressed in this passage? There is a popular chorus that claims: "Every promise in the Book is mine." Pious though it sounds, the concept is hermeneutically invalid. Certainly we would not want to claim *all* the promises of Scripture (e.g., Matt. 23:29-33)! Nor would we want to claim all the commands given to believers, such as the command to Abraham to sacrifice his son (Gen. 22:3). The humorous anecdote of the young man who was searching frantically for God's will and decided to follow the leading of whatever Scripture he opened to is well known: the first passage that fell open was Matthew 27:5 ("Judas . . . went and hanged himself," KJV); the second passage was Luke 10:37 ("Go, and do thou likewise," KJV); and the third, John 13:27 ("That thou doest, do quickly," KJV).

Though we smile at the folly of applying a text without regard to its context, a significant number of Christians use this method to determine God's will for their lives. A more valid hermeneutical procedure is to ask the questions discussed above. Who is speaking? Is the teaching normative or intended for specific individuals? To whom is the passage directed?

Promises and commands are usually directed to one of three groups: national Israel, Old Testament believers, or New Testament believers. Normative promises and commands directed to New Testament believers are those most likely to apply to contemporary Christians. Some of the promises and commands directed to Old Testament believers also apply, depending on context and content (see chapter 5). Some commentators "spiritualize" the physical promises and commands made to national Israel and then apply them also to contemporary settings, but this practice is difficult to justify since it violates authorial intent.

Chapter Summary

The following steps are involved in historical-cultural and contextual analysis:
1. Determine the general historical and cultural milieu of the writer and his audience.
   a. Determine the general historical circumstances.
   b. Be aware of cultural circumstances and norms that add meaning to given actions.
   c. Discern the level of spiritual commitment of the audience.
2. Determine the purpose(s) the author had in writing a book.
   a. Note explicit statements or repeated phrases.
   b. Observe parenetical or hortatory sections.
   c. Observe issues that are omitted or focused on.
3. Understand how the passage fits into its immediate context.
   a. Identify the major blocks of material in the book and show how they fit into a coherent whole.

b. Show how the passage fits into the flow of the author's argument.

c. Determine the perspective which the author intends to communicate—noumenological (the way things really are) or phenomenological (the way things appear).

d. Distinguish between descriptive and prescriptive truth.

e. Distinguish between incidental details and the teaching focus of a passage.

f. Identify the person or category of persons for whom the particular passage is intended.

Resources for Further Information

J. McKee Adams. *Biblical Backgrounds.*

Denis Baly. *The Geography of the Bible.*

C. K. Barrett. *The New Testament Background: Selected Documents.*

Roland DeVaux. *Ancient Israel.*

Alfred Edersheim. *The Life and Times of Jesus the Messiah.*

James Freeman. *Manners and Customs of the Bible.*

R. K. Harrison. *Old Testament Times.*

E. W. Heaton. *Everyday Life in Old Testament Times.*

Martin Noth. *The Old Testament World.*

C. F. Pfeiffer, ed. *The Biblical World: A Dictionary of Biblical Archeology.*

James B. Pritchard, ed. *The Ancient Near East in Pictures Relating to the Old Testament.*

James B. Pritchard, ed. *Ancient Near Eastern Texts Relating to the Old Testament.* 2nd ed.

Merrill C. Tenney. *New Testament Times.*

John A. Thompson. *The Bible and Archeology.*

W. M. Thomson. *The Land and the Book.*

Edwin Yamauchi. *The Stones and the Scriptures.*

For several examples of good contextual and historical-cultural analysis, see W. C. Kaiser, ed., *Classical Evangelical Essays in Old Testament Interpretation.*

Exercises

BT4: By now you have the knowledge necessary to know how to find the correct answer to this question posed earlier in the chapter. See what you can do.

BT5: Do you see a relationship between the Jewish hermeneutical fallacy of letterism and interpretation that fails to distinguish between teaching focus and incidental detail? If you do, describe the nature of this similarity.

BT6: Among Christian counselors, there are differences of opinion regarding the meaning and usefulness of dreams in counseling. Ecclesiastes 5:7 says that "when dreams increase, empty words grow many" (RSV). Use your knowledge of hermeneutics to discern as accurately as you can the meaning of this verse, and then discuss the implications of the meaning of that verse for your use of dreams in counseling.

BT7: A Christian author was discussing the way to discover God's will for one's life and made the point that inner peace was an important indicator. The sole verse he used to anchor his argument was Colossians 3:15 ("Let the peace of Christ rule in your hearts"). Would you agree with his use of this verse to make this point? Why, or why not?

BT8: You are discussing with a person the need for a personal relationship with Jesus Christ as the only means of salvation. He claims that living a moral life is what God expects of us, and shows you Micah 6:8 to validate his point.

> He has showed you, O man, what is good. And what does the Lord require of you? To act justly and to love mercy, and to walk humbly with your God.

Will you argue that this verse is consistent with your point of view, and if so, how will you do it? If you take the point of view that salvation was by works in the Old Testament (as this verse seems to suggest), how will you reconcile this with Paul's statement in Galatians 2:16 that "by works of the law shall no one be justified" (RSV)?

BT9: A popular Christian counselor, talking about the problem some people have of saying yes when they mean no and then finally exploding in anger because of all the pent-up frustration, said:

Always being Mr. Nice-Guy, and then turning your real feelings into stomach acid is self-defeating. You may get what you want—for the moment—by lathering others, but you don't like yourself for it.

Consider putting out what you're feeling in simple honesty. As Jesus put it, "Let your yes be a clear yes, and your no, no." Anything else spells trouble.[5]

Do you agree with this author's use of Scripture (paraphrase of Matt. 5:33-37) to make this point? Why, or why not?

BT10: A Christian man lost his job during the economic recession of 1974-1975. He and his wife interpreted Romans 8:28 ("All things work together for good") to mean that he lost his job in order that God might give him a better-paying one. Consequently he turned down several lower- or equal-paying job opportunities and remained on unemployment for over two years before returning to work. Do you agree with his way of interpreting this verse? Why, or why not?

BT11: Hebrews 10:26-27 states: "If we deliberately keep on sinning after we have received the knowledge of the truth, no sacrifice for sins is left, but only a fearful expectation of judgment and of raging fire that will consume the enemies of God." A person comes to you extremely depressed. A week ago she willfully and deliberately stole some merchandise from a local store, and now on the basis of the above verses believes that there is no possibility of repentance and forgiveness. How would you counsel her?

BT12: A favorite verse used in Christmas carols and some sympathy cards is Isaiah 26:3 ("Thou dost keep him in perfect peace whose mind is stayed on thee," RSV). Are these valid uses of this Scripture?

BT13: A person comes to you at the request of her husband. She says she has had a vision that instructed her to leave her husband and family and go to Bulgaria as a missionary. Her husband has tried to reason with her that this vision must have some other explanation than being sent from God since: (1) her children and husband need her, (2) God has not given the rest of the family a similar call, (3) she has no financial support, and (4) the mission boards to whom she has applied have not accepted her. Her continuing response to all this is to quote Proverbs 3:5-6 ("Trust in the Lord with all

5. David Augsburger, *Caring Enough to Confront* (Glendale: Regal, 1974), p. 32.

your heart and lean not on your own understanding; in all your ways acknowledge him, and he will make your paths straight"). How would you
counsel her, particularly regarding this verse, since it seems to be a mainstay
of her obsession?

BT 14: You have just finished telling someone that you do not agree with the
oracular use of Scripture (consulting the Bible by opening it and applying
the first words one reads as God's instructions to him), because it generally
interprets words without regard to their context. This person argues that God
has often used just this method to bring him comfort and guidance. How
would you reply?

chapter four

Lexical-Syntactical Analysis

When this chapter is completed, you should be able to:

1. Identify two major reasons why lexical-syntactical analysis is important.
2. Recall seven steps involved in lexical-syntactical analysis.
3. Identify three methods of determining the meanings of ancient words, and compare the validity of each method.
4. Recall five methods of determining which one of the several possible meanings of a word was actually intended by an author in a given context.
5. Identify and describe the three major types of parallelism found in Hebrew poetry.
6. Explain the difference between verbal parallels and real parallels.
7. Define the following terms: lexical-syntactical analysis, syntax, lexicology, denotation, connotation, and figures of speech.
8. Explain the usage of and be able to use the following lexical tools:
   a. Hebrew, Greek, and English concordances
   b. Lexicons
   c. Theological wordbooks
   d. Bullinger's *Figures of Speech Used in the Bible*
   e. Interlinear Bibles
   f. Analytical lexicons
   g. Hebrew and Greek grammars

93

Definition and Presuppositions

Lexical-syntactical analysis is the study of the meaning of individual words (lexicology) and the way those words are combined (syntax), in order to determine more accurately the author's intended meaning.

Lexical-syntactical analysis does not encourage blind literalism: it recognizes when an author intends his words to be understood literally, when figuratively, and when symbolically, and then interprets them accordingly. Thus when Jesus said "I am the door," "I am the vine," and "I am the bread of life," we understand these expressions to be metaphors, as He intended. When He said "Be on your guard against the yeast of the Pharisees and Sadducees" He intended *yeast* to be symbolic of the teaching of those groups (Matt. 16:5-12). When He said to the paralytic, "Get up, take your mat and go home," He expected the paralyzed man to literally obey His command, which the man did (Matt. 9:6-7).

Lexical-syntactical analysis is founded on the premise that, although words may take on a variety of meanings in different contexts, they have but one intended meaning in any given context. Thus, if I were to say "He is green," those words might mean that (1) he is inexperienced, or (2) he looks sick, or (3) he is envious. Although my words could mean any of these three things, the context usually will indicate which of these ideas I wish to communicate. Lexical-syntactical analysis helps the interpreter determine the variety of meanings that a word or group of words might possess, and then make a probability statement that meaning X is more likely than meaning Y or Z to be the author's intention in this specific passage.

The Need for Lexical-Syntactical Analysis

The need for this type of analysis is shown in the following quotations from two well-known theologians. Alexander Carson has aptly said:

No man has a right to say, as some are in the habit of saying, "The Spirit tells me that such or such is the meaning of a passage." How is he assured that it is the Holy Spirit, and not a spirit of delusion, except from the evidence that the interpretation is the legitimate meaning of the words?"[1]

John A. Broadus, a famed commentator, notes:

It is a mournful fact that Universalists . . . [and] Mormons can find an apparent support for their heresies in Scripture, without interpreting more loosely, without doing greater violence to the meaning and connection of the Sacred Text than is sometimes done by orthodox, devout, and even intelligent men.[2]

Lexical-syntactical analysis is needed because without it (1) we have no valid assurance that our interpretation is the meaning God intended to convey, and (2) we have no grounds for saying that our interpretations of Scripture are more valid than those of heretical groups.

Steps in Lexical-Syntactical Analysis

Lexical-syntactical analysis is sometimes difficult, but it often yields exciting and meaningful results. In order to make this complex process somewhat easier to understand, it has been operationalized into a seven-step procedure:

1. *Identify the general literary form.* The literary form an author uses (prose, poetry, etc.) influences the way he intends his words to be understood.

1. Alexander Carson, *Examination of the Principles of Biblical Interpretation.* Cited in Ramm, *Protestant Biblical Interpretation*, p. x-xi.
2. John A. Broadus, *A Treatise on the Preparation and Delivery of Sermons* (30th edition).

2. *Trace the development of the author's theme and show how the passage under consideration fits into the context.* This step, already begun as part of contextual analysis, gives a necessary perspective for determining the meaning of words and syntax.

3. *Identify the natural divisions of the text.* The main conceptual units and transitional statements reveal the author's thought process and therefore make his meaning clearer.

4. *Identify the connecting words within the paragraphs and sentences.* Connecting words (conjunctions, prepositions, relative pronouns) show the relationship between two or more thoughts.

5. *Determine what the individual words mean.* Any word that survives long in a language begins to take on a variety of meanings. Thus it is necessary to identify the various possible meanings of ancient words, and then to determine which of the several possible meanings is the one the author intended to convey in a specific context.

6. *Analyze the syntax.* The relationship of words to one another is expressed through their grammatical forms and arrangement.

7. *Put the results of your lexical-syntactical analysis into nontechnical, easily understood words that clearly convey the author's meaning to the English reader.*

The General Literary Form

The literary form of a writing influences the way an author meant it to be interpreted. A writer composing poetry does not use words in the same way that he does when writing prose. This fact takes on significance when we recognize that *one-third* of the Old Testament is written in the form of Hebrew poetry. To interpret these passages as if they were prose, a practice which has often been done, is to misinterpret their meaning.

For purposes of our analysis at this point, it is sufficient to speak of three general literary forms—prose, poetry, and apocalyptic literature. Apocalyptic writing, found most obviously in the visionary passages of Daniel and Revelation, frequently contains words used symbolically. Prose and poetry use words in literal and figurative ways: in prose the literal usage predominates; in poetry figurative language is used most often.

Discriminating between Hebrew poetry and prose is difficult for the English reader, particularly since Hebrew poetry is characterized by rhythm of ideas rather than rhythm of sound. (More about this later in the chapter.) For this reason the newer translations place poetry in verse form so that it can be distinguished easily from prose, a format which provides an important interpretive advantage over older translations.

Development of the Author's Theme

This step, already begun as part of contextual analysis, is important for two reasons. First, the context is the best source of data for determining which of several possible meanings of a word is the meaning the author intended. Second, unless a passage is put into the perspective of its context there is always the danger of becoming so involved in the technicalities of a grammatical analysis that one loses sight of the primary idea(s) the words actually convey.

The Natural Divisions of the Text

The verse and chapter divisions which are so much a part of our thinking today were not an original part of the Scriptures; these divisions were added many centuries after the Bible was written, as an aid in locating passages for easy reference. Although verse divisions serve this purpose well, the standard verse-by-verse division of the text has the distinct disadvantage of dividing the author's thoughts unnaturally.

In modern prose style we are accustomed to the division of thoughts into conceptual units through the use of sentences and paragraphs. The first sentence in a paragraph serves either as a transition from one concept to the next or as a thesis which is elaborated in subsequent sentences. Since we are accustomed to understanding written concepts in this way, several of the newer translations have retained the verse numberings but placed the ideas in sentence and paragraph structure, making it easier for the modern reader to follow the flow of the author's conceptual process.

Connecting Words Within the Paragraphs and Sentences

Connecting words, including conjunctions, prepositions, relative pronouns, etc., often aid in following the author's progression of thought. When a relative pronoun is used, it is important to ask, "What is the noun being discussed?" A "therefore" often provides the connecting link between a theoretical argument and the practical applications of that argument.

By way of illustration, Galatians 5:1 says: "Stand fast therefore, and do not submit again to a yoke of slavery" (RSV). Taken by itself the verse could have any one of several meanings: it could refer to human slavery, political slavery, slavery to sin, etc. The "therefore" indicates, however, that this verse is an application of a point Paul had made in the previous chapter. A reading of Paul's arguments (Gal. 3:1–4:30) and his conclusion (4:31) clarifies the meaning of the formerly ambiguous 5:1. Paul is encouraging the Galatians not to become enslaved again to the bonds of legalism (i.e., trying to win salvation through good works).

Word Meanings

Most words that survive long in a language acquire many denotations (specific meanings) and connotations (additional implications). Besides their specific meanings, words often have a variety of popular denotations, i.e., usages found in ordinary conversation. Consider a few of the popular designations of the word *done*.

"I'm done"—meaning "I've completed some work."
"I'm done in"—meaning "I'm completely tired out."
"The cake is done"—meaning "The cake is thoroughly baked."

Words or phrases may have both popular and technical denotations. The phrase "foot-and-mouth disease," for example, has one meaning when used as a medical term and a very different meaning when used popularly.

Literal denotations may eventually lead to metaphoric denotations. When used literally, green designates a color; used metaphorically, its meaning can be extended from the literal color of an unripe apple to the idea of an immature, or inexperienced person.

Words also have connotations, implied emotional meanings not explicitly stated. To say that someone is incorrigible does not have the same connotation as to say that he has the courage of his convictions. Incorrigibility carries with it an unstated (but deniably present) negative connotation; to have the courage of one's convictions has a more positive, or at least a neutral, connotation.

A word that has more than one denotation may also have more than one connotation. When green is used as a color, it has relatively neutral connotations for most people; when used metaphorically, it has a pejorative cast to it.

Methods of Discovering the Denotations of Ancient Words

To discover the variety of meanings a word may have, three methods are commonly used. The first method is to study the ways a word was used in other ancient literature—secular literature, the Septuagint (the Greek translation of the Old Testament made before the time of Christ), and other biblical writings by the same or a different author.

The second method is to study synonyms, looking for points of comparison as well as contrast. Earlier students of lexicology often drew up fairly rigid distinctions between words that had similar but not exactly equivalent meaning. The trend today seems to be toward suggesting that some synonyms generally had certain shadings of meaning which contrast with the general usage of other words. For example, two of the Greek words for love (*agapao* and *phileo*) generally do have distinctive meanings (e.g., Jn. 21:15-17); however, they occasionally also appear to have been used as synonyms (Mt. 23:6; 10:37; Lk. 11:43; 20:46).

The third method for determining word meanings is to study etymology—considering the meaning of the historical roots of the word. Extensive etymological studies are used less frequently today than previously because of two disadvantages: (1) the historical roots of words are often conjectural, and (2) the meanings of words often change radically with the passage of time, so that little or no apparent connection remains between the original meaning of the root word and its meaning a few hundred years later.

Several examples from the English language illustrates this change. The English word *enthusiasm* originally meant "possessed by a god" and was so used until the early 1800s. When I pick a dandelion from my lawn I am not literally picking a "lion's tooth," although this is the meaning of the French phrase (*dent de lion*) from which the word is derived. When I describe someone as nice I do not mean that he is ignorant, even though this is the meaning of the Latin word *nescius* from which the word *nice* has developed.

Thus an author may have had no intention of conveying the meaning that a word possessed two hundred years prior to his time; in fact, he probably was unaware of these former denotations. Hence an exegesis that depends heavily on etymological derivations possesses questionable validity; as a result, etymological derivations are used less than in previous centuries.

A related expository method that is even less valid hermeneutically than expositions based on etymological derivations of Hebrew or Greek words are expositions based on etymological discussions of the English words into which those Greek or Hebrew words have been translated. For example, one occasionally hears a sermon on a text that includes the word *holy* in which the preacher does an etymological exposition of the *Anglo-Saxon roots* of the word *holy.* Similar expositions are sometimes done with the word *dunamis* and its historical connections with our English word *dynamite.* Obviously, such expositions have very dubious validity because, interesting though they may be, they often import meaning onto the text which the author did not intend. The most valid method of determining word meanings is to discover the various denotations a word possessed at the time it was used by the writer.

Several kinds of lexical tools are available which enable the modern student of Scripture to ascertain the various possible meanings of ancient words. While a knowledge of Hebrew and Greek certainly enhances one's ability to do word studies, an increasing number of these lexical tools are being keyed numerically to *Strong's Exhaustive Concordance,* making it possible for the person who has no knowledge of Hebrew or Greek (or whose knowledge is "rusty") to do word studies in these languages. The most important kinds of lexical tools are described below.

Concordances. A concordance contains a listing of all the times a given word is used in Scripture. To examine the various ways a given Hebrew or Greek word was used, consult a Hebrew or Greek concordance, which lists all the passages in which the word appears.

An English concordance lists all the passages in which various Hebrew and Greek words were translated into a given

English word. For example, *Strong's Exhaustive Concordance* shows us that the word *peace* occurs more than four hundred times in our English Bibles, and lists each reference. By use of a numbering system, it also identifies the various Hebrew and Greek words which are translated into our English word *peace* (there are ten Hebrew words and six Greek words). With the use of Strong's numbering system it is a relatively simple matter to turn to the back of the concordance and find the Hebrew or Greek root word used in any particular passage. The back of the concordance also includes brief definitions of the meaning of each Hebrew and Greek word.

English, Hebrew, and Greek concordances can be used together to do word studies. For example, if you wished to study a particular kind of *fear* found in a given passage, you could use *Strong's* to identify the Hebrew or Greek root word. Using the same numbers from *Strong,* you could then go to the *Englishman's Hebrew and Chaldee Concordance* or the *Englishman's Greek-English Concordance* and find a listing of all the passages where that Hebrew or Greek word was used. By analyzing these passages, you could make your own conclusions about the exact denotation(s) of that word.

Lexicons. A lexicon is a dictionary of Hebrew or Greek words. Like an English dictionary, it lists the various denotations of each word found in it. Many lexicons survey the usage of words in both secular and biblical literature, giving specific examples. Words are often listed in Hebrew and Greek alphabetical order, so it is helpful to know the Hebrew and Greek alphabets in order to use these tools.

Two of the most widely used Hebrew lexicons are:

Brown, Driver, and Briggs. *A Hebrew and English Lexicon of the Old Testament.*

Gesenius. *Hebrew and Chaldee Lexicon to the Old Testament.*

Widely used Greek lexicons include:

Bauer. *A Greek-English Lexicon of the New Testament and Other Early Christian Literature.* Translated and edited by Arndt and Gingrich.

Moulton and Milligan. *The Vocabulary of the Greek Testament: Illustrated from the Papyri and Other Non-Literary Sources.*

Thayer. *Greek-English Lexicon of the New Testament.*

Recent editions of some of these works are so constructed that the person with little or no Hebrew or Greek can use them. Recent editions of both Gesenius's and Thayer's lexicons are keyed to the numbering system found in *Strong's Exhaustive Concordance.* An Index to Bauer's lexicon, in a separate volume by John R. Alsop, makes it readily usable by someone with a knowledge of the Greek alphabet.

Midway between an English dictionary and a Greek lexicon are E. W. Bullinger's *Critical Lexicon and Concordance* and W. E. Vine's *Expository Dictionary of New Testament Words.* These volumes list English words (in English alphabetical order) and beneath each word list the various Greek words translated into that particular English word. With each Greek word is a short definition of its meaning. Both of these volumes are easily used with little or no knowledge of Greek.

Those interested in the study of synonyms will find R. B. Girdlestone's *Synonyms of the Old Testament* and R. C. Trench's *Synonyms of the New Testament* helpful. Both books were originally published in the late 1800s and therefore do not include information from recent archeological discoveries; nevertheless they remain in wide use.

Theological Wordbooks. These books give more extensive definitions of words than are found in lexicons or books of synonyms. The most well-known is the ten volume *Theological Dictionary of the New Testament* (TDNT), edited by Kittel and Friedrich. This monumental work provides an extensive examination of the usages of important Greek New Testament words. A typical article will discuss the role of that word in (1) secular Greek sources, (2) the Old Testament, (3) Philo,

Josephus, pseudepigraphical and rabbinical literature, (4) the various New Testament books, and (5) the apostolic fathers.

While this dictionary will probably remain the standard reference work for academic theologians, there are a number of disadvantages of TDNT for the average pastor or evangelical Christian who wishes to do word studies. First, the frequent appearance of Hebrew and Greek words in the text makes TDNT difficult reading for those who are not familiar with these languages. Second, the entries are extensive (fifteen or more pages on many important words) and often do not include summaries that would help put the discussion into perspective. Third, the theological position of its authors varies considerably, and the influence of liberal presuppositions on some of the articles is significant. Fourth, the price of this ten-volume set places it beyond the reach of many students of Scripture.

The *New International Dictionary of New Testament Theology,* edited by Colin Brown, is a three-volume reference work that gives word studies midway between the concise definitions of a lexicon and the very extensive discussions of the TDNT. The articles are scholarly and up-to-date, and appear generally to be written by orthodox theologians. Frequent references and summaries from TDNT are made. Most of the text is in English and in regular-sized print (in contrast to the small print in TDNT). The average length of a word discussion is three to five pages; the total price of the three-volume set is approximately one-third the price of TDNT. For these reasons the *New International Dictionary* set probably represents a more usable tool for the average pastor and student of Scripture than does TDNT.

Methods of Discovering the Denotation Intended in a Specific Context

Having discovered the variety of meanings a word possessed in its contemporary culture, the next major task is to ascertain which of those denotations the author intended when he used the word in the passage under study.

An objection occasionally voiced is that the author may have intended more than one denotation simultaneously, and that therefore he was communicating a variety of meanings concurrently. However, personal introspection reveals that the simultaneous use of more than one denotation of a word runs counter to all normal communication (with the exception of puns, which are humorous precisely because they do use words in two senses simultaneously). Also, if we press words in all their denotations, we soon produce heretical exegesis. For example, the Greek word *sarx* may have these meanings:

- the solid part of the body excepting bones (1 Cor. 15:39)
- the whole substance of the body (Acts 2:26)
- the sensuous nature of man (Col. 2:18)
- human nature as dominated by sinful desires (Rom. 7:18)

Although this is only a partial list of its denotations, we can see that if all these meanings were applied to the word as it is found in John 6:53, where Christ talks about His own flesh, the interpreter would be attributing sin to Christ.

Optional BT: If you are still not convinced that words should not be understood in all their denotations in each context, try the following exercise:

Write out a three-sentence communication similar to statements you normally make. Then, using a regular dictionary, write out each of the denotations for the nouns, verbs, adjectives, and adverbs you used in these three sentences. Combine those various denotations in all their possible arrangements and write out the resulting sentences. Is the meaning expressed in your first three sentences the same as the meaning expressed by all the combinations?

There are several methods for discerning the specific denotations intended by an author in a particular context:

First, look at definitions or explanatory phrases that the authors themselves give. For example, 2 Timothy 3:16-17 states that the Word of God was given so that "the man of God might be *perfect*" (KJV). What does the author mean by "perfect" here? Does he mean sinless? Incapable of error? Incapable of error or sin in some specific area? The best answer is supplied by his own explanatory phrases immediately following—"that the man of God may be perfect, throughly furnished unto all good works." In this context Paul meant for this word, translated into our language as *perfect*, to convey the idea of being thoroughly equipped for godly living.

Similarly the author of Hebrews says in 5:14, "But strong meat belongeth to them that are perfect" (KJV). Again the author makes his intention clear with an explanatory phrase immediately following: "But strong meat belongeth to them that are perfect, even those who by reason of use have their senses exercised to discern both good and evil." Here the word means *mature,* and refers to those "who by constant use have trained themselves to distinguish good from evil." (NIV) Thus the author's own explanatory phrases often serve as an important way of ascertaining his intended denotation.

Second, the subject and predicate of a sentence may mutually explain each other. For example, the Greek word *moranthei* found in Matthew 5:13 can mean either "to become foolish," or "to become insipid." How do we determine the intended denotation? In this instance the subject of the sentence is *salt,* and so the second denotation ("if the salt has lost its savor") is selected as the correct one.

Third, look at parallelism if it occurs within the passage. As mentioned earlier, one-third of the Old Testament (and some of the New Testament) is poetry. Hebrew poetry is characterized by parallelism, a feature which may shed light on the meaning of words that are in question.

Hebrew parallelism can be categorized into three basic types: synonymous, antithetic, and synthetic. In *synonymous parallel-*

ism the second line of a stanza repeats the content of the first, but in different words. Psalm 103:10 is an example:

> He does not treat us as our sins deserve
> > or repay us according to our iniquities.

In *antithetic parallelism* the idea of the second line sharply contrasts with that of the first line. Psalm 37:21 provides an example:

> The wicked borrow and do not repay
> > but the righteous give generously.

In *synthetic parallelism* the second line carries further or completes the idea of the first line. Psalm 14:2 is an example:

> The Lord looks down from heaven on the sons of men
> > to see if there are any who understand,
> > > any who seek God.

Thus, if a passage is poetry, recognition of the type of parallelism employed may give clues to the meaning of the word in question.

Fourth, determine if the word is being used as part of a figure of speech. Sometimes words or phrases are used in ways which deviate from simple, normal speech in order to produce a fanciful or vivid impression. Such phrases are often called figures of speech, and are intended to have a meaning different from the literal. If a figure persists and becomes widely accepted within a culture it is called an idiom. Some English examples of figures of speech or idioms are:

> His eyes were bigger than his stomach.
> This fog is as thick as pea soup.
> I'm broke.
> The White House said . . .

We'll hit Athens about 2 P.M.

The thermometer is going up.

The furnace has gone out.

She made the cake from scratch.

Take a bus.

I'd better get off the phone so I don't tie up the line.

Figures of speech, as can be seen from the above list, are ubiquitous—we use them frequently in everyday speech, as did the biblical authors. In addition, figures of speech convey a definite meaning just as surely as do literal usages. To say that something is a figure of speech does not imply that the meaning of the phrase is ambiguous. Figures of speech convey a single intended meaning just as other speech does.

An interpretation of a figure of speech using the normal denotations of a word will usually result in a radical misunderstanding of the author's intended meaning. For example, if I were to interpret literally the phrases "his eyes were bigger than his stomach" or "it's raining cats and dogs," I would seriously misinterpret the meaning of these phrases. For this reason, those who proudly boast that they believe everything in the Bible literally (if by this they mean that they fail to recognize figures of speech and special features of poetry and prophecy) may be doing a disservice to the very Scripture they respect so highly.

Figures of speech are common in the biblical text. A good procedure to follow whenever doing an in-depth study of a passage is to consult Bullinger's *Figures of Speech Used in the Bible*. Index III of Bullinger's book will indicate whether or not there are any figures of speech in a passage, and will provide appropriate explanations of them. Bullinger's book must be used with discretion (it represents his personal judgments and knowledge of Hebrew and Greek figures of speech), but it does provide a large amount of important and useful information.

Fifth, study parallel passages. In order to understand the meaning of an obscure word or phrase, look for additional data in clearer parallel passages. It is important, though, to distinguish between verbal parallels and real parallels. Verbal parallels are those which use similar words but refer to different concepts. The concept of God's Word as a sword, found in Hebrews 4 and Ephesians 6, is an example of a verbal, but not a real, parallel. Hebrews 4 speaks of the Bible's function as a divider which differentiates between those who are truly obedient to its message and those who profess obedience but inwardly remain disobedient. In Ephesians 6, Paul also speaks of the Bible-as-a-sword, but in this instance refers to it as a defensive weapon to be used against the temptations of Satan (v. 11). (Christ used the Word in this way when Satan tempted Him in the desert.)

Real parallels, in contrast, are those which speak of the same concept or same event. They may use different words, and frequently add additional data not found in the passage under study. The marginal references found in most Bibles are designed to yield real parallels, although occasionally such parallels seem to be more verbal than real. A careful examination of the context is the best indicator of whether the passages are verbal or real parallels.

In summary, five ways of ascertaining the specific intended denotation of a word in a given passage are: (1) Look at definitions or explanatory phrases that the author gives; (2) use the subject and predicate to explain each other; (3) look at parallelism if it occurs in the passage; (4) determine if the word or phrase was intended as a figure of speech; and (5) study parallel passages.

Syntax

Syntax deals with the way thoughts are expressed through grammatical forms. Each language has its own structure, and one of the problems that makes learning another language so difficult is that the learner must master not only the word definitions and pronunciations of the new language, but also new ways of arranging and showing the relationship of one word to another.

English is an analytic language: word order is a guide to meaning. For example, nouns normally precede verbs, which normally precede direct objects or predicate adjectives. We say "the tree is green" rather than some other combination of those words. Hebrew is also an analytic language, but less so than English. Greek, in contrast, is a synthetic language: meaning is understood only partially by word order and much more by word-endings or case-endings.[3]

There are several tools that are helpful in discovering what information syntax can contribute to your understanding of the meaning of a passage.

Interlinear Bibles. These Bibles contain the Hebrew or Greek text with the English translation printed between the lines (hence the name *interlinear*). By juxtaposing the two sets of words, they enable you to identify easily the Greek or Hebrew word(s) which you wish to study further. (Those more proficient in Hebrew and Greek can, of course, go directly to the Hebrew or Greek texts rather than to interlinears.)

Analytical Lexicons. Many times the word you encounter in the text is some variation of the root form of the word. For example, in English you might encounter various forms of the verb *to speak:*

spoke

spake

had spoken

will speak

will have spoken

3. Bernard Ramm, *Protestant Biblical Interpretation*, 3rd rev. ed. (Grand Rapids: Baker, 1970), p. 136.

Nouns likewise may take on different forms and play different roles within sentences.

An analytical lexicon does two primary things: (1) it identifies the root word of which the word in the text is a variation, and (2) it identifies which part of speech the variation is. For example, if the word you wished to study was the Greek word *thumon,* by looking in an analytical Greek lexicon you would find that this is the accusative singular of the word *thumos,* which means "anger" or "wrath."

Hebrew and Greek Grammars. If you are unfamiliar with the meaning of the term "accusative singular" to describe the form of a word, a third set of syntactical aids will be valuable. Hebrew and Greek grammars explain the various forms that words can take in their respective languages, and the meaning of the words when they appear in one of these forms. Well-respected Hebrew grammars include Gesenius's *Hebrew Grammar* and J. Weingreen's *Practical Grammar for Classical Hebrew.* Greek grammars include A. T. Robertson's *Grammar of the Greek New Testament in the Light of Historical Research* and Blass and Debrunner's *Greek Grammar of the New Testament and Other Early Christian Literature.* Most seminary courses in exegesis will describe the above processes in much more detail.

It is important to know how to go through the above process when there is need to do so. However, much of this work has already been done and compiled. For example, exegetical commentaries such as A. T. Robertson's *Word Pictures in the New Testament* do lexical-syntactical analyses of nearly every important word and phrase in the New Testament. Expository commentaries, such as the *Tyndale New Testament Commentaries,* attempt to do both a historical-cultural/contextual analysis and a lexical-syntactical analysis.

Restatement

Put the results of your lexical-syntactical analysis into non-technical, easily understood words that clearly convey the author's intended meaning to the English reader. There is always the danger in lexical-syntactical analysis of becoming so involved with technical details (e.g., Bullinger's technical names or grammatical case names) that we lose sight of the *purpose of the analysis,* namely, to communicate the author's meaning as clearly as possible. There is also the temptation to impress others with our erudition and profound exegetical abilities. People need to be fed, not impressed. Technical study needs to be done as part of any exegesis, but it should be part of the *preparation* for exposition: the majority of it need not appear in the product (except in the case of academic or technical theological papers).[4]

Laborious technical discussions often succeed only in putting an audience to sleep. A good exposition is easily recognized, not by its massive technical discussions, but because it "rings true"—the audience senses that it fits naturally into its context—and because it represents an exposition of the original writer's ideas rather than those of the interpreter.

Chapter Summary

The following seven steps have been suggested for doing a lexical-syntactical analysis:

1. Identify the general literary form.
2. Trace the development of the author's theme and show how the passage under consideration fits into the context.

---

4. When technical documentation is necessary in written material, it can be inserted as a footnote to avoid distracting the reader from the exposition. However, Hebrew or Greek words can be introduced into a written text by transliteration. Transliteration involves transforming a Hebrew or Greek word into English letters which have the same sound as the original word. Transliteration can be done easily by anyone who knows the sounds of the Hebrew and Greek letters. Transliterations of all Hebrew and Greek words in Scripture can be found in the back of *Strong's Exhaustive Concordance.* When a transliterated word is included in a written text it is usually underlined or placed in italics.

3. Identify the natural divisions (paragraphs and sentences) of the text.
4. Identify the connecting words within the paragraphs and sentences and show how they aid in understanding the author's progression of thought.
5. Determine what the individual words mean.
   a. Identify the multiple meanings a word possessed in its time and culture.
   b. Determine the single meaning intended by the author in a given context.
6. Analyze the syntax to show how it contributes to the understanding of a passage.
7. Put the results of your analysis into nontechnical, easily understood words that clearly convey the author's intended meaning to the English reader.

Exercises

(Note: these exercises, and the ones in following chapters, incorporate hermeneutical skills learned in all previous chapters.)

BT 15: A pastor preached a sermon using 1 Corinthians 11:29 as a pre-communion text. He interpreted the phrase "not discerning the Lord's body" (KJV) as a reference to Christ's body, the church. His message from the text was that we are not to partake of communion when we have unresolved negative feelings toward a brother or sister, because to do so would be to eat and drink without "discerning the Lord's body." Is this a valid use of this text?

BT 16: A devout young Christian became actively involved in the charismatic movement. Within this movement he was exposed to several powerful speakers who taught that every Spirit-filled Christian should possess all the spiritual gifts (glossolalia, interpretation of tongues, prophecy, healing, etc.). He prayed earnestly that God would give him these gifts so that he might be a more effective Christian. Even after several months, however, he still had not received some of them, and became angry and bitter toward God. Use your hermeneutical skills to analyze 1 Corinthians 12, and then outline the scriptural teachings of this passage that you would use in counseling with this person.

BT17: Most people assume that the girl spoken of in Matthew 9:18-26 was dead, but there is some reason to believe that she was comatose rather than dead.

   a. What lexical-syntactical factors would you consider as you attempt to answer this question?
   b. What factors suggest that she was dead? Evaluate the strength of these factors.
   c. What factors suggest that she was comatose rather than dead? Evaluate the strength of these factors.
   d. Do you think she was comatose or dead?

BT18: A great deal of discussion by Christians on the topic of anger has been based on Ephesians 4:26: ("Be angry . . ." NASB). Analyze the meaning of this verse and discuss whether or not it supports the positive view of human anger normally drawn from it.

BT19: In Matthew 5:22, Jesus says that one who calls a brother a fool is in danger of hell-fire, yet He calls the Pharisees fools in Matthew 23:17-19. How do you explain this apparent contradiction?

BT20: There has been much discussion concerning the nature of "worldly" (neurotic?) versus "godly" guilt (2 Cor. 7:10) among Christian psychologists. Applying your knowledge of hermeneutics to this particular text, differentiate the two as best you can.

BT21: Some Christian groups maintain a very strong stand on the issue that Creation took six literal 24-hour periods, believing that to do otherwise suggests a less-than-faithful adherence to the biblical record. Do a word study of the Hebrew word for *day (yom)* as used in the early chapters of Genesis, and state the conclusions. What does your word study indicate regarding the question of whether Creation occurred in six days or six periods of unspecified duration?

BT22: A well-known Christian psychologist in a Christian psychological journal published an article based on the thesis that since man is created in the image of God, we can learn about God by studying man. Two years later he published a second article using the thesis that since man is created in the image of God, we can learn about man by studying God. Do you agree with his theses? Why, or why not?

BT23: Using Romans 9:13 as a text ("Jacob I loved, but Esau I hated"), a well-known Bible teacher proceeded to do an analysis of these two brothers to show why God hated one and loved the other. Is this a valid use of this text? Why, or why not?

BT24: A Christian student was studying the psychological effects of conversion. In his study of 2 Corinthians 5:17 ("If anyone is in Christ, he is a new creation"), he looked up other biblical usages of the word *creation (ktisis)* and found that this word is almost always used of the creation of the world, implying the creation of something out of nothing (*ex nihilo*). If this is so, he reasoned, the psychological characteristics of the new Christian are something new that did not exist before. However, in studying the psychological literature he could find no evidence of a new personality dimension in Christians that is not present in non-Christians. (There does seem to be in some cases a reorganization of the preexisting personality patterns, but no newly created personality dimension has been detected.) How would you help him reconcile the psychological data with his understanding of 2 Corinthians 5:17?

BT25: There is much discussion today among Christians about whether Scripture speaks of man as trichotomous (three parts — body, soul, and spirit), dichotomous (two parts — body and soul-spirit), or holistic (a unit — with body, soul, and spirit as different aspects, different ways of viewing that total unit). What are the hermeneutical principle(s) that should be applied when attempting to resolve this question?

chapter five

Theological Analysis

After completing this chapter, you should be able to:

1. Identify five steps in the process called theological analysis.
2. Define the following terms:
   a. Theological analysis
   b. Analogy of Scripture
   c. Analogy of faith
3. Identify five major positions on the nature of God's relationship to man, and summarize each in a few sentences.
4. State a personal position on the nature of the divine-human relationship, summarizing the reasons for your decision in one or two pages.

Two Basic Questions

The basic question asked in theological analysis is "How does this passage fit into the total pattern of God's revelation?" It immediately becomes evident that another question must first be answered, namely, "What *is* the pattern of God's revelation?" This prior question is so important (and so infrequently asked) that the greater part of this chapter will be spent discussing it. Once the pattern of divine revelation has been dealt with, the question of how a particular passage fits into that total pattern becomes much easier to answer.

There are a number of theories regarding the best way to conceptualize the nature of God's relationship to man. Within salvation history (defined in this book as the history of God's saving work for humanity), some theories see significant discontinuity; others stress the continuity within salvation history. Probably most lay dispensationalists (but not necessarily dispensational theologians) view the nature of God's relationship to man as basically discontinuous, with a secondary emphasis on continuity; most covenantal theologians view the divine-human relationship as primarily continuous, with a minimal emphasis on discontinuity.

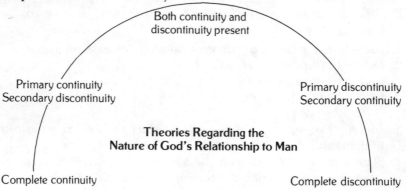

Both continuity and
discontinuity present

Primary continuity
Secondary discontinuity

Primary discontinuity
Secondary continuity

**Theories Regarding the
Nature of God's Relationship to Man**

Complete continuity

Complete discontinuity

Hypotheses about the pattern of God's relationship to man are necessary, for they provide an organizational framework around which the biblical data can be understood. Without some sort of organizing principle, the bulk of data would be too great to comprehend. However, there are at least two major dangers in accepting a certain system or hypothesis about the nature of divine revelation. First, there is the danger of imposing one's own system *onto* the biblical data rather than deriving the system *from* the data. F. F. Bruce has cautioned:

> There is a great danger, when once we have adhered to one particular school of thought or adopted one particular system of theology, of reading the Bible in the light of that school or system and finding its distinctive features in what we read.[1]

A second and perhaps even greater danger is that of accepting a theory about the pattern of divine revelation without even recognizing it as a theory, or without looking at other theories to see which theory fits the data best. Quite frequently, for example, those who have been taught in a church that adopts one of these positions is not aware that the position is a theory or that there are other ways of organizing the biblical data.

The first part of this chapter presents five of the most common conceptual systems that have been proposed to explain the nature of God's relationship to man. Following this is a recommendation; a methodology for deciding whether God's methods of dealing with man have been primarily continuous or discontinuous. The final part of the chapter identifies the steps and principles with which to do theological analysis.

The Relevance of the Continuity-Discontinuity Issue

Chapter 3 emphasized the importance of ascertaining the recipient of a given passage or command. Those who understand salvation history as primarily continuous generally view all Scripture as relevant for the believer today, since they see a basic unity between themselves and believers throughout

---

1. F. F. Bruce, "Foreword," in *God's Strategy in Human History*, ed. R. Forster and V. Marston (Wheaton: Tyndale, 1973), p. vii.

Old and New Testament history. Those who see salvation history as primarily discontinuous tend to consider that only the Book of Acts and the Church Epistles possess primary relevance for the church today, since the remainder of Scripture was directed to people who were under a different biblical economy.[2] Since the Epistles comprise only 10 percent of the Bible, the issue of whether the remaining 90 percent possesses primary relevance to contemporary believers is one of paramount importance.

Many significant theological issues, as well as many significant Christian counseling issues, are also affected by the way one resolves this question. Specific examples of the effect of this question on Christian counseling theory are found in two recent well-known books. Bruce Narramore and William Counts' book, *Guilt and Freedom*, is based on the assumption that law and grace represent two antithetical systems of salvation. The book develops two contrasting psychologies concerning man's relationship to God based on these assumptions. Those who see the relationship between law and grace differently would have a correspondingly different view of the psychological implications of these biblical concepts. Dwight Small in his book, *The Right to Remarry*, postulates a discontinuity between the context in which Christ's commands on divorce were given and the present-day situation for believers. His conclusions on divorce, based on this postulate, are therefore significantly different from the conclusions of those who see a basic continuity between the contexts.

On a more general level, the attitude one takes toward the continuity-discontinuity issue significantly affects both Sunday school teaching and preaching. In contrast to the discontinuity theorists, those who believe there is a basic continuity between

2. Lewis Sperry Chafer, in *Dispensationalism*, (Dallas: Dallas Seminary Press, 1951) p. 34, states that the only Scriptures addressed specifically to Christian believers are the Gospel of John (particularly the Upper Room Discourse), the Book of Acts, and the Epistles.

the Old and New Testaments tend (1) to use the Old Testament more frequently in teaching and preaching, and (2) to find examples of Old Testament principles which possess continuing relevance for Christians today.

Other examples could be given, both in general theological issues as well as specific counseling issues, and the conclusion is inescapable: the way we resolve this question will have major implications for our own lives as well as for the lives we influence.

Representative Theoretical Systems

The "Theologies but No Theology" Model

Liberal theologians, as mentioned in earlier chapters, typically view Scripture as a product of the evolutionary development of Israel's religion. As Israel's religious consciousness became more sophisticated, so did its theology. Consequently, liberal theologians see in Scripture a variety of theologies—writings that reflect different levels of theological sophistication, sometimes conflicting with one another. Rather than viewing the Bible as God's truth revealed by God to man, they believe Scripture to be man's thoughts about God. Since men's thoughts changed over time, they believe that Scripture reveals a number of developing theological ideas and movements rather than any single, unified theology. As such, they tend to see biblical history as discontinuous, with a lesser emphasis on continuity (although no generalization is valid for every person within this group). E. W. Parson's book, *The Religion of the New Testament*, is an example of the application of this type of theory to the New Testament.

Dispensational Theory

Another theory that places primary emphasis on discontinuity and less emphasis on continuity, though for very different reasons than the "theologies but no theology" movement, is dispensational theory. Whereas liberal theologians see discontinuity in the biblical record as a reflection of man's struggles to understand God, dispensationalists are nearly always orthodox in their view of inspiration, believing that any discontinuity in the pattern of salvation history is there because God intended it to be there.

Dispensationalism is one of those theories that people seem either to "swear by" or "swear at"; few take a neutral position. It has been called "the key to rightly dividing the Scriptures"[3] and alternately "the most dangerous heresy currently to be found within Christian circles."[4]

A dispensation was defined by Scofield as "a period of time during which man is tested in respect of obedience to some *specific* revelation of the will of God."[5] The pattern of salvation history is seen as three regularly recurring steps: (1) God gives man a specific set of responsibilities or pattern for obedience, (2) man fails to live up to this set of responsibilities, and (3) God responds in mercy by giving a different set of responsibilities, i.e., a new dispensation.

Dispensationalists recognize between four and nine dispensations: the usual number is seven (or eight if the tribulation period is considered a separate dispensation). The following description of the seven dispensations, summarized from Charles C. Ryrie,[6] is typical, but there are many variations within this school.

Dispensation of Innocency or Freedom. This dispensation included the time Adam and Eve were in a state of innocency,

3. C. I. Scofield, *Rightly Dividing the Word of Truth* (Findlay, Ohio: Dunham, 1956).

4. John W. Bowman, "The Bible and Modern Religions, II. Dispensationalism," *Interpretation* 10 (April 1956): 172.

5. Scofield Reference Bible (New York: Oxford University Press, 1917), p. 5. Most contemporary dispensational writers stress the concept of various stewardship arrangements rather than time periods.

6. Charles C. Ryrie, *Dispensationalism Today* (Chicago: Moody Press, 1965), pp. 57-64.

before the fall, and terminated at the time they sinned through disobedience. It is described in Genesis 1:28–3:6.

Dispensation of Conscience. During this period "obedience to the dictates of conscience was man's chief stewardship responsibility." It ended as man became increasingly wicked and God brought judgment through the flood. This dispensation is described in Genesis 4:1–8:14.

Dispensation of Civil Government. During this dispensation God gave man the right to capital punishment, implying with it the right to develop human government. Instead of scattering and filling the earth, man expressed his rebellion by building the tower of Babel. God's judgment came through the confusion of languages. This period is described in Genesis 8:15–11:9.

Dispensation of Promise. This interval covered the time of the patriarchs and was given its name because of God's promise to Abraham of a land and of subsequent blessings. The disobedience of Jacob in leaving the land of promise and going to Egypt resulted in slavery. This period is described in Genesis 11:10–Exodus 18:27.

Dispensation of Mosaic Law. This period lasted from Moses until the death of Christ. During this time God gave commandments covering all phases of life and activity. Israel's failure to abide by these commandments led to division of the kingdom and to bondage. The dispensation of law is described in Exodus 18:28–Acts 1:26.

Dispensation of Grace. During this period (which includes the present) man's responsiblity is to accept God's gift of righteousness. This age will end with man's rejection of God's gracious gift, leading to the tribulation. The dispensation of grace is described in Acts 2:1–Revelation 19:21.

Dispensation of the Millennium. During the millennial kingdom, man's responsibility will be obedience to the personal rule of Christ. At the end of this period a final rebellion will break out and end in the final judgment. The best-known biblical passage describing this period is Revelation 20.

A display of dispensations as presented by Edwin Hartill, shown on pages 126–27, varies somewhat from the description of Ryrie's who does not consider the tribulation to be a separate dispensation. The two descriptions show the similarities as well as differences between various dispensational writers.

One of the points of difference is whether the dispensational regulations represent various means of salvation or various guidelines for obedient living *after* salvation. A common belief among dispensational laymen is that the dispensations of law and grace represent alternative means of salvation. This belief is based, in part, on some of the notes in the Scofield Reference Bible. For example, the note accompanying John 1:17 states:

> As a dispensation, grace begins with the death and resurrection of Christ (Rom. 3:24-26; 4:24, 25). The point of testing is no longer legal obedience as the *condition* of salvation, but acceptance or rejection of Christ, with good works as a fruit of salvation [emphasis added].

The majority of dispensational theologians, however, would probably agree with Ryrie's statement that

> The *basis* of salvation in every age is the death of Christ; the *requirement* for salvation in every age is faith; the *object* of faith in every age is God; the *content* of faith changes in the various dispensations [italics his].[7]

For the majority of dispensational theologians the primary change between dispensations is not in the means of salvation, but in the specifications for obedient living that follow a person's commitment to accept God's salvation.

Another point of disagreement, and often a fair amount of ambiguity, is the degree of relevance of commands given in

7. Ibid., p. 123.

one dispensation for believers in another dispensation. At one extreme would be Charles C. Cook's viewpoint:

> In the Old Testament there is not one sentence that applies to the Christian as a Rule of Faith and Practice— not a single command that is binding on him, as there is not a single promise there given him at first hand, except what is included in the broad flow of the Plan of Redemption as there taught in symbol and prophecy.[8]

Although a number of other dispensational writers have made similar statements, probably the majority of contemporary dispensational theologians see much more continuity between the dispensations than does Cook. H. P. Hook states: "Most theologians holding this [dispensational] position state that in the progress of revelation there is unfolded the will of God in various economies. Rather than being terminated as a principle they grow or evolve into the next economy."[9] In my view, one of the major challenges facing dispensationalism today is the development of a position which clearly specifies how the commands of a former dispensation apply to believers in a successive one. Clearly, if dispensational theory is correct, then it represents a powerful hermeneutical tool, and a crucial tool if one is to interpret biblical promises and commands rightly. On the other hand, if dispensational theory is incorrect, then the person who teaches such distinctions could be in serious jeopardy of bringing the judgments of Matthew 5:19 down on himself. The second section of this chapter presents biblical evidence that bears on this question.

For further reading on this important theory, the following six books contain much useful information. The first three are written by authors who agree with dispensational theory; the last three present critiques of this theory.

8. Charles C. Cook, *God's Book Speaking for Itself* (New York: Doran, 1924), p. 31.
9. H. P. Hook, "Dispensation," in *Zondervan Pictorial Encyclopedia of the Bible*, ed. Merrill Tenney (Grand Rapids: Zondervan, 1975), 2:144.

Chart of the Eight Dispensations

DESIGNATION	INNOCENCE	CONSCIENCE	HUMAN GOV'T.	PROMISE	LAW	GRACE	TRIBULATION	KINGDOM
CITATION	Gen. 1:26-28; 2:23	Gen. 3:8 & 23	Gen. 8:1	Gen. 12:1; Ex. 19:8.	Ex. 19:8	Jn. 1:17	Dan. 12:1 Jer. 30:7	Eph. 1:1
LIMITATION	Creation to fall	Fall of man to Flood	Flood to Tower of Babel.	Call of Abraham to Exodus.	Ex. to Cross. Sinai to Calvary.	Descent of H.S. to descent of Christ.	Ascent of Church to descent of Christ.	Descent of Christ to Great W. Throne.
DURATION	Unknown	1656 yrs.	427 yrs.	430 yrs.	1491 yrs.	1900 yrs.	7 yrs.	1000 yrs.
CONDITION	Man in innocence. Not ignorant.	In sin — Gen. 6:5, 6.	Noah now righteous leader. Man governing.	Idolatry and nation scattered.	Bondage to obedience and disobedience.	All the world guilty before God.	Intense suffering.	Living in Kingdom of Glory.
OBLIGATION	Not to eat of the tree of knowledge of good and evil.	Do good and choose right— Gen. 4:6, 7	Govern for God— Gen. 9:5, 6.	To stay in land of promise — Gen. 12:5.	To keep the law.	To accept Christ, believing.	Worship God & refuse to worship Beast.	To submit to the Son.
TRANSGRESSION	Disobeyed and ate. Lust of flesh, eyes, pride of life.	Did evil— Matt. 24:37, 38, 39.	Building Tower of Babel— Gen. 11:4.	Went into Egypt.	Failed to keep the law.	Failed to accept Christ.	Repented not. Worshiped Beast.	Feigned obedience.
CONDEMNATION	Curse on man—Gen. 3:14-19.	God destroyed flesh— Gen. 6:13.	Tongues confused— Gen. 11:7.	Slavery.	Division of No. & So. Kingdoms. I King 11:29-40.	Judgment & eternal damnation.	Battle of Armageddon. Destruction.	Fire devours them— Rev. 20:9.

CULMINATION	Expulsion from garden— Gen. 3:24.	Flood— 8 saved.	People scattered— Gen. 11:8.	In Egypt under Pharaoh.	Calvary. Christ fulfilled law.	Rapture of church from world.	Armageddon.	Cast into Lake of Fire.
PREDICTION	Promise of the Redeemer. Gen. 3:15.	Ark— salvation— Gen. 6:18. New Covenant with Noah.	Confusion in government.	Promise of seed thru Abraham. More definite now— Gen. 22:18.	Isa.9:6, 7. "For unto us a child is born."	I Thess. 4:16, 17.	Matt. 24:29-31.	New heavens and new earth.
CORRECTION OR INSTRUCTION	They would not be as God (as Satan said).	Conscience not sufficient to bring man to God.	No hope in human government.	God did not abandon world when He chose Abraham.	The law will not save.	Eph. 2:8-9.		

Edwin Hartill, *Principles of Biblical Hermeneutics* (Grand Rapids: Zondervan, 1947), p. 18.

Lewis Sperry Chafer. *Dispensationalism*.

C. C. Ryrie. *Dispensationalism Today*.

C. I. Scofield. *Rightly Dividing the Word of Truth*.

Louis Berkhof. *Systematic Theology*, pp. 290-301.

William E. Cox. *An Examination of Dispensationalism*.

George Eldon Ladd. *Crucial Questions about the Kingdom of God*.

Lutheran Theory

Luther believed that for a proper understanding of Scripture we must carefully distinguish between two parallel and ever-present truths of Scripture: Law and Gospel. As mentioned in chapter 2, *Law* refers to God in His hatred of sin, His judgment, and His wrath. *Gospel* refers to God in His grace, His love, and His salvation.

Both aspects of God's nature exist side by side in Scripture throughout both the Old and New Testaments. The Law reflects the holiness of God's character; were He to dispense with it, He would become an amoral rather than a holy God. Grace is God's response to the fact that man can never meet the standard of holiness that the Law demands.

One way of distinguishing Law and Gospel is to ask, "Is this speaking judgment on me?" If so, it is Law. In contrast, if a passage brings comfort, it is Gospel. Using these criteria, determine whether the following passages would be considered Law or Gospel:

1. Genesis 7:1: "The Lord then said to Noah, 'Go into the ark, you and your whole family, because I have found you righteous in this generation.'" *Grace*
2. Matthew 22:37: "Jesus replied: 'Love the Lord your God with all your heart and with all your soul and with all your mind.'" *Law*
3. John 3:36: "Whoever believes in the Son has eternal life, but whoever rejects the Son will not see life, for God's wrath remains on him." *grace*

(Answers: (1) Gospel, (2) Law, and (3) Gospel; Law)

For Lutheran theologians, Law and Gospel reveal two integral aspects of God's personality: His holiness and His grace. Thus they see Law and Gospel as inseparable parts of salvation history, from the story of Adam and Eve's sin to the close of the millennium.

Law and Gospel have continuing purposes in the lives of both unbelievers and believers. For the unbeliever the Law condemns, accuses, and shows him his need for the Lord. For the believer the Law continues to demonstrate the need for grace, and gives guidelines for daily living. The Gospel shows the unbeliever a way of escape from condemnation; for the believer it serves as a motivation to keep God's moral law.

The careful differentiation between, but maintenance of both Law and Gospel has been an important hermeneutical tool and hallmark of orthodox Lutheran preaching. The Lutheran position places strong emphasis on continuity. God continues to respond to man with both Law and Grace as He has from the very beginning of human history. Law and Grace are not two different epochs in God's dealing with man, but are integral parts of His every relationship. For further reading on the Lutheran position, the following two books are recommended:

P. Althaus. *The Theology of Martin Luther.*

C.F.W. Walther. *The Proper Distinction between Law and Gospel.*

Covenantal Theory

Another theory that focuses on continuity rather than discontinuity in salvation history is covenantal theory. Covenantal theologians view all biblical history as covered by two covenants, a covenant of works until the fall and a covenant of grace from the fall to the present.[10] The covenant of works is described as that agreement between God and Adam which promised Adam life for perfect obedience and death as the penalty for disobedience. The covenant of grace is the agreement between God and a sinner in which God promises salvation through faith, and the sinner promises a life of faith and obedience.[11] All Old Testament believers as well as contemporary believers are part of the covenant of grace.

A charge against covenantal theology is that it is an oversimplification to classify the Old and New Testaments under the single category, covenant of grace. Several verses of Scripture appear to indicate an older and newer covenant, corresponding roughly to our Old and New Testaments. For example, Jeremiah 31:31-32 says:

> "The time is coming" declares the Lord,
>   "When I will make a new covenant
> with the house of Israel
>   and with the house of Judah.
> It will not be like the covenant
>   I made with their forefathers
> when I took them by the hand
>   to lead them out of Egypt,
> because they broke my covenant
>   though I was a husband to them."

Several verses in the Book of Hebrews seem to make a similar distinction:

> But the ministry Jesus has received is as superior to theirs
> as the covenant of which he is mediator is superior to the

10. Some Reformed theologians speak of a third covenant—the covenant of redemption—which was formed in eternity past. This was an agreement between the Father and the Son, in which the Father pronounced the Son as Head and Redeemer of the elect, and the Son voluntarily agreed to die for those whom the Father had given Him.

11. Louis Berkhof, *Systematic Theology*, 4th rev. and enl. ed. (Grand Rapids: Eerdmans, 1941), pp. 211-218, 265-271.

old one, and it is founded on better promises. . . . By
calling this covenant "new," he has made the first one
obsolete; and what is obsolete and aging will soon dis-
appear (Heb. 8:6, 13).

Covenantal theologians respond to this issue by making several points: First, Old Testament believers were saved by grace
just as New Testament believers; therefore they can both be
accurately considered as part of the covenant of grace. Second,
the many comparisons between the Old and New Testaments
in the Book of Hebrews never describe them as antithetic.
The relationship is seen as that between a good covenant relationship and an even better one. The good covenant which
God had offered in the Old Testament (a covenant of grace)
had been rejected by the idolatrous Israelites. God replaced
it with a new covenant of grace even more gracious than the
former one. The relationship is further described as that between a system that looked forward to its fulfillment, and the
fulfillment itself. The blood of bulls and goats could never
take away sin finally and absolutely, but simply acted as a
downpayment until Christ came as the perfect atonement
(Heb. 10:1-10). Therefore, covenantal theologians conclude,
the Old and New Testament covenants are synthetic rather
than antithetic. Both are covenants of grace, one built on the
gracious promises of its predecessor.

A second charge leveled at covenantal theory is that the
Old Testament speaks of several covenants: a preflood Noahic
covenant (Gen. 6:18), a post-flood Noahic covenant (Gen.
9:8-17), an Abrahamic covenant (Gen. 15:8,18; 17:6-8), a
Mosaic covenant (Exod. 6:6-8), a Davidic covenant (Ps. 89:3,
4,26-37), and a new covenant (Jer. 31:31-34). In light of this,
is it proper to speak of a covenant of grace rather than specific
covenants? If there are several covenants, is not the covenantal
theory almost the same as the dispensational theory?

Although covenantal theologians recognize each of these
individual covenants, there are several basic differences be-

tween covenantal and dispensational conceptions of salvation history. In response to the first issue above, the covenantal conception of salvation history emphasizes continuity: a general covenant of grace overshadowed each of the specific covenants. Human beings have been called by grace, justified by grace, and adopted into the family of God by grace ever since the fall. Thus covenantal theologians believe it is accurate to group these individual covenants under the more general heading of the covenant of grace.

Dispensational theologians place relatively more emphasis on discontinuity. While most of them would agree that salvation has always been by grace, they also believe that there are significant changes regarding God's commands for obedient living that occur across the dispensations. Although contemporary dispensational theologians are now stressing the continuity between dispensations, previous dispensational theologians emphasized the differences between dispensations. Humanity's responsibilities within each dispensation were seen as a different type of test from the previous one. Thus when humans failed to be obedient to God when given the responsibility of following conscience (second dispensation), God gave them the responsibility of obedience through government.

Covenantal theologians place relatively more emphasis on the additive rather than the disjunctive nature of the covenants. For example, the postflood Noahic covenant was consistent with the preflood covenant; it simply filled in more details of the grace relationship. Similarly, the Mosaic covenant did not abolish the Abrahamic one; rather, the Mosaic covenant added to the Abrahamic (Gal. 3:17-22). Thus, starting from exactly the same biblical data and very similar views of inspiration and revelation, dispensational and covenantal theologians have arrived at somewhat different views of the nature of salvation history, views which are consequently reflected in their theological analysis of all passages other than the Epistles.

The following four books present further information on covenantal theory: the first three are written by covenantal theologians and the fourth is a critique of these views.

Louis Berkhof. *Systematic Theology*, pp. 262-301.

J. Oliver Buswell, Jr. *Systematic Theology* 1:307-320.

E. W. Hengstenberg. "The New Covenant," in *Classical Evangelical Essays in Old Testament Theology*, ed. W. C. Kaiser, Jr.

C. C. Ryrie. *Dispensationalism Today*, pp. 177-191.

Epigenetic Model

The epigenetic theory views divine revelation as analogous to the growth of a tree from a seed, to a seedling, to a young tree, and then to a fully grown tree. This concept can be contrasted with one which likens divine revelation to the building of a cathedral piece by piece. A cathedral when half built is an imperfect cathedral. A tree when half grown is a perfect tree. The epigenetic theory views God's self-disclosures as never being imperfect or errant, even though later disclosures may add further information.

The term *epigenetic theory* has not been widely used. It is referred to frequently by other terms, such as the *organic unity* of Scripture,[12] where *organic* refers to the concept of living growth.

The idea of progressive revelation, which is almost unanimously held by evangelical scholars, is highly consistent with the epigenetic theory. Progressive revelation is the concept that God's revelation gradually increased in definiteness, clarity, and fullness as it was revealed over time, even as a tree increases its girth and root and branch structures over time.

12. See, for example, Louis Berkhof, *Principles of Biblical Interpretation* (Grand Rapids: Baker, 1950), p. 134; J. I. Packer, *Fundamentalism and the Word of God* (Grand Rapids: Eerdmans, 1958), p. 52; John Wenham, *Christ and the Bible* (Downers Grove, Ill.: InterVarsity, 1972), pp. 19, 103-104.

As the trunk and branches of a tree may grow in several directions concurrently, so also the concepts of God, Christ, salvation, and the nature of man grew simultaneously as God's revelation progressed.

In some ways the epigenetic model may be viewed as a middle road between dispensationalism and covenantal theology. Covenantal theologians often criticize dispensationalists for minimizing the essential unity of Scripture. Dispensationalists contend that covenantal theologians fail to maintain important distinctions that should be maintained (e.g., the difference between Israel and the church). A model that is responsive to both criticisms would emphasize the unity of salvation history but allow for valid differentiation as well. The epigenetic model, with its unified trunk but variegated branch structure, provides this balance.

Kaiser suggests that the concept of God's *promise* might serve as the central organizing concept within the epigenetic model. He describes the promise as God's pledge to do or be something for Old Testament Israelites, then for future Israelites, and eventually for all nations. The promise thus extends from the past to the present and into the future.

The promise doctrine is not the only possible central organizing principle that could be suggested for the epigenetic which gradually become more defined and differentiated. Branches of the promise include: (1) material blessings for all men and animals; (2) a special seed to humankind; (3) a land for a chosen nation; (4) spiritual blessings for all nations; (5) a national deliverance from bondage; (6) an enduring dynasty and kingdom that will one day embrace a universal dominion; (7) a forgiveness of sin; and others.[13]

The promise doctrine is not the only possible central organizing principle that could be suggested for the epigenetic model. Lutherans would probably want to suggest that Christ

13. Walter C. Kaiser, Jr., *Toward an Old Testament Theology* (Grand Rapids: Zondervan, 1978), p. 14.

be the central concept. J. Barton Payne might have suggested "God's testament" as a candidate.[14] Others might suggest God's grace, in all its manifestations, as a possibility.

A Methodology for Deciding Among Models

Which of these five models or hypotheses about the nature of divine revelation most accurately reflects the biblical data? No one doubts that there is movement from the Old Testament to the new. The Old Testament believers looked forward to a promised Redeemer; New Testament believers either saw personally or looked back to their Redeemer. The new covenant was superior to the old. The Jews rejected the gospel and it was taken to the Gentiles. And so the question remains: Has God's method of dealing with men been primarily continuous or primarily discontinuous? Is the nature of these various epochs within human history basically disjunctive or additive?

It is difficult to view objectively the merits of our own position or of other positions from the center of our own position. An alternative method of evaluating various models is to first organize the biblical data around several key concepts (concepts that are independent of the models being compared), and then to analyze each model in terms of how well it fits and accounts for the data.

Some of the most important concepts found throughout Scripture include: (1) *God's principles*, manifested through His laws; (2) *God's grace*, manifested in His response to a humanity that repeatedly breaks His principles; (3) *God's salvation*, manifested in His provision of a means of reconciliation between humanity and Himself; and (4) *God's work in individuals*, mani-

14. J. Barton Payne, *The Theology of the Older Testament* (Grand Rapids: Zondervan, 1962), pp. 71-96.

fested through the ministry of the Holy Spirit. Each of these four concepts will be discussed in the following pages, beginning with God's grace. At the end of the chapter you will be asked to come to your own conclusion regarding which model of God's relationship to man most adequately accounts for the biblical data.

The Concept of Grace

A common conception of many evangelical believers is that law and grace reveal opposite sides of God's nature. Law reveals the angry, stern side of God, the Old Testament side of Him; grace reveals the merciful, loving, New Testament side of Him.

Many are surprised to find that grace and the gospel are very much Old Testament concepts. Speaking of the Old Testament Israelites who were led from Egypt to Canaan by Moses, Hebrews 4:1-2 says: "Therefore, since the promise of entering his [Christ's] rest still stands, let us be careful that none of you be found to have fallen short of it. For we also have had *the gospel* preached to us, *just as they did*; but the message they heard was of no value to them, because those who heard did not combine it with faith" (emphasis added).

Similarly, we find that the gospel was preached to Abraham. Paul says in Galatians 3:8-9: "The Scripture foresaw that God would justify the Gentiles by faith, and announced the gospel in advance to Abraham: 'All nations will be blessed through you.' So those who have faith are blessed along with Abraham, the man of faith." Paul mentions in another epistle that Abraham and David were examples of men who were justified by faith (Rom. 4:3-6).

But do these passages refer to the same gospel that we are saved by? Although the Greek word (*evangelion*) for gospel is the same in all these references, might it not be referring to a different gospel from the New Testament covenant? It seems possible that this might be the case, for there are several descriptive titles in the Bible, such as: "the gospel of peace" (Eph. 6:15), "the gospel of Christ" (1 Cor. 9:12), "the gospel of the grace of God" (Acts 20:24), "this gospel of the kingdom" (Matt. 24:14), and "an eternal gospel" (Rev. 14:6). Since there are different descriptive titles, are there different gospels?

Paul's answer in Galatians 1:6-9 is an emphatic *no*.

> I am astonished that you are so quickly deserting the one who called you by the grace of Christ and are turning to a different gospel—which is really no gospel at all. Evidently some people are throwing you into confusion and are trying to pervert the gospel of Christ. But even if we or an angel from heaven should preach a gospel other than the one we preached to you, let him be eternally condemned! As we have already said, so now I say again: If anybody is preaching to you a gospel other than what you accepted, let him be eternally condemned!

It is hard to escape the conclusion that Paul believed quite strongly that there was only one gospel, with the resulting inference that the various titles mentioned above are descriptive of the same gospel.[15] Abraham and David looked forward to the fulfillment of the gospel even as we look backward to its completion in Christ. This is not to say that Old Testament believers understood Christ's atonement as clearly as we do now, but that they had faith that God would provide reconciliation for them, and God honored their faith by granting them redemption.

Perhaps there is gospel in the Old Testament, but what about grace? Is not the God of the Old Testament a stern God of judgment in contrast to the gracious God of the New Testament? This question brings us to one of the most beautiful

15. For a discussion of the view that there are actually four forms of the gospel, see the note on Revelation 14:6 in the Scofield Reference Bible. Part 3 of this note asserts that the various forms of the gospel are not to be identified with one another. The parallel note in the New Scofield Reference Bible modifies the above position, saying that there is only one gospel of salvation, with various aspects.

concepts in the Old Testament, and one of the least understood.

When the RSV translators were translating the Bible, there was one word that occurred in the Old Testament some 250 times for which they were unable to find a suitable English word. In the Hebrew this word is *hesed*: the King James translators had frequently translated this as "lovingkindness," as in the oft-repeated phrase "for his lovingkindness endureth forever." The RSV translators were not satisfied that even this phrase adequately translated the richness and depth of God's *hesed* for His people. After finishing the entire Bible, the translators were still struggling to find a word. They finally settled on "steadfast love" because this phrase speaks of the loyal love of God to His covenantal promise. And besides *hesed* there are a wide variety of other words in the Old Testament that refer to God's abundant mercy, goodness, and long-suffering.[16]

There is evidence of God's grace in every dispensation. When Adam and Eve sinned, God graciously intervened, promised a Redeemer, and made immediate provision for their acceptance before Him in their sinful condition. In the dispensation of conscience Noah found grace in the sight of God (Gen. 6:8); God graciously intervened, saving Noah and his family. In the dispensation of civil government man rebelled by building the tower of Babel. God did not destroy the rebellious creation, but continued to work in the hearts of men like Abraham and Melchizedek by extending a gracious promise that He would bless the whole world through Abraham. In the dispensation of Mosaic law, God continued to deal graciously with Israel despite the many and continued periods of declension and backsliding. In the dispensation of grace He continues to deal graciously with humankind.[17]

16. Walter C. Kaiser, Jr. *The Old Testament in Contemporary Preaching* (Grand Rapids: Baker, 1973), pp. 22-23.

17. Charles C. Ryrie, *Dispensationalism Today* (Chicago: Moody, 1965), pp. 57-64.

Many other evidences demonstrate that the God of the Old Testament is a God of grace. Psalms 32 and 51 remind us that an adulterer and even a murderer can find forgiveness with God. Psalm 103 sings of God's mercy and steadfast love in words unparalleled in all Scripture. Thus the God of the Old Testament is not an ungracious Being: His grace, mercy, and love are as much in evidence in the Old Testament as they are in the New.

The Concept of Law

A concept closely intertwined with grace is the concept of law. Even as some Christians believe that the basic nature of God as revealed in the Old Testament is dissimilar from His nature as revealed in the New, so also some Christians believe that the means of gaining salvation in the Old Testament differs from that in the New Testament. The most common view is that salvation was by law in the Old Testament and by grace in the New.[18]

Context of the Giving of the Law. Examination of the context in which the law was given provides clues concerning its intended purpose. First, the law was given within the context of a gracious covenant: God had made a covenant of grace with Abraham, a covenant which the giving of the law never nullified (Gal. 3:17). Second, God had graciously rescued Israel from Egypt and providentially sustained the people with manna and other miracles during their sojourn in the desert. Third, the law was given after Israel had, as a body of believers, made a commitment to serve the Lord (Exod. 19:8). Thus

18. The well-known note in the Scofield Reference Bible (John 1:17), which seemed to suggest that there were two ways of salvation, has been cited earlier in the text. It may be of interest to the reader that this note and others which seemed to suggest two means of salvation have been significantly reworded in the New Scofield Reference Bible. The revised Scofield notes are generally consistent with the view that salvation has always been by grace, though the rules for obedient living may change across dispensations.

the law was given, not as a means of justification, but as a guideline for living after Israel's commitment to serve the Lord.

Was the law given even hypothetically as a means of justification (salvation)? The New Testament informs us that the law could never serve as a means of salvation. Paul teaches that no one can earn righteous standing before God by the works of the law (Gal. 3:11,21,22).[19] Romans 4:3 teaches that Abraham was saved on the basis of his faith, not his works, and the subsequent verses (13-16) teach that the promise was extended to Abraham's descendants, not on the basis of their works, but because of their faith.[20]

How then do we understand Paul's teaching that we are no longer under the dominion of the law (Rom. 6:14; 7:4) but have been delivered from it (Rom. 7:6) because Christ has fulfilled the righteousness of the law in us? The answer to this can be understood in light of Scripture's teaching on the aspects and the purposes of the law.

Three Aspects of the Law. Ezekiel Hopkins has suggested that the Old Testament law can be meaningfully divided into three aspects: the *ceremonial* (those ritual observances that pointed forward to the final atonement in Christ), the *judicial or civil* (those laws God prescribed for use in Israel's civil government), and the *moral* (that body of moral precepts that possess universal, abiding applicability for all humanity).[21]

19. See also Rom. 11:6; Gal. 2:15,16,21; 5:3,4; Eph. 2:8,9; Phil. 3:9.

20. For further substantiation of the idea that law was never offered as a means of salvation, see Geerhardus Vos, *Biblical Theology* (Grand Rapids: Eerdmans, 1948), p. 143; Walter C. Kaiser, Jr., "Leviticus 18:5 and Paul: 'Do this and You Shall Live (Eternally?),'" *Journal of the Evangelical Theological Society*, 14 (1971):19; James Buswell, Jr. *Systematic Theology* (Grand Rapids: Zondervan, 1962), 1:313; Anne Lawton, "Christ: The End of the Law. A Study of Romans 10:4-8," *Trinity Journal*, 3 (Spring, 1974):14-30. For an alternative viewpoint, see Richard Longenecker, *Paul: Apostle of Liberty* (New York: Harper and Row, 1964), p. 121; Charles Hodge, *Systematic Theology* (Grand Rapids: Eerdmans, 1946), 2:117-122.

21. Ezekiel Hopkins, "Understanding the Ten Commandments," in *Classical Evangelical Essays in Old Testament Interpretation*, ed. Walter C. Kaiser, Jr. (Grand Rapids: Baker, 1972), p. 43.

Some have argued against the validity of the above distinctions on the bases that the Old Testament Israelites did not understand their law according to these three categories, and the New Testament does not explicitly make such distinctions. Old Testament believers probably did not divide their law according to these categories: such division would have been superfluous since all three aspects of the law applied to them. As New Testament believers we must decide whether or not the New Testament validates these distinctions. In addition, while the New Testament may not *explicitly* make such distinctions, much of our theological study involves making explicit what is implicit in the biblical record. David Wenham says:

> We have to distinguish those laws which may be said to point forward to Christ and which are therefore unnecessary after his coming (e.g., the ceremonial laws according to Hebrews) and the moral laws, which do not so obviously point forward to Christ (though they were explained more fully by him) and which continue to be binding moral truths for the Christian. The moral laws are "fulfilled" by Christ in a very different sense from the ceremonial laws: they are not superseded, but rather are included in the New Christian framework of reference. So although the New Testament may not spell out the distinction between the moral and ceremonial law, in practice it seems to recognize it.[22]

The *ceremonial aspect* of the law encompasses the various sacrifices and ceremonial rites that served as figures or types pointing to the coming Redeemer (Heb. 7-10). A number of Old Testament texts confirm that the Israelites had some conception of the spiritual significance of these rites and ceremonies (Lev. 20:25,26; Pss. 26:6; 51:7,16,17; Isa. 1:16). Several

22. David Wenham, "Jesus and the Law: An Exegesis on Matthew 5:17-20," *Themelios* 4 (April 1979):95.

New Testament texts differentiate the ceremonial aspect of
the law and point to its fulfillment in Christ (e.g., Mark 7:19;
Eph. 2:14-15; Heb. 7:26-28; 9:9-11; 10:1,9).

Regarding the ceremonial aspect of the law, one New Testament passage (Heb. 10:1-4) raises a significant question that
merits discussion here. The passage reads:

> The law is only a shadow of the good things that are
> coming—not the realities themselves. For this reason it
> can never, by the same sacrifices repeated endlessly year
> after year, make perfect those who draw near to worship.
> If it could, would they not have stopped being offered?
> For the worshipers would have been cleansed once for
> all, and would no longer have felt guilty for their sins.
> But those sacrifices are an annual reminder of sins, be-
> cause it is impossible for the blood of bulls and goats to
> take away sins.

At first glance this passage seems to contradict certain Old
Testament passages which indicate that Old Testament believers were indeed forgiven on the basis of repentance and appropriate offerings. Perhaps this problem can be most easily
explained by a modern analogy. The Old Testament sacrifices
can be compared to a check that is used to pay a bill. In one
sense, the bill is paid when a check is made out to its recipient;
but in another sense, the bill is not paid until the cash transfer
is made for which the check is a symbol. In a similar manner
the Old Testament sacrifices cleansed believers of sins, but
only received final clearance when Christ died and cleared the
balance on which the Old Testament sacrifices were only
promissory notes. It is important to stress that the ceremonial
law was fulfilled, not annulled or abolished (Matt. 5:17-19).

The *civil, or judicial, aspect* of the law encompasses the precepts given to Israel for the government of its civil state. Although many Gentile governments have adopted principles
from this portion of the law as their own, these civil laws seem

to have been intended for the government of the Jewish people, and believers from other nations are commanded to be obedient to the civil laws of their own government.[23]

The *moral aspect* of the law reflects the moral nature and perfection of God. Since God's moral nature remains unchanging, the moral law remains unchanging and is as relevant for the believer today as for the believers to whom it was given. The Christian is dead to the condemning power of the law (Rom. 8:1-3), but still very much under its command of obedience as a guide to right living before God (Rom. 3:31; Rom. 6; 1 Cor. 5; 6:9-20).

The Purposes of the Law. Several Scriptures speak of the purposes of the law. Galations 3:19 teaches that it was given "because of transgressions" or, as the NEB translates it, "to make wrongdoing a legal offense." Thus one primary purpose of the law was to make humans consciously aware of the distinction between good and evil, between right and wrong.

A related reason is found in 1 Timothy 1:8-11, which teaches that the law is good if one uses it lawfully. From the context it becomes evident that a "lawful use of the law" was the restraint of evildoing. Thus by making humans aware that some actions are morally wrong, the law serves at least to some degree as an inhibitor of evildoing.

A third purpose of the law is to act as a custodian to bring individuals to Christ (Gal. 3:22-24). By showing them their sinfulness, the law serves as a guide or tutor. It shows them that their only hope for justification is through Christ.

A fourth purpose of the law is to serve as a guideline for godly living. The original context of the giving of the law immediately followed the Israelites' commitment to be faithful to the true God. The law was a guide to reveal how they could remain true to their commitment while surrounded by idolatrous and grossly immoral nations on every side.

23. Hopkins, "Understanding the Ten Commandments," p. 46.

In the New Testament as well, obedience is never considered an optional part of the believer's life. Jesus said, "If you love me, keep my commandments" (John 14:15). In John 15:10 He is quoted as saying, "If you keep my commandments, you shall abide in my love." First John 3:9 teaches that a true believer does not make sin the practice of his life, and the entire Epistle of James is devoted to teaching that true faith will result in godly behavior. The motive for obedience is love rather than fear (1 John 4:16-19), but salvation by grace in no way obviates the fact that obedience to God's moral law is an intrinsic *result* of true saving faith.

Knowing these aspects and purposes of the law, we can better understand Paul's writings on the law. Paul's arguments in Galatians were not against the law, but against *legalism*—that perversion of the law which says that salvation can be obtained by keeping the law. The Judaizers were attempting to persuade the Galatian believers to mix salvation by grace with salvation by law—two mutually incompatible systems. Paul traced Israel's history, showing that believers from Abraham on had been saved by grace, and that no one ever could be saved by keeping the law, since the law was not meant to bring salvation. On the other hand, Paul argued just as forcefully for the right use of the law—as an indicator of God's moral standards, as a restraint against evildoing, as a custodian to bring individuals to Christ, and as the believer's guide to godly living.

The New Testament believer is not "under law" in three senses: (1) he is not under the ceremonial law because this has been fulfilled in Christ, (2) he is not under Jewish civil law because this was not intended for him, and (3) he is not under the condemnation of the law because his identification with the vicarious atoning death of Christ frees him from it.

In summary, then, the law continues to perform the same functions in the New Testament that it did in the Old Testament. The misunderstanding that law was actually a second means of salvation is based on the fact that the Israelites themselves misunderstood the law similarly, and turned the law from its proper purpose into legalism, the attempt to earn salvation by keeping it. The biblical evidence seems to support the Lutheran belief that law and grace remain as continuing, inseparable parts of salvation history from Genesis to Revelation.

The Concept of Salvation

Salvation throughout the Old and New Testaments has already been mentioned several times in the discussion of law and grace, so this section will function basically as a summary of points made in those sections. In the Old Testament as in the New, atonement came by the shedding of blood (Lev. 17:11; Heb. 9:22). The shedding of animal blood in the Old Testament had efficacy because it pointed to the final atonement on Calvary (Heb. 10:1-10).

Old Testament believers were justified by faith even as New Testament believers (Gal. 2:15–3:29) and are called saints (i.e., sanctified ones) even as New Testament believers (Matt. 27:52).

God reveals the law *and* His grace throughout both the Old and New Testaments simultaneously, not as mutually exclusive means of salvation, but as complementary aspects of His nature. The law reveals His moral nature, which He cannot compromise and still remain a moral God; grace reveals His loving plan to provide a means of reconciling human beings to Himself even though they are imperfect, without compromising His own nature.

Faith in God's provision of a sacrifice remains the basis for salvation throughout the Old and New Testaments. The accuracy of the Old Testament believer's conception of the object of that faith changed over time—from Eve's first dim understanding to Isaiah's more complete conceptions, to the apostles' post-resurrection understanding—but the ultimate object of that faith, God the Redeemer, remains the same across the thousands of years of Old Testament history. In the

Judeo-Christian religion as in no other, salvation always remains a gift of God, not a work of man. Thus it is probably accurate to conclude that salvation throughout the Bible is basically continuous, with only a secondary emphasis on discontinuity.

The Ministry of the Holy Spirit

A fourth topic that has implications for the general question of continuity versus discontinuity across the Old and New Testaments is the ministry of the Holy Spirit: Is His work the same in both Testaments, or has His work been different since Pentecost?

Theologians are in considerable disagreement on this matter. Paul K. Jewett exemplifies a discontinuous perspective when he says: "The church age may be called the age of the Spirit, and the time that preceded it may be cited as a time when the Spirit was 'not yet given' (John 7:39). The difference between the Spirit's manifestation before and after Pentecost was so great that it may be stated in absolutes, though such absolutes should not be pressed literally."[24]

In contrast, Walters concludes that the ministry of the Holy Spirit demonstrates continuity throughout the Old and New Testaments. He says:

> There is no irreconcilable antithesis, as some would suggest, between the teaching of the Old Testament and the teaching of the New on this subject. Just as no dichotomy exists between the Old Testament emphasis on the providential nature of God's dealings with men and the New Testament teaching concerning His grace, or between the activity in creation of the pre-incarnate Logos, on the one hand, and the work of redemption of the incarnate Son, on the other, so it is with the teaching of Scripture concerning the Holy Spirit. It is the same Fa-

24. Paul K. Jewett, "Holy Spirit." in *Zondervan Pictorial Encyclopedia of the Bible*, ed. Merrill Tenney (Grand Rapids: Zondervan, 1976), 3:186.

ther and the same Son who is active in both Testaments, and it is the same Holy Spirit who is at work throughout the ages. True, we have to wait for the New Testament revelation before we are given a detailed picture of His activity. But this fuller teaching given by our Lord and His apostles conflicts in no way with what we learn from the Old Testament writers.[25]

Many evangelical Christians view the Holy Spirit as a rather inactive member of the Trinity throughout the Old Testament, one who did not commence significant intervention in human affairs until Pentecost.[26] There are, in fact, several passages which appear to indicate a significant change in the activity of the Holy Spirit after Pentecost. John 7:39 says that the Holy Spirit had not been given at the time of Christ's earthly ministry. John 14:26 uses the future tense to speak of the coming of the Holy Spirit. In John 16:7 Christ says that the Holy Spirit will not come unless He (Christ) goes away, and in Acts 1:4-8 He commanded the disciples to wait in Jerusalem until the Holy Spirit had come on them.

There are, on the other hand, several passages that speak of an active Holy Spirit ministry in the Old Testament. For example, the Holy Spirit dwelt among the Israelites in Moses' day (Isa. 63:10-14). The Holy Spirit dwelt in Joshua (Num. 27:18); He empowered and guided Othniel (Judg. 3:10); He gave skilled craftsmen their ability (Exod. 31:1-6). The Holy Spirit empowered Samson (Judg. 13:25; 14:6; 15:14); He moved King Saul to prophesy (1 Sam. 10:9-10); and He indwelt David (Ps. 51:11). All the Old Testament prophets (writers) prophesied as they did because of the Holy Spirit's

25. G. Walters, "Holy Spirit," in *The New Bible Dictionary*, ed. J. D. Douglas (Grand Rapids: Eerdmans, 1962), p. 531.

26. It has been suggested by several evangelical theologians that the reason God did not reveal the concept of the Trinity in the Old Testament to the degree which He did in the New was that ancient Israel was surrounded by polytheistic nations and cults. Introduction of the concept would have allowed rapid assimilation of the polytheistic pagan religion into Israel's worship of the one true God.

energizing (1 Peter 1:10-12; 2 Peter 1:21). The Holy Spirit dwelt among the Israelites who returned from the Babylonian captivity (Hag. 2:5).

There are several references to the Holy Spirit's activity before Pentecost in the New Testament also. John the Baptist was filled with the Holy Spirit from his mother's womb (Luke 1:15). Zechariah, his father, was filled with the Holy Spirit, resulting in the prophecy found in Luke 1:67-79. The Holy Spirit was on Simeon (the tense implies continuously), inspiring him to prophesy when he beheld the baby Jesus (Luke 2:25-27). Jesus told His apostles at the Last Supper that they knew the Holy Spirit, because He was already dwelling with them (John 14:17). In one of his post-resurrection appearances before Pentecost, Jesus bestowed the Holy Spirit on His apostles (John 20:22).

How then shall we reconcile these verses which indicate that the Holy Spirit was active before Pentecost in the lives of both Old and New Testament believers, with Christ's command that the apostles wait at Jerusalem for the Holy Spirit to come on them (Acts 1:4-5)? The apparent contradictions can be made more evident by juxtaposing several verses for comparison:

Set 1	*Set 2*
1. John 7:39: The Holy Spirit had not yet been given them.	1. John 14:17: The Holy Spirit was (already) dwelling among them.
2. John 16:7: The Holy Spirit would not come unless Christ went away.	2. John 20:22: Christ bestowed the Holy Spirit on them while He was still with them.
3. Acts 1:4-8: The apostles were to wait at Jerusalem until the Holy Spirit came.	

At least three methods have been suggested to reconcile these apparent contradictions. The first method proposes that the Holy Spirit's activity before Pentecost was similar to His activity after Pentecost, but that His action in the lives of men was sporadic rather than constant. One of the major difficulties with this view is that in some of the ministries of the Holy Spirit (as in giving of craftsmanship abilities, or more importantly, in the believer's growth process), a constant rather than sporadic ministry is required.

A second method distinguishes between the Holy Spirit's ministry of being "upon" (or "among") and "in" God's people. According to this view, the Holy Spirit was among and upon believers before Pentecost, but did not reside in them until Pentecost (John 14:17). A major difficulty with this hypothesis, of course, is the question of whether the believer's sanctification can be accomplished with only an external sporadic working of the Spirit or whether the spiritual growth process requires a more continuous, internal relationship between the believer and the Holy Spirit.

A third method focuses on the meaning of "coming" and "going" when applied to God. When referring to God (excepting Christ in His earthly state) the concept of coming and going does not refer to movement from one physical location to another, because God as a spiritual Being is omnipresent. For example, when Isaiah said: "Oh, that you would rend the heavens and come down" (Isa. 64:1), the context shows that Isaiah knew that God was with him in his ministry, and that what he was asking God for was a special manifestation of His presence. Similarly, when David asked God to come down in Psalm 144:5, the context indicates that David knew that God was protecting him from those seeking his life, but David needed a special manifestation of God's deliverance. Other verses could be given, but both the biblical and logical evidence regarding God's existence as a spiritual Being (a Being for whom time and space parameters do not mean the same thing they mean for us), indicate that the concept of God's coming and going does not refer to His movement from one location to another. Rather, "coming" as applied to God often refers to God's manifestation of Himself in some special way.

Thus when Christ commanded His apostles to wait for the coming of the Holy Spirit, we can understand this as a command to wait for a special manifestation of the Holy Spirit's presence, a manifestation that would empower them to initiate the missionary program for this age. (*Baptizing* them and *coming on* them are used as synonyms in this instance: Acts 1:5,8.)

This understanding of the word *coming* also helps us reconcile the passages which indicate that the disciples had already received the Holy Spirit (John 20:22) with the fact that they were still to wait for His coming. They were still to wait for a special manifestation of His presence that would transform them from fainthearted disciples into courageous apostles, even though He was already present in their lives.

This interpretation can also be used to understand the meaning of John 7:37-39. This difficult passage reads:

> On the last and greatest day of the Feast, Jesus stood and said in a loud voice, "If a man is thirsty, let him come to me and drink. Whoever believes in me, as the Scripture has said, streams of living water will flow from within him." By this he meant the Spirit, whom those who believed in him were later to receive. Up to that time the Spirit had not been given, since Jesus had not yet been glorified.

What does verse 39 mean by the phrase, "the Spirit had not been given"? John 14:17 teaches that He was dwelling among the disciples then. The context gives us the most important clues concerning the meaning of this phrase. Verse 39 states that the event would not happen until Jesus was glorified. In the Gospel of John Jesus' glorification refers to His offering of Himself on the cross and the completion of His earthly work. The passage suggests that the Holy Spirit had not manifested Himself in a way that could be spoken of as streams of living water flowing from the hearts of believers, and would not manifest Himself in this way until Christ had finished His earthly ministry.

The metaphor "streams of living water" suggests, in a desert country such as Palestine, a reason for rejoicing and praise. The most likely reference to the fulfillment of this passage is the special manifestation of the Holy Spirit at Pentecost. The metaphor fits, for the first glossolalic utterances were praise (Acts 2:11). If this analysis is correct, then this passage is not teaching that the Holy Spirit was not present at that time (an interpretation which would contradict other biblical passages as shown above), but rather that the Holy Spirit would not manifest Himself in this special way until Christ had been glorified. A similar analysis can be done with the John 16 passage.

For the purpose of theological analysis, the question is, "Is the Holy Spirit's work in the Old and New Testament primarily continuous, increasing perhaps in quantity but remaining qualitatively the same, or is His work basically discontinuous, changing after Pentecost?" The biblical evidence suggests that the Holy Spirit ministered in similar ways throughout the Old and New Testaments, convicting people of sin, leading them to faith, guiding and empowering them, inspiring them to make verbal or written prophecies, giving them spiritual gifts, and regenerating and sanctifying them.[27]

Other Factors

Two other factors have implications for the continuity-discontinuity question. The first of these is collective quotations, i.e., quotations that have been drawn from several Old Testament passages to make a point. Such quotations are found, for example, in Romans 3:10-18, and Hebrews 1:5-13; 2:6-8,12,13. The phenomenon of collective quotations makes

27. For a discussion of the gifts of the Spirit manifested throughout the Old Testament, see Arnold Bittlenger, *Gifts and Graces*, trans. Herbert Klassen (Grand Rapids: Eerdmans, 1967), pp. 27-53; for discussion of the regeneration and sanctification of Old Testament believers, see John Stott, *The Baptism and Fullness of the Holy Spirit* (Downers Grove, Ill.: InterVarsity, 1964), pp. 15-16.

more sense if salvation history is a unity rather than a series
of discontinuous theologies.

The second is the teaching of 2 Timothy 3:16-17. This passage seems more consistent with a continuous rather than a
discontinuous view of salvation history. Compare Paul's teaching with a paraphrase of several statements of faith used by
various churches:

2 Timothy 3:16-17 (RSV)	Statement of Faith
All Scripture is inspired by God and profitable for teaching, for reproof, for correction, and for training in righteousness.	All Scripture is inspired by God and the New Testament is profitable for teaching, for reproof . . . .

The difference between these is especially interesting because
the young Christian pastor to whom 2 Timothy was written
probably had a Bible composed of thirty-nine Old Testament
books and four New Testament books.[28] Yet Paul tells him
that all these books are profitable for Christian teaching, reproof, correction, and training in righteousness. It is important to rethink our attitude toward the Old Testament in light
of Paul's teaching in this passage.

Chapter Summary

Theological analysis asks the question, "How does this passage fit into the total pattern of God's revelation?" Before
answering that question we must have some understanding of
the pattern of revelational history.

28. Victor Walter, "The Measure of our Message," *Trinity Journal*, 3 (Spring,
1974):72.

Various views have been offered—from those which emphasize major discontinuities within biblical history to those which emphasize almost total continuity. Five such theories were identified and discussed in relation to the continuity-discontinuity continuum.

Four major Biblical concepts—grace, law, salvation, and the ministry of the Holy Spirit—were also discussed in terms of the continuity-discontinuity issue, and the reader is encouraged to spend some time at this point coming to his own conclusions about the nature of salvation history. This process forms the basis for doing theological analysis.

The steps in theological analysis are:

1. *Determine your own view of the nature of God's relationship to man.* The collecting of evidence, the framing of questions, and the understanding of certain texts presented in this chapter are undoubtedly biased by the author's conceptions of a biblical view of salvation history. The conclusion of this step is too important to assume from someone else without carefully and prayerfully considering the evidence yourself.

2. *Identify the implications of this view for the passage you are studying.* For example, a position on the nature of God's relationship to man that is primarily discontinuous will view the Old Testament as less relevant for contemporary believers than the New Testament.

3. *Assess the extent of theological knowledge available to the people of that time.* What previous knowledge had they been given? (This previous knowledge is sometimes referred to in hermeneutics textbooks as the "analogy of Scripture.") Good biblical theology texts may prove helpful in this regard.

4. *Determine the meaning the passage possessed for its original recipients in the light of their knowledge.*

5. *Identify the additional knowledge about this topic which is available to us now because of later revelation.* (This is sometimes referred to in hermeneutics textbooks as the "analogy of faith.") *Nave's Topical Bible* and systematic theology texts will often prove helpful in acquiring this type of information.

Summary of General Hermeneutics

Historical-Cultural and Contextual Analysis	Lexical-Syntactical Analysis	Theological Analysis

1. Determine the general historical and cultural milieu of the writer and his audience.
  a. Determine the general historical circumstances.
  b. Be aware of cultural circumstances and norms that add meaning to given actions.
  c. Discern the level of spiritual commitment of the audience.
2. Determine the purpose the author had in writing a book by:
  a. Noting explicit statements or repeated phrases.
  b. Observing parenetical or hortatory sections.
  c. Observing issues that are omitted or focused on.
3. Understand how the passage fits into its immediate context.
  a. Identify the major blocks of material in the book and show how they fit into a coherent whole.
  b. Show how the passage fits into the flow of the author's argument.
  c. Determine the perspective which the author intends to communicate—noumenological or phenomenological.
  d. Distinguish between descriptive and prescriptive truth.
  e. Distinguish between incidental details and the teaching focus of the passage.
  f. Identify the person or category of persons for whom the particular passage is intended.
	1. Identify the general literary form.
	2. Trace the development of the author's theme and show how the passage under consideration fits into the context.
	3. Identify the natural divisions (paragraphs and sentences) of text.
	4. Identify the connecting words within the paragraphs and sentences and show how they aid in understanding the author's progression of thought.
	5. Determine what the individual words mean.
	  a. Identify the multiple meanings a word possessed in its time and culture.
	  b. Determine the single meaning intended by the author in a given context.
	6. Analyze the syntax to show how it contributes to the understanding of the passage.
	7. Put the results of your analysis into nontechnical, easily understood words that clearly convey the author's intended meaning.
		1. Determine your own view of the nature of God's relationship to man.
		2. Identify the implications of this view for the passage you are studying.
		3. Assess the extent of theological knowledge available to the people of that time.
		4. Determine the meaning the passage possessed for its original recipients in the light of their knowledge.
		5. Identify the additional knowledge about this topic which is available to us now because of later revelation.

Exercises

BT26: Carefully think through the continuity-discontinuity issue, using the text, recommended readings, and your own resources to examine the question further. Write out a summary of your own position. Your position will probably be tentative at this point, open to modification as new information becomes available.

BT27: A couple in deep conflict comes to you for counseling about a certain matter. The husband says that they need a new car and wants to finance it through their local bank, since they don't have the money to pay for it in cash. His wife, basing her argument on Romans 13:8 ("Owe no man anything"), believes it is wrong to borrow money to purchase the car. The husband says he doesn't think that the verse refers to their situation and wants to know what you think. What will you do?

BT28: At least one Protestant denomination refuses to have a paid clergy on the basis of 1 Timothy 3:3. Do you agree with the scriptural basis of their practice? Why, or why not?

BT29: A married couple you have been counseling reveals that the husband has been having an affair. The husband professes to be a Christian, so you ask him how he reconciles his behavior with the biblical teaching on marital faithfulness. He replies that he loves both persons, and justifies his behavior on the basis of 1 Corinthians 6:12 ("All things are lawful for me," RSV). What will you do?

BT30: You are part of a Bible study discussion group in which someone offers a point based on an Old Testament passage. Another person responds with: "That's from the Old Testament, and therefore doesn't apply to us as Christians." As discussion leader that night, how would you handle the situation?

BT31: A sincere young Christian attended a teaching series based on Psalm 37:4 ("Delight yourself in the Lord, and he will give you the desires of your heart") and Mark 11:24 ("Whatever you ask for in prayer, believe that you have received it, and it will be yours"). Based on the teaching, he began to write checks "on faith," and was rather dismayed when they "bounced." How would you counsel him regarding the teaching he had received concerning these verses?

BT32: Your cousin, now attending a neoorthodox seminary, argues against the approach toward hermeneutics that carefully considers historical, cultural, contextual, and grammatical matters because "the letter kills, but the Spirit gives life" (2 Cor. 3:6). He goes on to state that interpretations should be in line with "the spirit of Christianity," and that your method of interpretation often results in exegesis that is no longer consistent with the gracious spirit of Christ. How would you respond?

BT33: Some writers have suggested that there is an inconsistency between the doctrine of Paul (as found in Gal. 2:15-16; Rom. 3:20,28) and the doctrine of James (as found in James 1:22-25; 2:8,14-17,21-24). Do you believe these can be reconciled? If so, how would you reconcile them?

BT34: Paul's experience in Romans 7:7-25 has long been a source of discussion among Christians with important implications for counselors. The main question has been: Is his experience the struggle of a believer or is it a preconversion struggle only? Using your knowledge of hermeneutics, compare the arguments for each interpretation. You may present an alternative interpretation if it can be justified exegetically. What are the implications of your interpretation for Christian mental health and counseling?

chapter six

Special Literary Methods:

Similes, Metaphors, Proverbs, Parables, and Allegories

After completing this chapter, you should be able to:

1. Describe in one to three sentences each of the literary terms mentioned in the chapter title.
2. Identify these literary methods when they occur in the biblical text.
3. Describe the interpretive principles necessary to determine the author's intended meaning when he uses any of the above literary devices.

Definitions and Comparisons of Literary Methods

Chapters 3, 4, and 5 have discussed those methods used in the interpretation of all texts, and generally labelled "general hermeneutics." This chapter and the following one focus attention on special hermeneutics, which studies the interpretation of special literary forms. Good communicators use a variety of literary devices for illustration, clarification, emphasis, and maintenance of audience interest. Biblical writers and speakers also used such devices. Some of their common methods included similes, metaphors, proverbs, parables, and allegories.

E. D. Hirsch likens various types of literary expression to games: to understand them properly it is necessary to know what game you are playing. It is also necessary to know the rules of that game. Disagreements arise in interpretation because (1) there is a question over what game is being played, or (2) there is confusion about the proper rules for playing that game.[1] Fortunately for the modern Bible student, careful literary analysis has yielded a substantial body of knowledge concerning the characteristics of these literary forms and the principles necessary to interpret them properly.

Two of the simplest literary devices are similes and metaphors. A *simile* is simply an expressed comparison: it typically uses the words *like* or *as* (e.g., "the kingdom of heaven is like . . ."). The emphasis is on some point of similarity between two ideas, groups, actions, etc. The subject and the thing with which it is being compared are kept separate (i.e., not "the kingdom of heaven is . . ." but rather "the kingdom of heaven is like . . .").[2]

A *metaphor* is an unexpressed comparison: it does not use the words *like* or *as*. The subject and the thing with which it is being compared are intertwined rather than kept separate. Jesus used metaphors when He said, "I am the bread of life," and "You are the light of the world." Although the subject and its comparison are identified as one, the author does not intend his words to be taken literally: Christ is no more a piece of bread than Christians are photon-emitters. In both similes and metaphors, because of their compact nature, the author

1. E. D. Hirsch, *Validity in Interpretation* (New Haven: Yale University Press, 1967), p. 70.
2. Many of the points discussed here and later in this chapter were received from Dr. Walter C. Kaiser, Jr., Professor of Old Testament at Trinity Evangelical Divinity School, Spring, 1974.

usually intends to stress a single point (e.g., that Christ is the source of sustenance for our spiritual lives, or that Christians are to be examples of godly living in an ungodly world).

A *parable* can be understood as an extended simile. The comparison is expressed, and the subject and the thing compared, explained more fully, are kept separate. Similarly an *allegory* can be understood as an extended metaphor: the comparison is unexpressed, and the subject and the thing compared are intermingled.

A parable generally proceeds by keeping the story and its application distinct from each other: usually the application follows the story. Allegories intermingle the story and its application so that an allegory carries its own interpretation within itself. The following examples of a parable and an allegory illustrate this distinction:

Parable (Isaiah 5:1-7)
¹I will sing to the one I love
   a song about his vineyard:
My loved one had a vineyard
   on a fertile hillside
²He dug it up and cleared it of stones
   and planted it with the choicest vines.
He built a watchtower in it
   and cut out a winepress as well.
Then he looked for a crop of good grapes,
   but it yielded only bad fruit.
³Now you dwellers in Jerusalem and men of Judah,
   judge between me and my vineyard.
⁴What more could have been done for my vineyard
   than I have done for it?
When I looked for good grapes,
   why did it yield only bad?
⁵Now I will tell you
   what I am going to do to my vineyard:
I will take away its hedge,
   and it will be destroyed;

I will break down its wall,
and it will be trampled.
⁶I will make it a wasteland
neither pruned nor cultivated,
and briars and thorns will grow there.
I will command the clouds
not to rain on it.
⁷The vineyard of the Lord Almighty
is the house of Israel,
and the men of Judah
are the garden of his delight.
And he looked for justice, but saw bloodshed;
for righteousness, but heard cries of
distress.

Allegory (Psalm 80:8-16)
⁸You brought a vine out of Egypt;
you drove out the nations and planted it.
⁹You cleared the ground for it,
and it took root and filled the land.
¹⁰The mountains were covered with its shade,
the mighty cedars with its branches.
¹¹It sent out its boughs to the Sea,
its shoots as far as the River.
¹²Why have you broken down its walls
so that all who pass by pick its grapes?
¹³Boars from the forest ravage it
and the creatures of the field feed on it.
¹⁴Return to us, O God Almighty!
Look down from heaven and see!
¹⁵Watch over this vine,
the root your right hand has planted,
the son you have raised up for yourself.
¹⁶Your vine is cut down, it is burned with fire;
at your rebuke your people perish.

In the parable the story is found in verses one to six and the application in verse seven. In the allegory the story and its application are intermingled and proceed together.

A *proverb* may be conceived as a compressed parable or allegory, sometimes partaking of characteristics of both. Schematically the relationship between these five literary devices is presented below:

$$\text{Simile} \xrightarrow{\text{extended}} \text{Parable}$$
$$\downarrow \text{compressed}$$
$$\text{Proverb}$$
$$\uparrow \text{compressed}$$
$$\text{Metaphor} \xrightarrow{\text{extended}} \text{Allegory}$$

To summarize: In similes and parables the comparisons are expressed and kept separate, while in metaphors and allegories they are unexpressed and intermingled. In a parable there is a conscious separation of the story and its application, whereas in an allegory there is an intermingling of the two. Proverbs can be viewed as either compressed parables or compressed allegories. The following sections will discuss the nature and interpretation of proverbs, parables, and allegories at greater length.

Proverbs

Walter C. Kaiser has described proverbs as sayings that are "terse, brief, have a little 'kick' to them, and a little bit of salt as well."[3] Many people view proverbs as nice slogans—good mottos to hang on one's wall. Few recognize the tremendous beauty and wisdom often contained in these sayings.

One of the greatest problems of religion is the lack of practical integration between our theological beliefs and daily living. It is possible to divorce our religious life from practical decisions we make each day. Proverbs can provide an important antidote, for they demonstrate true religion in specific, practical, and meaningful terms.

3. W. C. Kaiser, Jr., *The Old Testament in Contemporary Preaching* (Grand Rapids: Baker, 1973), p. 119. This section on Proverbs is taken largely from his discussion, pp. 118-120.

The general focus in the Book of Proverbs is the moral aspect of the law—ethical regulations for daily life phrased in universally abiding terms. Specific foci include wisdom, morality, chastity, control of the tongue, associations with others, laziness, and justice. "As Deuteronomy preaches the Law, the Wisdom Books put it into short, understandable phrases that are both quotable and easily digested."[4]

Many of the proverbs are concerned with wisdom, a concept which provides the context for all of them. Wisdom in Scripture is not synonymous with knowledge. It begins with "the fear of the Lord." The fear of the Lord is not normal fear, or even that more profound type known as "numinous awe," but is basically a stance, an attitude of the heart that recognizes our rightful relationship to the Creator-God. Wisdom and wise living proceed from this proper stance, this recognition of our rightful place before God. Within this context the proverbs no longer remain pious mottos to be hung on the wall, but become intensely practical, meaningful ways of inspiring a close walk with the Lord.

From an interpretive standpoint it is good to recognize that because of their highly condensed form, proverbs usually have a single point of comparison or principle of truth to convey. Pressing a proverb in all of its incidental points usually results in going beyond the author's intention. For example, when King Lemuel says of the virtuous woman that "she is like the merchants' ships" (Prov. 31:14), he probably did not intend this to be a statement about her girth; she is like the ships of the merchants because she goes various places gathering food for the needs of her household. Thus, proverbs (like similes and metaphors) usually convey a single intended thought or comparison.

Parables

Our word *parable* is related to the Greek word *paraballo* which means "to throw or place alongside." Thus, a parable

4. Ibid., p. 119.

is something placed alongside something else for the purpose of comparison. The typical parable uses a common event of natural life to emphasize or clarify an important spiritual truth.

Jesus, the master teacher, used parables regularly as He taught. The Greek word for parable occurs nearly fifty times in the synoptic gospels in connection with His ministry, suggesting that parables were one of His favorite teaching devices.

Purpose of Parables

Scripture reveals two basic purposes of parables. The first of these is to reveal truth to believers (Matt. 13:10-12; Mark 4:11). Parables can cause a lasting impression often far more effectively than ordinary discourse. For example, Christ could have said, "You should be persistent in your prayer life." a statement that His hearers would probably have shrugged off and quickly forgotten. Instead He told them of a widow who kept begging an unjust judge to help her, until the judge finally decided to answer her petitions to stop her complaining. Christ then taught the lesson of the parable: if an unjust judge who cares nothing about a widow can be swayed by persistent begging, how much more will a loving heavenly Father answer those who consistently pray to Him. Similarly, Christ could have said, "You should be humble when you pray." Instead He told His audience of the Pharisee and the tax collector who went up to the temple to pray (Luke 18:9-14). The ridiculousness of the Pharisee's pride and the authenticity of the tax collector's humility teach Christ's lesson in a simple but unforgettable way.

In revealing truth parables are also used effectively in Scripture to confront believers with wrongdoing in their lives. If a believer possesses basically sound moral standards cognitively, and yet fails to live up to those standards in some area of his life, a parable can be an effectual means of pointing out this discrepancy. Consider the case of David and Nathan as told in 2 Samuel 12:1-7. The context of this incident is that

David had just had Uriah killed in order that he might marry
Uriah's wife Bathsheba. The text reads:

> The Lord sent Nathan to David. When he came to
> him, he said, "There were two men in a certain town, one
> rich and the other poor. The rich man had a very large
> number of sheep and cattle, but the poor man had noth-
> ing except one little ewe lamb he had bought. He raised
> it, and it grew up with him and his children. It shared his
> food, drank from his cup and even slept in his arms. It
> was like a daughter to him.
> "Now a traveler came to the rich man, but the rich
> man refrained from taking one of his own sheep or cattle
> to prepare a meal for the traveler who had come to him.
> Instead, he took the ewe lamb that belonged to the poor
> man and prepared it for the one who had come to him."
> David burned with anger against the man and said to
> Nathan, "As surely as the Lord lives, the man who did
> this deserves to die! He must pay for that lamb four times
> over, because he did such a thing and had not pity."
> Then Nathan said to David, "You are the man!"

David, a man of moral principle, easily identified with the
great wrong that had been done to the poor man in the story,
and when the parable was applied to his own behavior, he
quickly repented of his wrong.

In addition to clarifying and emphasizing spiritual truths
for believers, parables have a second purpose—one that seems
diametrically opposed to the first. A parable hides truth from
those who have hardened their hearts against it (Matt.
13:10-15; Mark 4:11-12; Luke 8:9-10). It may seem difficult
to reconcile this purpose with our conception of God as a
loving Being who announces truth rather than hides it.

Perhaps the answer to this apparent dilemma can be found
in the scriptural passages discussed in connection with spiritual factors in the perceptual process (chapter 1). It may be
that as man resists truth and yields to sin, he becomes less and

less able to understand spiritual truth. Thus the same parables that brought insight to faithful believers were without meaning to those who were hardening their hearts against the truth. Such an understanding of the above-mentioned verses is compatible with a careful exegesis of them, and removes from God any responsibility for the Pharisees' spiritual blindness.

Principle for the Interpretation of Parables

Historical-Cultural and Contextual Analysis

The same type of analysis that is used in interpreting narrative and expository passages should be used in the interpretation of parables. Since parables were used to clarify or emphasize a truth that was being discussed in a specific historical situation, an examination of the topics under discussion in the immediate context of a passage often sheds valuable light on the meaning.

For example, the Parable of the Laborers in the Vineyard (Matt 20:1–16) has been given a number of interpretations, many of which have little or no relationship to the context within which this parable was spoken. Immediately preceding Jesus' telling of this parable, the rich young ruler had come to Jesus and asked Him what he must do to inherit eternal life. Jesus perceived that the greatest obstacle that prevented this young man from total commitment to God was his riches, and told him to give away what he possessed and become a disciple. The young man went away sorrowful, unwilling to part with his riches.

Peter asked the Lord, "We have left everything to follow you! What then will there be for us?" Jesus assured Peter that they would be amply rewarded for their service, but then went on to tell the Parable of the Laborers. In this context it can be seen that Jesus' story was a gentle rebuke to Peter, a rebuke of the self-righteous attitude which says, "See how much I have done (I was not unwilling to give up *all* and follow You as this young man was). I should certainly get a large reward for my great sacrifice." Jesus was gently rebuking Peter for possessing the attitude of a hireling—"What am I going to get out of this?"—rather than recognizing that the motive for service in the kingdom is to be love.[5] Interpretations of a parable which fail to consider the historical occasion within which it occurs may pose interesting hypotheses, but are highly unlikely to be stating Jesus' intended purpose.

Sometimes the intended meaning is stated explicitly in the introduction to the parable, either by Jesus or by the biblical author. At other times the intended meaning is conveyed through the application that is made of the parable (see Matt. 15:13; 18:21,35; 20:1-16; 22:14; 25:13; Luke 12:15,21; 15:7,10; 18:1,9; 19:11 for examples). At other times, placement of the parables within the chronology of Jesus' life adds further meaning. The intended purpose of the Parable of the Wicked Tenants (Luke 20:9-18) is fairly obvious, but it certainly must have possessed greater poignancy as Jesus told it shortly before His crucifixion.

In addition to historical and contextual clues, knowledge of cultural details often sheds important light on the meaning of a parable. For example, harvests, weddings, and wine were Jewish symbols of the end of the age. The fig tree was a symbol of the people of God. Lamps were put under baskets to extinguish them; thus to light a lamp and put it under a bushel meant to light it and immediately put it out.[6] Jeremias' book, *The Parables of Jesus*, abounds with information about cultural details such as this, and explains the meaning these stories and symbols had for Jesus and His original hearers.[7]

5. R. C. Trench, *Notes on the Parables of Our Lord* (reprinted, Grand Rapids: Baker, 1948), pp. 61-66.

6. Ramm, *Protestant Biblical Interpretation*, p.282.

7. J. Jeremias, *Parables of Jesus*, Rev. ed. (New York: Scribner's, 1971). Jeremias' literary analysis of the nature of parables is questioned by many evangelical scholars. His work remains valuable, nevertheless, because of his rich knowledge of Hebrew culture and customs.

Lexical-Syntactical Analysis

The same rules of lexical-syntactical analysis that apply to other forms of prose should also be applied to parables. The same tools mentioned in chapter 4—lexicons, concordances, grammars, and exegetical commentaries—can all be used with profit in the exposition of parables.

Theological Analysis

There are three main theological questions that an expositor must answer before he can interpret most of the parables Jesus used. First he must define, on the basis of the available evidence, the terms "kingdom of heaven" and "kingdom of God" and then decide whether or not these terms are synonyms. Since a very large percentage of Jesus' teaching, including His parables, refers to these kingdoms, their proper identification is an important question.[8]

Those who believe that these two kingdoms are to be distinguished from each other, hold various proposals regarding the identities of the two kingdoms. A common view is that the kingdom of God refers to all intelligent beings who are willingly subject to God, both in heaven and on earth, whereas the kingdom of heaven includes all human beings who profess allegiance to God, whether that profession is genuine or spurious.[9]

Those who interpret these two names to be synonymous usually explain the use of different phrases in the following way: Matthew, writing primarily to Jews, preferred the term "kingdom of heaven" as a respectful term equivalent to "king-

8. "Modern scholarship is quite unanimous in the opinion that the Kingdom of God was the central message of Jesus." George E. Ladd, *A Theology of the New Testament* (Grand Rapids: Eerdmans, 1974), p. 57.

9. See the note on Matthew 6:33 in the Scofield Reference Bible for an example of a position that clearly differentiates the kingdom of God from the kingdom of heaven. The corresponding note in the New Scofield Reference Bible states that these two terms are in many cases used synonymously, but are to be distinguished in some instances.

dom of God," due to the tendency within Judaism to avoid the direct use of the name of God. Mark and Luke, writing to Gentiles, used the term "kingdom of God" because it would convey the idea better to their audiences.[10]

Several parallel passages within the Synoptics use the term "kingdom of God" when referring to a particular incident and the term "kingdom of heaven" when referring to a very similar incident mentioned in one of the other Gospels. The following list gives examples.

Reason for Parables	Matt. 13:10-15; cf. Mark 4:10-12 and Luke 8:9-10
Mustard Seed	Matt. 13:31-32; cf. Mark 4:30-32 and Luke 13:18-19
Leaven	Matt. 13:33; cf. Luke 13:20-21
The Beatitudes	Matt. 5:3; cf. Luke 6:20

If these two are actually separate kingdoms, then Jesus would have been ascribing two entirely different meanings to highly similar parables told on separate occasions. He may have done this, but it hardly seems likely, particularly in the first set of comparisons.

The parallelism of Matthew 19:23-24 also supports the hypothesis that Jesus meant these two terms to be understood as the same kingdom. Here He is recorded as saying:

> I tell you the truth, it is hard for a rich man to enter the *kingdom of heaven*. Again I tell you, it is easier for a camel to go through the eye of a needle than for a rich man to enter the *kingdom of God* (emphasis mine).

For these and other reasons the majority of evangelical expositiors have understood these terms as synonyms. Further excellent discussions on the kingdom are found in the *New Bible Dictionary* and George Eldon Ladd's books, *Crucial Questions about the Kingdom* and *A Theology of the New Testament* (chapter 4).

10. H. Ridderbos, "Kingdom of Heaven," *The New Bible Dictionary*, ed. J. D. Douglas (Grand Rapids: Eerdmans, 1962), p. 693.

A second question involving the kingdom (and the interpretation of the parables) is almost unanimously agreed on by
evangelical scholars. This is that in some senses the kingdom
has come, in other senses it is continuing, and in some senses
it will not ultimately come until the eschatological completion
of this age.[11]

Christ taught that in one sense the kingdom was already
present during His sojourn on earth (Matt. 12:28 and parallels; Luke 17:20-21), that it could be entered by the new birth
(John 3:3), and that it was being entered by tax collectors and
harlots because they were repenting and believing (Matt.
21:31).

Parables also speak of the continuing ministry of the kingdom. They tell of sowing and reaping, small seeds growing
into magnificent trees, a great net being let down into the sea
and not pulled up until the end of the age, and grain and
tares growing together. They speak of wise and foolish com-
mitments, and of industrious versus slothful use of abilities.

In a third sense, many parables look forward to their ultimate fulfillment when God's kingdom rule will be realized
fully, not only in the hearts of believers, but in His complete
triumph over evil. No longer will God approach man in the
form of a servant, but as the Ruler, the ultimate Judge, the
final Divider.

A third theological issue that affects one's interpretation of
parables relates to the *postponed-kingdom theory*. This theory
suggests that Jesus originally intended to institute an earthly
kingdom, and that His early teachings (e.g., Matt. 1–12) were
instructions regarding this kingdom. According to the
postponed-kingdom theory, it was only midway through His
teaching ministry that Jesus recognized that He would be rejected and eventually go to the cross.

11. See Bernard Ramm, *Protestant Biblical Interpretation*, 3rd rev. ed. (Grand
Rapids: Baker, 1970), pp. 280-281.

If the postponed-kingdom theory is correct, it can be argued that the parables which Jesus spoke before realizing that He was to be rejected were intended as rules for governing His earthly kingdom. Since this earthly kingdom has been postponed until the future millennial era, the instructions and parables He spoke prior to Matthew 13 should not be considered relevant for church age believers.

The contrasting viewpoint to the postponed-kingdom theory is that Jesus had no illusions about setting up an earthly kingdom. Simeon's prophecy (Luke 2:34-35) and Isaiah's messianic prophecy (Isaiah 53), which Jesus was certainly aware of, would have left little doubt in Jesus' mind that His earthly ministry would end in His atoning death rather than in the establishment of an earthly kingdom (cf. John 12:27). Those who believe that Jesus spent His entire ministry aware that He was going to the cross usually believe that all His teachings and parables are directed to New Testament believers, and do not await a future application in the millennial kingdom. The necessity of making a decision on the postponed-kingdom theory is obvious, then, in the process of interpreting Jesus' early parables.

There is one other aspect of theological analysis that is important in the interpretation of parables. Parables can serve the important purpose of fixing doctrine in our memories in a particularly striking fashion. However, orthodox expositors unanimously agree that no doctrine should be grounded on a parable as its primary or only source. The rationale for this principle is that clearer passages of Scripture are always used to clarify more obscure passages, never vice versa. Parables are by nature more obscure than doctrinal passages. Thus doctrine should be developed from the clear prose passages of Scripture, and parables used to amplify or emphasize that doctrine.

Church history illustrates the heresies of those who failed to observe this caution. One example suffices to show how easily this can occur: Faustus Socinus argued from the Parable of the Unmerciful Servant (Matt. 18:23-35), that as the king pardoned his servant merely on the basis of his petition, so in the same way God, without requiring sacrifice or intercessor, pardons sinners on the ground of their prayers.[12] Socinus thus makes this parable the basis for doctrine rather than interpreting it in the light of doctrine. Trench notes a second caution—one that is important in the interpretation of all of Scripture, including parables—namely, that "we are not to expect, in every place, the whole circle of Christian truth to be fully stated, and that no conclusion may be drawn from the absence of a doctrine from one passage which is clearly stated in others."[13]

Literary Analysis

Throughout history a central question regarding parables has been "How much is significant?" Chrysostom and Theophylact argued that there is but one central point in a parable; all the rest is drapery or ornament. Augustine, while agreeing with their principle, in practice often extended his interpretations to even the minutest fibers of the narrative. In more recent times, Cocceius and his followers have strongly affirmed that *every* part of a parable is significant.[14] Thus there have been scholars on both sides of the question throughout history.

Fortunately for us, on the first two occasions recorded in which Jesus spoke in parables, He interpreted their meaning (The Sower: Matt. 13:1-23; The Wheat and the Tares: Matt. 13:24-30,36-43). His interpretations appear to be midway between the extreme views mentioned above: in Jesus' own analyses it is possible to discern both a central, focal idea, and a significant emphasis on details *as they relate to that focal idea*.

---

12. Trench, *Notes on the Parables of Our Lord* (reprinted, Grand Rapids: Baker, 1948), p. 41.

13. Ibid., pp. 17-18.

14. Ibid., pp. 15,33.

Jesus' analysis of the details of the parable is in contrast with the practice of those who give significance to the details in such a manner that the details teach an additional lesson unrelated to the central point of the parable.

For example, the central concept in the Parable of the Sower is that God's Word will meet with varying receptions in different people. The details illustrate these: (1) the person who fails to understand, (2) the enthusiast who soon loses his courage, (3) the person whose ability to respond is choked by worldly cares and riches, and (4) the person who hears, responds, and becomes a productive member of God's kingdom. The focal point of the Parable of the Tares is that within the kingdom regenerate men and imitators will exist side by side throughout this age, but God's final judgment is sure. The details give further information about the origin and nature of these imitators and the relationship of the believer to them.

Thus, if any inferences can be drawn from Christ's interpretations of His own parables, they are that (1) there is a central, focal point of teaching in Christ's parables, and (2) the details have significance as they relate to that focal teaching. The details are not to be given meaning that is independent of the main teaching of the parable.

Interpreters have likened the focal teaching of a parable to the hub of a wheel, and its details to the spokes. When the right interpretation has been found, a natural symmetry and closure will result.

Trench, in his classic work on parables, says:

> An interpretation, besides being thus in accordance with its context, must be so without the use of any very violent means; even, as generally, the interpretation must be easy—if not always easy to be discovered, yet being discovered easy. For it is here as with the laws of Nature; genius may be needful to discover the law, but being discovered it throws light back upon itself, and commends itself unto all. Again, as it is the proof of the law that it explains *all* the phenomena, so it is tolerable evidence

that we have found the right interpretation of a parable,
if it leaves none of the main circumstances unexplained.[15]

Trench and a number of other commentators suggest that
the correct interpretation of a parable will commend itself
because it fits easily and naturally, and because it explains all
the main details. False interpretations betray themselves by
being out of harmony with some important details of the parable or its context.

Resources for Further Reading

R. C. Trench. *Notes on the Parables of our Lord.*
M. S. Terry. *Biblical Hermeneutics*, pp. 276-301.
J. Jeremias. *The Parables of Jesus.*
Bernard Ramm. *Protestant Biblical Interpretation*, 3rd rev. ed., pp. 276-288.

Allegories

As a parable is an extended simile, so an allegory is an
extended metaphor. An allegory differs from a parable, as
noted before, in that a parable typically keeps the story distinct
from its interpretation or application, while an allegory inter-
twines the story and its meaning.

Interpretively, parables and allegories differ on another
major point: in a parable there is one focus, and the details
are significant only as they relate to that focus; in an allegory
there are generally several points of comparison, not necessarily centered around one focus. For example, in the Parable
of the Mustard Seed (Matt. 13:31-32) the central purpose is
to show the spread of the gospel from a tiny band of Christians (the mustard seed) to a worldwide body of believers (the
full-grown tree). The relationship between the seed, the tree,

15. Ibid., p. 17.

the field, the nest, and the birds is casual; and these details achieve significance only in relationship to the growing tree. However, in the allegory of the Christian's armor (Eph. 6), there are several points of comparison. Each part of the Christian's armor is significant, and each is necessary for the Christian to be "fully armed."

Principles for Interpreting Allegories

1. Use historical-cultural, contextual, lexical-syntactical, and theological analyses as with other types of prose.
2. Determine the *multiple* points of comparison intended by the author by studying the context and the points that he emphasized.

Literary Analysis of Allegory

Many allegories are found throughout Scripture. The allegory of Christ as the True Vine (John 15:1-17) is analyzed here to show the relationship of the several points of comparison to the meaning of the passage. There are three foci in this allegory. The first of these is the vine as a symbol of Christ.[16] The whole passage emphasizes the importance of the vine: the pronouns *I*, *me*, and *my* occur thirty-eight times in the seventeen verses, and the word *vine* three times, underscoring the centrality of Christ in the spiritual fruitbearing of the Christian. This focus is summed up in verse 4: "No branch can bear fruit by itself; it must remain in the vine. Neither can you bear fruit unless you remain in me."

The second focus of the allegory is the Father, symbolized as the vine-dresser. In this illustration the Father is actively concerned with fruitbearing. He prunes some branches that they may be more fruitful, and eliminates those which produce no fruit.

16. Discussion of these points can be found in A. B. Mickelsen, *Interpreting the Bible* (Grand Rapids: Eerdmans, 1963), pp. 232-234.

The third focus of the allegory is found in the branches, the disciples themselves. "Abiding" speaks metaphorically of relationship, and the present tense speaks of *continuing* relationship as a necessity for fruitbearing. Obeying God's commands is a necessary part of relationship, and loving fellow believers is an integral part of that obedience. The allegory portrays the need for a continuous, living relationship with the Lord Jesus, coupled with obedience to His Word, as the essence of discipleship and fruitbearing.

The Problem of Paul's Allegorization

One passage that has caused a great deal of perplexity for evangelicals is Paul's allegorizing in Galatians 4. Liberal theologians have been quick to seize on this as an illustration of Paul's adoption of the illegitimate hermeneutical methods of his day. Evangelicals have often retreated in embarrassed silence, for it does seem that in these verses Paul used illegitimate allegorization. If Paul did indeed use illegitimate methods, this would certainly have significant implications for our doctrine of inspiration.

On this passage several evangelical scholars have taken a position similar to G. W. Meyer, who in his *Critical Commentary on Galatians* says:

> At the conclusion of the theoretical portion of his epistle, Paul adds a quite peculiar ... disquisition—a learned rabbinico-allegorical argument derived from the law itself—calculated to annihilate the influence of the pseudo-apostles with their own weapons, and to root them out on their own ground.[17]

Thus Meyer considers that Paul used allegorization, not to give it legitimacy as a method of exegesis, but as an *argumen-*

17. G. W. Meyer, *Critical Commentary on Galatians*, cited in M. S. Terry, *Biblical Hermeneutics* (Grand Rapids: Zondervan, 1974), p. 321.

tum ad hominem against his opponents who were using these same methods to turn a proper use of the law into a system of legalism.

Alan Cole paraphrases the passage in the following way:

> Tell me, do you not listen to what the law says—you who want to be under law as a system? Scripture says that Abraham had two sons, one by the slave-wife and the other by the freeborn wife. The slave-wife's son was born perfectly naturally, but the son of the freeborn wife was born in fulfilment of God's promise. All this can be seen as a symbolic picture [an allegory] for these women could represent two Covenants. The first (i.e., the slave-wife) could stand for the covenant made at Mount Sinai; all her children (i.e., those under that covenant) are in spiritual bondage. That is Hagar for you. So the scriptural character "Hagar" could also stand for Mount Sinai in Arabia. Sinai stands in the same category as the Jerusalem that we know, for she is certainly in slavery, along with her "children." But the heavenly Jerusalem stands for the freeborn wife—and she is our "mother." For Scripture says:
>
> > "Be glad, you woman who is not in childbirth;
> > Break into a shout of triumph, you who are not in
> >   labour;
> > For the abandoned wife has more children
> > Than the wife who has her husband."
>
> Now you, my fellow-Christians, are children born in fulfilment of God's promise, like Isaac was. But just as in those days the son born in the course of nature used to bully the son born supernaturally, so it is today. But what does Scripture say to that? "Expel the slave-wife and her son; for the slave-wife's son is certainly not going to share the inheritance with the freeborn wife's son." And so my summing-up is this: We Christians are not children of the slave-wife, but of the freeborn wife. Christ has given us

our freedom; stand firm, and do not allow yourselves to
be harnessed again to the yoke that spells slavery.[18]

Paul immediately differentiated his method from that of
the typical allegorist by recognizing the grammatical-historical
validity of the events. In verses 21-23 he indicates that Abraham had two sons, one by a slave woman and the other by a
free woman.

Paul went on to say that these things could all be allegorized, and then he developed a series of correspondences:

corresponds to

a	1 Hagar, bondmaid = Old Covenant	The present Jerusalem
	2 Sarah, freewoman = New Covenant	Jerusalem above
b	1 Ishmael, child of flesh	Those in bondage to law
	2 Isaac, child of promise	We, Christian brethren (v. 28)
c	1 Ishmael persecuted Isaac	So now legalists persecute Christians
	2 Scripture says: Cast out bondmaid and son	I say (vv. 31; 5:1): Be not entangled in a yoke of bondage (legalism)[19]

Lotto Schmoller, in *Lange's Biblework* [*Commentary on the Holy
Scriptures*, ed. John Peter Lange], remarks:

Paul to be sure allegorizes here, for he says so himself.
But with the very fact of him saying this himself, the
gravity of the hermeneutical difficulty disappears. He
means therefore to give an allegory, not an exposition; he
does not proceed as an exegete, and does not mean to
say (after the manner of the allegorizing exegetes) that
only what he now says is the true sense of the narrative.[20]

18. Alan Cole, *The Epistle of Paul to the Galatians, Tyndale New Testament Commentaries*, ed. R. V. G. Tasker (Grand Rapids: Eerdmans, 1965), pp. 129-130.
19. M. S. Terry, *Biblical Hermeneutics*, p. 322.
20. Cited in Terry, *Biblical Hermeneutics*, p. 323.

To sum up, the following factors suggest that Paul is using
allegorization to confound his hypocritical opponents:

1. Paul had made a series of very strong arguments against
the Judaizers, arguments that by themselves would substantiate his case. This final argument was not needed; it stands
more as an example of using the pseudo-apostles' own weap-
ons against them.

2. If Paul regarded allegorizing as a legitimate method,
then it seems almost certain that he would have used it in
some of his other epistles, but he did not.

3. Paul differed from the typical allegorist when he admitted the historical validity of the text, rather than saying that
the words of the text were only a shadow of the deeper (and
truer) meaning. He admitted that these events happened historically and then went on to say that they can be allegorized.
He did not say "this is what the text means" nor claim that he
was giving an exposition of the text.

Resources for Further Reading

A. B. Mickelsen. *Interpreting the Bible*, pp. 230-235.

M. S. Terry. *Biblical Hermeneutics*, pp. 302-328.

Chapter Summary

The following steps incorporate general and special
hermeneutics:

1. Do a historical-cultural and contextual analysis.
2. Do a lexical-syntactical analysis.
3. Do a theological analysis.
4. Identify the literary form and apply an appropriate analysis.

a. Look for explicit references that indicate the author's intent regarding the method he was using.

b. If the text does not explicitly identify the literary form of the passage, study the characteristics of the passage deductively to ascertain its form.

c. Apply the principles of literary devices carefully but not rigidly.

(1) Metaphors, similes, and proverbs—look for the single point of comparison.

(2) Parables—determine the focal teaching and the details of significance surrounding it.

(3) Allegories—determine the multiple points of comparison intended by the author.

5. State your understanding of the meaning of the passage.

6. Check to see if your stated meaning "fits" into the immediate context and total context of the book. If it doesn't, recycle the process.

7. Compare your work with that of others.

Exercises

BT35: Allegories and Allegorizing

From the time of Christ until the time of Luther a major hermeneutical tool was the practice of allegorization. Today most evangelical scholars reject allegorization as an illegitimate hermeneutical device.

a. Define allegorization and show why this long-used method of interpreting Scripture is now repudiated.

b. Contrast the genre of allegory with the method of allegorizing and show why one is considered legitimate and the other illegitimate.

BT36: Use your knowledge of literary methods to identify and interpret the meaning of John 10:1-18. (In order to gain experience for yourself, don't consult reference Bible study notes or commentaries until after you have completed your interpretation.)

BT37: Romans 13:1-5 commands Christians to be obedient to their governmental authorities. This command has caused conflicts for Christians who

have lived under governments such as in Nazi Germany and in some contemporary totalitarian regimes. What is the meaning of this text, and other
relevant passages, for Christians who encounter a government which commands them to act contrary to their consciences?

BT38: Some Bible teachers believe that Christians should not experience
illness and disease, basing their arguments in part on 3 John 2. Analyze this
passage and state whether or not you think it is intended to teach that Christians should not experience illness.

BT39: The Parable of the Wheat and the Tares (Matt. 13:24-30) appears
to teach that error within the church should not be judged for fear of "up-
rooting the wheat." How would you reconcile this with the apparent teaching
of Matthew 7:15-20, Titus 3:10, and other verses that appear to teach that
the church is to judge evil and error within itself?

BT40: In the Parable of the Unmerciful Servant (Matt. 18:23-35), the first
servant was forgiven a large sum of money by his lord, and then refused to
forgive his fellow servant a small amount. A well-known Christian psychiatrist,
counselor, and educator stated that this parable shows that it is possible to
be forgiven (by God) without being forgiving (towards one's fellow man). Do
you agree? Why or why not?

BT41: Many Christians understand the story of Lazarus and the rich man
(Luke 16:19-31) as an actual event and derive a theology of the afterlife from
it. Some evangelical scholars are reluctant to do this for hermeneutical reasons. What would be their reasons?

BT42: In the Old Testament there are at least two familiar passages that seem
to contradict what we believe about God's justice. One passage refers to God
hardening Pharaoh's heart (Exod. 4:21) and then His punishment of Pharaoh
for having a hard heart. The second is when He caused David to take a
census (2 Sam. 24:1) and then punished David for doing so. How do you
explain these passages?

BT43: Nearly every Christian counselor has some clients who come to him
believing they have committed the unpardonable sin (Matt. 12:31-32 and
parallels). Throughout history this sin has been identified in a number of
ways. Ireneus saw it as a rejection of the gospel; Athanasius equated it with
denial of Christ. Origen said it was a mortal sin committed after baptism, and

Augustine identified it as persistence in sin until death. Perhaps the most common thought held by counselees is that this sin is one of unwittingly insulting Jesus and His works. Use your hermeneutical skills to determine the identity of this sin.

chapter seven

Special Literary Methods

Types, Prophecy, and Apocalyptic Literature

After completing this chapter, you should be able to:

1. Define the terms *type* and *antitype*.
2. Distinguish typology from symbolism and allegory.
3. Identify three distinguishing characteristics of a type.
4. Name five classes of types mentioned in Scripture.
5. Interpret correctly the meaning of typological allusions from Scripture.
6. Name three kinds of biblical prophecy.
7. Identify seven general differences between prophecy and apocalyptic literature.
8. Recognize six controversial issues in the interpretation of prophecy.
9. Define the terms *progressive prediction*, *developmental fulfillment*, and *prophetic telescoping*.
10. Define the terms *premillennialism*, *postmillennialism*, and *amillennialism*.

Types

The Greek word *tupos*, from which the word *type* is derived, has a variety of denotations in the New Testament. The basic ideas expressed by *tupos* and its synonyms are the concepts of resemblance, likeness, and similarity. From an inductive study of scriptural usage of this concept, the following definition of type has been developed: a *type* is a preordained representative relationship which certain persons, events, and institutions bear to corresponding persons, events, and institutions occurring at a later time in salvation history. Probably most evangelical theologians would find themselves in basic agreement with this definition of biblical typology.

A well-known example of a biblical type is found in John 3:14-15, where Jesus says, "Just as Moses lifted up the snake in the desert, so the Son of Man must be lifted up, that everyone who believes in him may have eternal life." Jesus pointed out two corresponding resemblances: (1) the lifting up of the serpent and of Himself, and (2) life for those who responded to the object lifted up.[1]

Typology is based on the assumption that there is a pattern in God's work throughout salvation history. God prefigured His redemptive work in the Old Testament, and fulfilled it in the New; in the Old Testament there are shadows of things which shall be more fully revealed in the New. The ceremonial laws of the Old Testament, for example, demonstrated to Old Testament believers the necessity of an atonement for their sins: these ceremonies pointed forward to the perfect atonement to be made in Christ. The prefigurement is called the *type*; the fulfillment is called the *antitype*.[2]

Types are similar to symbols and can even be considered a special kind of symbol. However, there are two differentiating characteristics. First, symbols serve as signs of something they represent, without necessarily being similar in any respect, whereas Types resemble in one or more ways the things they prefigure. For example, bread and wine are symbols of Christ's body and blood; the seven golden lampstands (Rev. 2:1) are

1. A. B. Mickelsen, *Interpreting the Bible* (Grand Rapids: Eerdmans, 1963), p. 237.
2. *Antitype* as a literary term does not always correspond to the Greek word *antitupos*, which appears occasionally in Scripture (e.g., Heb. 9:24).

symbols of the churches in Asia. There is no necessary similarity between the symbol and the thing it symbolizes, as there is between a type and its antitype. Second, types point forward in time; whereas symbols may not. A type always precedes historically its antitype, whereas a symbol may precede, exist concurrently with, or come after the thing which it symbolizes.

Typology is also to be distinguished from allegorism. Typology is the search for linkages between historical events, persons, or things within salvation history; allegorism is the search for secondary and hidden meanings underlying the primary and obvious meaning of a historical narrative. Typology rests on an objective understanding of the historical narrative, whereas allegorizing imports subjective meanings onto it.

For example, in the typological allusion found in John 3:14-15 we recognize the existence of a real serpent and a real Christ, one as a type, the other as an antitype. The historical circumstances surrounding both present the key to understanding the relationship between them. In contrast, in allegorism the interpreter attributes meaning to a story which would ordinarily not be deduced from a straightforward understanding of it. For example, one allegorization of the story of Herod's massacre of the infants in Bethlehem states that "the fact that only the children of two years old and under were murdered while those of three presumably escaped is meant to teach us that those who hold the Trinitarian faith will be saved whereas Binitarians and Unitarians will undoubtedly perish."[3]

Characteristics of a Type

Three primary characteristics of types can be identified.[4] The first of these is that "there must be some notable point

3. Cited in G. Lampe, and K. Woolcombe, *Essays in Typology* (Napeville: Allenson, 1957), pp. 31-32.
4. The three characteristics are quoted from M. S. Terry, *Biblical Hermeneutics* (reprinted, Grand Rapids: Zondervan, 1974), pp. 337-338.

of resemblance or analogy" between the type and its antitype. This does not imply that there are not many points of dissimilarity as well: Adam is a type of Christ, yet Scripture speaks of more points of dissimilarity than similarity (see Rom. 5:14-19).

Second, "there must be evidence that the type was appointed by God to represent the thing typified." There is some disagreement among scholars regarding how explicit God's declaration must be. Bishop Marsh's famous dictum regarding types stated that nothing may be considered a type unless it is explicitly stated to be one in Scripture. At the other end of the spectrum are those who classify as types anything that bears a resemblance to something later. A moderate view, and one held by the majority of scholars (e.g., Terry, Berkhof, Mickelsen, Eichrodt, Ramm, et. al.), is that for a resemblance to be a type there must be some evidence of divine affirmation of the corresponding type and antitype, although such affirmation need not be formally stated.

A third characteristic of a type is that it "must prefigure something in the future." Antitypes in the New Testament present truth more fully realized than in the Old Testament. The correspondence in the New reveals what was nascent in the Old. Typology is thus a special form of prophecy.

Jesus illustrated this principle by His frequent typological allusions. R. T. France summarizes Christ's usage of types in the following way:

> He uses *persons* in the Old Testament as types of himself (David, Solomon, Elijah, Elisha, Isaiah, Jonah) or of John the Baptist (Elijah); he refers to Old Testament *institutions* as types of himself and his work (the priesthood and the covenant); he sees in the *experiences* of Israel foreshadowings of his own; he finds the *hopes* of Israel fulfilled in himself and his disciples, and sees his disciples as assuming the *status* of Israel; in Israel's *deliverance* by God he sees a type of the gathering of men into his church, while the *disasters* of Israel are foreshadowings of

the imminent punishment of those who reject him, whose
unbelief is prefigured in that of the wicked in Israel and
even, in two instances, in the arrogance of the Gentile
nations.

In all these aspects of the Old Testament people of
God Jesus sees foreshadowing of himself and his work,
with its results in the opposition and consequent rejection
of the majority of the Jews, while the true Israel is now
to be found in the new Christian community. Thus in his
coming the history of Israel has reached its decisive points.
The whole of the Old Testament is gathered up in him.
He himself embodies in his own person the status and
destiny of Israel, and in the community of those who
belong to him that status and destiny are to be fulfilled,
no longer in the nation as such.[5]

In summary, then, in order for a figure to be a type there
must be (1) some notable resemblance or analogy between the
type and its antitype; (2) some evidence that the type was
appointed by God to represent the thing typified; and (3)
some future corresponding antitype.

Classifications of Types

Although there are some minor variations among writers
regarding the number and names of the various classes of
types, the five classes discussed below represent commonly
mentioned categories.

Typical persons are those whose lives illustrate some great
principle or truth of redemption. Adam is mentioned as a
type of Christ (Rom. 5:14): Adam was the representative head
of fallen humanity, while Christ is the representative head of
redeemed humanity.

5. R. T. France, *Jesus and the Old Testament* (Downers Grove: InterVarsity, 1971),
pp. 75-76.

Unlike the emphasis on the individual in our culture, the Jews identified themselves primarily as members of a group. Because of this, it is not unusual to find a representative person speaking or acting for the entire group. *Corporate identity* refers to that oscillation of thought between a group and an individual who represents that group, and was a common and accepted Hebrew thought form.[6] For example, Matthew 2:15 ("Out of Egypt I called my son") refers to Hosea 11:1, in which son is identified as the nation of Israel. In Matthew it was Christ Himself (as a representative of Israel) who was called out of Egypt, so the original words are applied to Him. Some of the Psalms also view Christ as representative of all humanity.[7]

Though contrary to our contemporary conceptions, these usages of the concepts of fulfillment and corporate identity possess the prerequisites of legitimate and valid hermeneutical devices; i.e., they were intended, used, and understood in that culture in certain culturally accepted ways. The fact that those concepts are somewhat different from our own only attests to the differences between cultures and says nothing about their validity or invalidity.

Typical events possess an analogical relationship to some later event. Paul uses the judgment on faithless Israel as a typological warning to Christian believers not to engage in immorality (1 Cor. 10:1-11). Matthew 2:17-18 (Rachel weeping for her slaughtered children) is mentioned as a typological analogy to the situation in Jeremiah's day (Jer. 31:15). In Jeremiah's day the event involved a national tragedy; in Matthew's time it involved a local one. The point of correspondence was the grief displayed in the face of personal loss.

6. A good discussion of the conceptions of human solidarity in the Old Testament and in early Jewish thought can be found in Russell Shedd, *Man in Community: A Study of St. Paul's Application of Old Testament and Early Jewish Conceptions of Human Solidarity* (London: Epworth Press, 1958), pp. 3-89.

7. John W. Wenham, *Christ and the Bible* (Downers Grove: InterVarsity, 1973), p. 107.

Typical institutions are practices that prefigure later salvation events. One example of this is atonement by the shedding of blood by lambs and later by Christ (Lev. 17:11; cf. 1 Pet. 1:19). Another is the Sabbath as a type of the believer's eternal rest.

Typical offices include Moses, who in his office as prophet (Deut. 18:15), was a type of Christ; Melchizedek (Heb. 5:6) as a type of Christ's continuing priesthood; and David as king.

Typical actions are exemplified by Isaiah's walking naked and barefoot for three years as a sign to Egypt and Ethiopia that Assyria would soon lead them away naked and barefoot (Isa. 20:2-4). Another example of a typical action was Hosea's marriage to a prostitute and his later redemption of her after her infidelity, symbolizing God's covenantal love to faithless Israel.

Principles for Interpretation of Types

Historical-cultural and contextual analysis. The most important place to begin the investigation of any two events in salvation history is the historical-cultural situation in which they occurred. Identification of proper names, geographical references, contemporary customs, and historical details and background are all necessary in order to understand how both a type and its antitype fit into the pattern of salvation history. The immediate context sometimes provides clues in this regard; at other times a study of the wider context (such as the purpose of the book) provides an understanding of the author's reason for including a certain event.

Lexical-syntactical analysis. Are the words being used literally, figuratively, or symbolically? (A further discussion of the symbolic use of words will be given later in this chapter under Prophecy). The same principles of lexical-syntactical analysis discussed in chapter 4 apply in the interpretation of types.

Theological analysis. The proper interpretation and understanding of types often leads to an increased appreciation of the unity of Scripture and the consistency with which God has dealt with man throughout salvation history. One's interpretation of a type will be affected, either consciously or unconsciously, by his view of the nature of salvation history. Interpretation cannot be divorced from the presuppositions one brings to the text.

Literary analysis. Once a type has been identified as such by using the three characteristics mentioned in the preceding section, two steps remain in the analysis: (1) search the text for the point(s) of correspondence, and (2) note the important points of difference between the type and its antitype.

As in any other kind of comparison, every incidental detail of the type and antitype was not intended by the author to be a point of correspondence. Some commentators, for example, have divined from the fact that the serpent was made of brass (a metal inferior to gold or silver) that this was a type of the outward plainness of the Savior's appearance. Other commentators have found in the acacia wood and gold of the tabernacle a type of the humanity and deity of Christ, and other types and symbols have been found in the boards, the sockets of silver, the heights of the doors, the linens, the coloring or lack of coloring of the draperies, etc.[8] Such practices seem dangerously akin to the allegorism of the Middle Ages, imputing meaning to the text which is highly unlikely to have been intended by the biblical author. The context and the analogy of faith (other related scriptural passages) remain the best source of discrimination between types and nontypes.[9]

Prophecy

The interpretation of prophecy is a highly complex subject, not so much because of disagreement regarding proper in-

8. C. I. Scofield, Scofield Reference Bible (New York: Oxford University Press, 1917), pp. 101-105.
9. A listing of biblical types can be found in J. Barton Payne's excellent volume, *Encyclopedia of Biblical Prophecy* (New York: Harper & Row, 1973), pp. 671-672.

terpretive principles, but because of differences of opinion over how to apply those principles. The following section identifies those principles about which there is general agreement and those issues which are still unresolved. Several books are listed at the end of the chapter for those who wish to study this topic further.

In both the Old and New Testaments "a prophet is a spokesman for God who declares God's will to the people."[10] Prophecy refers to three things: (1) predicting future events (e.g., Rev. 1:3; 22:7,10; John 11;51); (2) revealing concealed facts concerning the present (Luke 1:67-79; Acts 13:6-12), and (3) dispensing instruction, comfort, and exhortation in powerfully impassioned language (e.g., Amos; Acts 15:32; 1 Cor. 14:3,4,31).

If we accept the dates of the various books of the Bible that are commonly given by evangelical scholars, it would appear that a significant amount of the Bible is predictive prophecy (denotation 1). Payne calculates that of the Bible's 31,124 verses, 8,352 (27 percent) were predictive material at the time they were first spoken or written.[11] In Scripture, foretelling was usually in the service of forthtelling (denotation 3). The pattern frequently was: "In light of what the Lord is going to do (foretelling), we should be living godly lives (forthtelling)."

Predictive prophecy can serve a number of important functions. It can bring glory to God by testifying to His wisdom and sovereignty over the future. It can grant assurance and comfort to oppressed believers. It can motivate its hearers to stronger faith and deeper holiness (John 14:29; 2 Peter 3:11).[12]

Prophecy and Apocalyptic Literature

In the twentieth century, students of biblical prophecy have spent considerable time investigating a particular genre called

10. A. B. Mickelsen, *Interpreting the Bible* (Grand Rapids: Eerdmans, 1963), p. 280.
11. J. Barton Payne, *Encyclopedia of Biblical Prophecy*, p. 13.
12. Ibid., pp. 13-16.

"apocalyptic." The word is derived from the Greek word *apokalupsis* (found in Rev. 1:1), which means "uncovering" or "revelation." Apocalyptic literature's primary focus is the revealing of what has been hidden, particularly with regard to the end-times. Noncanonical apocalyptic writings are found from the time of Daniel until the end of the first century A.D., and share several characteristics in common. These features, as described by Leon Morris, include:

1. The writer tends to choose some great man of the past (e.g., Enoch or Moses) and make him the hero of the book.
2. This hero often takes a journey, accompanied by a celestial guide who shows him interesting sights and comments on them.
3. Information is often communicated through visions.
4. The visions often make use of strange, even enigmatic, symbolism.
5. The visions often are pessimistic with regard to the possibility that human intervention will ameliorate the present situation.
6. The visions usually end with God's bringing the present state of affairs to a cataclysmic end and establishing a better situation.
7. The apocalyptic writer often uses a pseudonym, claiming to write in the name of his chosen hero.
8. The writer often takes past history and rewrites it as if it were prophecy.
9. The focus of apocalyptic is on comforting and sustaining the "righteous remnant."[13]

George Ladd sees the development of apocalyptic as the result of three main factors. The first is "the emergence of a 'Righteous Remnant,' " a minority group, usually without substantial political power, who view themselves as remaining faithful to God while surrounded by those who are not. A second factor is "the problem of evil." As early as the Book of Job, the conception that God rewards the just and punishes evildoers had been recorded. How then could the Righteous Remnant reconcile the fact that they were oppressed by those

---

13. Leon Morris, *Apocalyptic* (Grand Rapids: Eerdmans, 1972), pp.34-61.

much more wicked than themselves? Third, "the cessation of prophecy" (recorded in the noncanonical Book of 2 Baruch 85:3) created a spiritual vacuum: the Righteous Remnant longed for a word from God but none was forthcoming. The apocalyptists attempted to bring a word of comfort and reassurance from God to the men of their day.[14]

Apocalyptic literature shares a number of points in common with biblical prophecy. Both are concerned with the future. Both frequently employ figurative and symbolic language. Both emphasize the unseen world that lies behind the action of the visible world. Both emphasize the future redemption of the faithful believer.

There are a number of differences as well. These include the following:

1. The initial presentation of prophecy was usually in spoken form and was put in writing at a later time. The initial presentation of apocalyptic was usually in writing.
2. Prophetic utterances most often are separate, brief oracles. Apocalyptic are often longer, more continuous; they have cycles of material repeated a second or third time in parallel form.
3. Apocalyptic tends to contain more symbolism, especially of animals and other living forms.
4. Apocalyptic places a greater stress on dualism (angels and the Messiah versus Satan and the Antichrist) than does prophecy.
5. Apocalyptic primarily comforts and encourages the Righteous Remnant. Prophecy often castigates the nominally religious.
6. Apocalyptic is generally pessimistic about the effectiveness of human intervention in changing the present. Prophecy focuses on the importance of human change.
7. Apocalyptic was usually written pseudonymously. Prophecy was usually written or spoken in the name of its author.[15]

The above distinctions are matters of degree and emphasis, rather than absolute differences. Exceptions can be cited to

14. George Eldon Ladd, "Apocalyptic," *Baker's Dictionary of Theology*, ed. E. F. Harrison (Grand Rapids: Baker, 1960).
15. Payne, *Encyclopedia of Biblical Prophecy*, pp. 86-87.

each of them; however, most conservative Bible scholars would agree with the distinctions.

Apocalyptic sections do occur within the canonical books, most notably in Daniel (chapters 7–12) and in Revelation. There are also apocalyptic passages in Joel, Amos, and Zechariah. In the New Testament, Jesus' Olivet Discourse (Matthew 24-25 and parallels) contains apocalyptic elements.

Biblical apocalyptic has many elements in common with the apocalyptic found in noncanonical books; differences have also been noted.[16] This overlap of characteristics affects the issue of inspiration. The question it raises is: "How does the use of an enigmatic, humanly developed genre such as apocalyptic affect the authority and trustworthiness of biblical passages in which it is found?"

In the study of literary forms, in previous chapters, we saw that God revealed His truth using literary forms familiar to the people of that time. The choice of a variety of literary devices to convey information does not affect the validity of that information. Our unfamiliarity with a particular genre such as apocalyptic does not affect the trustworthiness of the information contained in apocalyptic passages, but only our ability to interpret them with assurance. Perhaps as our understanding of intertestamental apocalyptic increases, our ability to interpret the end-time prophecies with assurance will increase proportionately.

Issues in the Interpretation of Prophecy and Apocalyptic Literature

Before interpretation of prophecy and apocalyptic literature can begin, a number of theoretical and practical issues must be decided. On some of these issues there is basic agree-

16. Morris, *Apocalyptic*, esp. pp. 51-54, 58-67; George Eldon Ladd, *Jesus and the Kingdom* (New York: Harper & Row, 1964), chapter 3.

ment among evangelicals; on others there are significant differences of opinion.

Hermeneutical principles. A basic question in the interpretation of prophecy and apocalyptic is whether this literature can be interpreted using the same hermeneutical principles that apply to other genres, or whether some special hermeneutical method is required.

The majority of evangelical scholars (Ramm, Berkhof, Tenney, Pentecost, Payne, et. al.) concur that the interpretation of prophecy starts with the procedures we have labeled as contextual, historical-cultural, lexical-syntactical, and theological analyses. An exposition of the apocalyptic portions of the Book of Revelation, for example, would begin with an attempt to understand as many of the historical circumstances of that time as possible. Then the context of the first three chapters would be examined for information relevant for the interpretation of what follows. Lexical-syntactical analysis would proceed as with other genres, with the recognition that both prophecy and apocalyptic tend to use words more frequently in symbolic, figurative, and analogical senses than do other genres. Theological analysis would ascertain how the prophecies fit into other parallel information in Scripture.

Deeper sense. A second major issue is whether or not a *sensus plenior* exists in prophecy. Is there an additional, deeper meaning in a prophetic text, a meaning intended by God but not clearly intended by the human author?

Both views on this issue can be illustrated by the case of Caiaphas the high priest, who prophesied that it was "better . . . that one man die for the people than that the whole nation perish" (John 11:50). Advocates of the *sensus plenior* view would suggest that Caiaphas obviously had no conception of Christ's atoning death and therefore was prophesying things he actually did not understand. Opponents of this view would argue that Caiaphas did understand what he prophesied (it *was* better that one man die than the whole nation), and only that he did not understand the full implications of what he said.

This, they argue, is a natural and frequently occurring phenomenon in communication: men often understand the meaning of what they say without understanding all of its implications. The biblical writers, in the same way, understood what they prophesied but probably did not understand all of the implications of their prophecies. Appendix C lists further readings on this issue.

Literal versus symbolic. A third, and very practical, issue in the interpretation of prophecy concerns how much of prophecy is to be interpreted literally, and how much symbolically or analogically. For example, a literal approach to prophecy often conceives the "beast" of Revelation as a person (note that even this is not *totally* literal); a symbolic approach views it as a personification of the lust for power. A literal approach conceives Babylon as an actual city (often considered to be Rome), whereas a symbolic approach views Babylon as the desire for economic gain. Literalists often view the last battle as an actual physical combat; symbolists see it as a representation of truth overcoming evil.

The question is not between a strictly literal versus a strictly symbolic approach; even the strictest literalist takes some things symbolically. For example, a literal understanding of the passage concerning the woman who sits on seven hills (Rev. 17:9) would suggest either that these were very small hills or that she had a very unusual figure. Conversely, even the most thoroughgoing symbolist interprets some things literally. Thus the differences between literalists and symbolists are relative rather than absolute, involving questions of "how much" and "which parts" of prophecy should be interpreted symbolically rather than literally.

In certain parts of prophecy some interpreters prefer an analogical approach, a sort of *via media* between the strictly literal and strictly symbolic. In this approach, statements are interpreted literally but then translated into their modern-day equivalents. The Battle of Armageddon, for example, is not fought with horses and spears but with modern analogues (perhaps tanks and artillery). The rationale underlying this interpretation is that if God had given John a vision of modern conveyances and equipment, the apostle would not have been able to understand what he saw nor to communicate it clearly to his audience.

The question of whether a word or phrase should be interpreted literally, symbolically, or analogically has no easy answer. The context and the historical usages of the words are the best general guides in making decisions concerning their usage within a specific passage.

Universality. A fourth issue, concerning the universality of certain apocalyptic symbols, is whether or not a symbol means the same thing each time it is used. Some older writers tended to ascribe universal symbolic significance to certain numbers, colors, or items; for example, oil was *always* a symbol of the Holy Spirit, leaven always a symbol of evil. Probably the majority of contemporary evangelical scholars reject the notion of universal symbols, but do accept the idea that there is a regularity in the symbolism of some biblical authors. Numbers frequently regarded as symbolic are 7, 12, and 40. (The issue of whether or not 1000 is symbolic is still unsettled.) Colors that frequently possess symbolic significance are white, red, and purple, often representing the concepts of purity, bloodshed, and royalty, respectively.[17]

Conditionality. A fifth issue is whether or not all prophetic statements are conditional, even when a conditional *if* is not stated. The problem can be illustrated in this way: On the basis of several biblical passages (e.g., Mal. 3:6; Heb. 6:17-18; James 1:17) we believe God to be immutable. On the other hand, we read on some occasions of God's repenting—changing His mind regarding a certain judgment—as in Exodus 32:14, Psalm 106:45, and Jonah 3:10. In the case of Jonah, God had apparently commanded Jonah to preach the message

17. See Mickelsen, *Interpreting the Bible*, pp. 272-278, for a fuller discussion of symbolic numbers, names, colors, metals, and jewels.

that Nineveh would be overthrown in forty days. There seemed to be no stated conditions by which that prediction could be averted; however, when the people of Nineveh repented, God also stayed His predicted judgment (Jonah 3:10).

These passages raise two questions. First, how do we reconcile the doctrine of God's immutability with the fact that Scripture records His change of mind in several instances? Second, since there was an unstated *if* in the prediction of Nineveh's coming judgment, do all prophecies contain an unstated conditional clause?

The answer to both questions is found, at least in part, in God's explanation to Jeremiah, found in Jeremiah 18:7-10, where He says:

> If at any time I announce that a nation or kingdom is to be uprooted, torn down and destroyed, and if that nation I warned repents of its evil, then I will relent and not inflict on it the disaster I had planned. And if at another time I announce that a nation or kingdom is to be built up and planted, and if it does evil in my sight and does not obey me, then I will reconsider the good I had intended to do for it.

These verses help us to qualify the concept of God's immutability more clearly. God occasionally changes His predicted actions so that He remains consistent in His character. Since men sometimes change their behavior and relationship to God, God changes His predicted actions toward them correspondingly, in order to remain consistent with His own character of love and righteousness. The same willingness to make national prophecies conditional on man's response is also found in the actions of God toward individuals who repent (e.g., 1 Kings 21:1-29). Thus it is probably wise to recognize that prophecies may carry with them an implied conditionality, even if the condition is not explicitly stated.[18]

Single versus multiple meaning. A final issue, and one about which there is considerable controversy among contemporary evangelicals, is whether prophetic passages have single or multiple meanings. Advocates of the multiple meaning position use a variety of terms to describe their position, such as "double meaning," "double reference," "manifold fulfillment," or "multiple sense." In earlier chapters we have already considered the theoretical and practical problems inherent in any system of exegesis which affirms that a passage may have a variety of meanings. Payne presents an excellent critique of the multiple meaning position, and also discusses prophetic interpretive principles that are consistent with the concept of a single intended meaning in each passage. His discussion forms the basis of the following paragraphs.[19]

To affirm that scriptural texts have a single *meaning* in no way negates the fact that that meaning may have a variety of *applications* in different situations. This same principle applies to prophetic passages and their fulfillments, as Payne illustrates:

> The NT epistles thus repeatedly quote OT prophecies, though not in reference to their actual fulfillments; for example, II Corinthians 6:16 cites Leviticus 26:11 (on God's presence with His people in the yet future testament of peace), 6:17 cites Isaiah 52:11 (on Israel's departure from unclean Babylon), and 6:18 freely renders Hosea 1:10 (on the inclusion of Gentiles in the family of God), all to illustrate the Christians' present enjoyment of the presence of God and our need to maintain separation from the uncleanness of the world, though only

18. Walter C. Kaiser, Jr., *The Old Testament in Contemporary Preaching* (Grand Rapids: Baker, 1973), pp. 111-114. For a further discussion of this issue, see Payne, *Encyclopedia of Biblical Prophecy*, pp. 62-68.

19. Payne, *Encyclopedia of Biblical Prophecy*, pp. 121-144.

the last, Hosea 1:10, had this originally in mind. Terry [M. S. Terry, *Biblical Hermeneutics*, p. 383] therefore makes it clear that, "We may readily admit that the Scriptures are capable of manifold practical *applications*; otherwise they would not be so useful for doctrine, correction, and instruction in righteousness (II Tim. 3:16)," though he remains firm in his insistence upon single fulfillment for Biblical prophecy.[20]

In place of the concept of multiple meanings, Payne substitutes the concepts of progressive prediction, developmental fulfillment, and prophetic telescoping. *Progressive prediction* refers to the fact that although each prophetic passage has a single intended fulfillment, often a series of passages exhibit a pattern of chronological progress in the prophetic enactment. Thus passage A may tell us about certain events, passage B about the events immediately following them, and passage C about the culminating events of the series. The combination of these various passages forms a whole which can be identified as progressive prediction. Sometimes these passages are presented as cycles within the same book, with each cycle presenting additional information. Two well-known examples of progressive predictions which occur in cycles are the Books of Zechariah and Revelation.

A second concept of prophetic meaning, *developmental fulfillment*, refers to the accomplishment of a generalized, comprehensive prophecy in several progressive stages. An example of this is the Genesis 3:15 prophecy, which speaks in quite general terms of the bruising of Satan's head. The progressive stages in the fulfillment of this prophecy begin with Christ's death, resurrection, and ascension (John 12:31-32; Rev. 12:5,10), continue in the church (Rom. 16:20), and end with Satan's imprisonment in the abyss (Rev. 20:3) and the lake of fire (Rev. 20:10).[21]

20. Payne, *Encyclopedia of Biblical Prophecy*, pp. 128-129.
21. Other examples of developmental fulfillment can be found in Payne, pp. 135-136.

A third concept of prophetic fulfillment is called *prophetic telescoping*, and refers to the well-known characteristic that "Biblical prophecy may leap from one prominent peak in predictive topography to another, without notice of the valley between, which may involve no inconsiderable lapse in chronology."[22] The telescoping that sometimes occurred when prophets blended the first and second advents of Christ is an example of this phenomenon.

Varieties of Eschatological Theories

Since there are many unresolved issues regarding the interpretation of prophecy, it is not surprising that there are a variety of eschatological theories. This section will briefly present some of those theories.

Premillennialism is the theory that Christ will return before the millennium (*pre*-millennium). He will descend to earth and set up a literal 1000-year earthly kingdom with its headquarters in Jerusalem.

Postmillennialism is the view that through evangelism, the world eventually will be reached for Christ. There will be a period in which the world will experience joy and peace because of its obedience to God. Christ will return to earth at the end of the millennium (*post*-millennium).

Amillennialism is conceptually a form of postmillennialism. The millennium, in this theory, is symbolic and refers to the time between Christ's first and second coming, not to a literal 1000-year period. During this time Christ rules symbolically in men's hearts. Christ's second coming will mark the end of the period. Some amillennialists believe that Christ will never have an earthly rule, even symbolically. For them the millennium refers to Christ's celestial rule in eternity.

Postmillennialism—the view that the church will eventually win the world for Christ and usher in the millennium—rap-

22. Ibid., p. 137.

idly lost popularity during the first half of the twentieth century. The carnage of the world wars was a grim reminder to most postmillennialists that the world was *not* being won for Christ. Hence the majority of evangelical Christians today identify themselves as either premillennialists or amillennialists.

Hermeneutically, the major issue that divides premillennialists from amillennialists is the question of how much of prophecy should be interpreted literally and how much symbolically. The premillennialist interprets most things literally. He believes that Christ will actually come to earth, set up a physical earthly kingdom, and reign for 1000 literal years. He believes that the promises to Israel and to the church should be kept separate, and that it is not valid to take physical promises made to Israel, spiritualize them, and apply them to the church. He bases his hermeneutical method on the principle that Scripture should be interpreted literally unless the context definitely suggests that the author intended it to be otherwise.

The amillennialist interprets things more symbolically, in view of the symbolic language used in prophetic passages. Ludwigson gives an example: "Christ bound Satan (symbolically): (1) by resisting him in the wilderness; (2) by paying the penalty of sin to redeem man; (3) by destroying the power of death in His resurrection; and (4) by offering salvation to the Gentiles, making it impossible for Satan to deceive the nations anymore. . . . Satan can still deceive individuals, [but] no longer can deceive nations.[23] Likewise, the amillennialist interprets Christ's millennial rule symbolically rather than literally: the kingdom is already present in the hearts of believers. New Testament believers represent spiritual Israel, and therefore Old Testament promises to Israel apply to the new Israel, the church.

There is a hermeneutical basis for both the premillennial and amillennial models of interpretation. It is correct, as the

23. R. Ludwigson, *A Survey of Bible Prophecy*, 2nd ed. (Grand Rapids: Zondervan, 1975), p. 109.

premillennialist asserts, to understand biblical passages literally unless the context suggests otherwise. However, the amillennialist is also correct in asserting that most prophecy and apocalyptic *is* symbolic, justifying a symbolic interpretation.

For those who wish to consider this issue more deeply, a bibliography on the subject is included below. In grappling with the issue, check the internal consistency of each position in turn in relation to all the biblical data. This "goodness of fit" method may be helpful in making a decision about the merits of the two theories. Ultimately, the most important spiritual implication of all eschatological study can be found in 1 John 3:2-3:

> Dear friends, now we are children of God, and what we will be has not yet been made known. But we know that when he appears, we shall be like him, for we shall see him as he is. Everyone who has this hope in him purifies himself, just as he is pure.

Principles for Interpreting Prophecy

Historical-cultural analysis. The wide variety of theories concerning the end-times arises not so much from a disagreement concerning principles of prophetic interpretation as from differences in application of those principles. Almost all commentators are agreed that a careful historical and contextual analysis is a prerequisite for accurate understanding of prophecy. Determination of the identity of all proper names, events, geographical references, etc., remains a crucial first step. Even when such references are used symbolically, as the city of Babylon often is, a knowledge of the historical city of Babylon provides important clues about its symbolic meaning. Careful historical analysis also remains the only way of determining whether or not a prophecy has already been fulfilled. An analysis of relevant cultural customs is no less important.

Lexical-syntactical analysis. A careful study of the context sometimes reveals whether an author intended his words to be understood literally, symbolically, or analogically. Even then, however, the task of interpreting may still be difficult, as Girdlestone observes:

> [What] makes the language of prophecy so vivid and yet so difficult is that it is always more or less figurative. It is poetry rather than prose. It abounds in peculiar words and expressions which are not usually to be found in prose writings of the same date. It is rich with allusions to contemporary life and to past history, some of which are decidedly obscure. The actions recorded in it are sometimes symbolical, sometimes typical. The present, the past, and the future, the declaratory and the predictive, are all combined and fused into one. The course of individuals, the rise and fall of nations, the prospects of the world at large, are all rapidly portrayed in realistic language.[24]

English words that have been translated from Hebrew, Aramaic, or Greek may possess a significantly different set of denotations from the original words. One example of this which is highly relevant to the study of prophecy is the word *fulfill*, or *fulfillment*. In the biblical languages this concept takes on a variety of meanings, including:

1. drawing out the full implications of something (Matt, 5:17; cf. verses 18-48);
2. completion of a fixed time (Mark 1:15; Luke 21:24);
3. satisfying a request or desire (Esther 5:8; Ps. 145:19; Prov. 13:19);
4. carrying out what is promised (Lev. 22:21);
5. conforming to or obeying a requirement (Gal. 5:14; James 2:8; Matt. 3:15);

24. Robert B. Girdlestone, *The Grammar of Prophecy* (reprinted, Grand Rapids: Kregel, 1955), p. 48. Cited in Ramm, *Protestant Biblical Interpretation,* p. 247.

6. correspondence of phrases, illustrations, or events between one historical period and another (Matt. 2:23, cf. Isa, 11:1; Jer. 31:15, cf. Matt. 2:17-18; Isa. 9:1-2, cf. Matt. 4:13-16).

Clearly, to apply our English denotations of the word *fulfill* to its occurrences in the biblical text will sometimes result in an interpretation unintended by its author.

Theological analysis. For the student interested in prophecy, there are usually a number of parallel passages which should be consulted. Sometimes such passages occur within the same book, as in those instances when prophecy is given in cycles. Frequently other prophets have spoken about the same topic, filling in additional details not contained in the passage under study. The index to Payne's *Encyclopedia of Biblical Prophecy* contains an alphabetic listing of subjects in prophecy, together with references to relevant biblical passages and discussions of those passages.

Literary analysis. Once it has been determined that the passage is prophetic or apocalyptic literature, the probability of symbolic and analogical allusions increases. The concepts of progressive prediction, developmental fulfillment, and prophetic telescoping can be applied to the understanding of the text as appropriate.

In interpretation of prophecy as in other types of biblical literature, comparison of one's work with that of others is important. The complexity of the topics, the wide range of parallel passages, and the multitude of unusual allusions make it imperative to draw from the wealth of knowledge of scholars who have studied this area in-depth.

Summary

The following steps for interpreting types and prophecy have been discussed:

Types	Prophecy and Apocalyptic Writing
1. Historical-cultural and contextual analysis: determine the significance within the time and culture of both the type and the antitype.	1. Historical-cultural and contextual analysis: determine the specific historical situation surrounding the composition of the writing. Study intervening history to see whether or not the prophecy has been fulfilled.
2. Lexical-syntactical analysis: follow the same principles as with other literary forms.	2. Lexical-syntactical analysis: expect more words to be used in symbolic and analogical senses.
3. Theological analysis: search the text for the points of correspondence between the type and its antitype as they relate to salvation history.	3. Theological analysis: study parallel passages or other cycles within the same prophecy for further information.
4. Literary analysis: a. Find some notable resemblance or analogy between the type and its antitype. b. Find some evidence that the type was appointed by God to represent the thing typified. c. Determine the point(s) of correspondence between the type and antitype—typical persons, events, institutions, offices, or actions. d. Note the important points of difference between the type and antitype.	4. Literary analysis: a. Be aware that the style is generally figurative and symbolic. b. Watch for supernatural elements such as information conveyed by the announcement of angels, by visions, or by other supernatural means. c. Notice the emphasis on the unseen world that lies behind the action of the visible world. d. Follow the action to its usual conclusion by a sovereign intervention of God. e. Analyze whether this passage is part of a progressive prediction, is capable of developmental fulfillment, or includes prophetic telescoping.
5. Compare your analysis with that of others; modify, correct, or expand your interpretation as appropriate.	5. Compare your analysis with that of others; modify, correct, or expand your interpretation as appropriate.

Resources for Further Reading

Louis Berkhof. *Systematic Theology*, Vol. 2, pp. 708-719.

Robert Clouse, ed. *The Meaning of the Millennium*.

Patrick Fairbairn. *The Typology of Scripture*.

G. Lampe & K. Woolcombe. *Essays on Typology*.

R. Ludwigson. *A Survey of Biblical Prophecy*.

A. B. Mickelsen. *Interpreting the Bible*, pp. 280-305.

Leon Morris. *Apocalyptic*.

J. Barton Payne. *Encyclopedia of Biblical Prophecy*.

J. Dwight Pentecost. *Things to Come*.

Bernard Ramm. *Protestant Biblical Interpretation* (3rd rev. ed.), pp. 241-275.

Merrill Tenney. *Interpreting Revelation*.

Milton S. Terry. *Biblical Hermeneutics*, pp. 405-448.

Exercises

BT44: It has been stated that the Bible prophesies the use of Christmas trees in Jeremiah 10:3-4. Is this a valid interpretation of this verse? Why or why not?

BT45: The Bible also foresees the use of jet airplanes, in Ezekiel 10:9-17, according to some interpreters. More specifically, this passage describes the hubcaps and wheels (vv. 9-11), the windows (v. 12), the jet turbines (v. 13), and a takeoff (vv. 15-16). Is this a valid interpretation? Why or why not?

BT46: According to some interpreters there is also a biblical prophecy of police cars, rushing to an emergency with their headlights beaming (Nahum 2:4). Discuss the validity of this interpretation.

BT47: Many Bible students have understood the seven churches of Revelation 2 and 3 as referring to both historical churches of John's time as well as seven successive epochs in the church history. Do you agree or disagree? Be able to give hermeneutical principles to justify your answer.

BT48: Interpret the Revelation 20 passage from both premillennial and amillennial viewpoints. What hermeneutical problems arise with each method?

208

BT49: Some of the fathers of the early church attempted to find a typological picture of the Trinity in the Old Testament by asserting that the three stories of the ark are types of the three persons of the Godhead. Is this valid typology? Why or why not?

BT50: A hermeneutics textbook made the following points from its study of typology of the OT tabernacle: Linen means the Righteous One, Jesus. Brass is always a symbol of judgment. Silver is always the symbol of redemption. In the tabernacle the pure linen (Jesus) was hung on the pillars of brass and was set in sockets of brass (judgment), but was held together with rods of silver hooks (redemption). Jesus could have come down from the cross, but He wouldn't. Our redemption held Him there (the silver hooks of redemption that held the linen to the brass).[25] Is this valid typology? Why or why not?

BT51: The same hermeneutics text makes the following points with regard to the typological meaning of badger skins (Exod. 26:14, KJV). The fact that these skins were not very pleasing to the eye is typical of the fact that "He hath no form nor comeliness." People outside could only see the outer covering of skins. To see the beautiful linen, one had to be inside. Correspondingly, the world sees only Christ's humanity and not His deity. From inside, one could see the purple, scarlet, blue, gold, and silver. The corresponding application is that we must get inside Christ to see His beauty.[26] Is this valid typology? Why or why not?

BT52: A minister preached a message on Ezekiel 37 (the vision of the dry bones). He said that although the message was initially to the nation of Israel, it could also be legitimately applied to the church. His message focused on the importance of developing relationships with others in the body of Christ (getting connected to the other bones). Is this a valid use of this text? Why or why not?

BT53: Another minister preached a message from Isaiah 18:1-7. He said that although the original intent was for Ethiopia, according to the "double fulfillment" theory of prophecy, it could also legitimately be applied to the United States. Some of his points were: (1) v. 1. The United States is one of the few countries with a bird as its national symbol; (2) v. 2 describes the

---

25. J. Edwin Hartill, *Principles of Biblical Hermeneutics* (Grand Rapids: Zondervan, 1947), p. 61.
26. Ibid., p. 62.

United States as a strong and mighty nation; (3) v. 3 refers to the raising of the American flag on the moon; and (4) v. 5 warns us that judgment is coming for the United States. Is this a legitimate use of this text? Why or why not?

BT54: Isaiah 14:12-15 has often been interpreted as a typological allusion to Satan. Discuss the hermeneutical pros and cons of such an interpretation.

BT55: In Matthew 16:19, Jesus prophesies that He will give to Peter the keys of the kingdom of heaven. What is the meaning of this prophecy?

BT56: Some believe that Paul's prophecy in 1 Corinthians 15:22 suggests that all will be saved ("For as in Adam all die, so in Christ all will be made alive"). How would you respond to this argument?

BT57: Some liberal commentators have claimed that Christ was mistaken regarding the time of His second coming, because of verses such as Matthew 24:34 which seem to indicate that He would return within one generation. Are there other legitimate ways of understanding this verse?

chapter eight

Applying the Biblical Message:

A Proposal for the Transcultural Problem

In the first seven chapters we studied the practices of traditional hermeneutics to answer the basic question: "What was the author's meaning when he wrote a particular text?" This chapter will address another question: "What are the implications of that meaning for us in a different time and culture?"

There are two main categories of Scripture to which the above question must be addressed. The first are the narrative portions of Scripture. How can we make these portions of the Bible useful for teaching, reproof, correction, and instruction in righteousness in a hermeneutically valid way?

Second, how do we apply the normative commands of Scripture? Do we transfer them wholesale into our time and culture, regardless of how archaic or peculiar they might seem to us? Or should we transform them? What guidelines do we follow to answer these questions?

This chapter is divided into two parts. The first part describes a method—principlizing—that is a hermeneutically legitimate way of showing the relevance of the narrative portions of Scripture for contemporary believers. The second half of the chapter proposes a model for translating biblical commands from one culture to another.

Principlizing: An Alternative to Allegorizing Biblical Narratives

As we saw in chapter 2, allegorism developed from a proper motive: the desire to make Old Testament passages relevant to the New Testament believer. Allegorism has been rejected, however, because it imports meaning onto the text which the author never intended to be there. Thus a method is needed for making the long historical sections of Scripture relevant for the contemporary believer.[1]

A simple recounting of the narrative is an insufficient and ineffective expository method. By itself such a method leads to a "B.C. message," a message that may have possessed relevance for believers at the time of the writing, but fails to seem applicable to believers today. What is needed, then, is an expository method that makes the narrative portions of Scripture relevant for contemporary believers without making the text say something the original author did not intend it to say. One method of doing this is called principlizing.

Principlizing is an attempt to discover in a narrative the spiritual, moral, or theological principles that have relevance for the contemporary believer. It is based on the assumption that the Holy Spirit chose those historical incidents that are re-

---

1. This statement is not meant to imply that narrative portions never teach doctrine directly and explicitly. The Gospel accounts of Jesus' teaching ministry are examples of narrative portions of Scripture that contain significant amounts of direct, explicit, doctrinal teaching. Narrative accounts of men acting in a prophetic capacity as spokesmen for God also often contain doctrinal teaching.

corded in Scripture for a purpose: to give information, to
make a point, to illustrate an important truth, etc. Principlizing is a method of trying to understand a story in such a way
that we can recognize the original reason it was included in
Scripture, the principles it was meant to teach.

Unlike allegorizing, which gives a story new meaning by
assigning its details symbolic significance not intended by the
original author, principlizing seeks to derive its teachings from
a careful understanding of the story itself. Unlike demythologizing, principlizing recognizes the validity of both the historical details of a narrative and the principles those details attempt
to teach.

Methodologically, the approach is the same as in the exegesis of any biblical passage. The historical circumstances and
the cultural customs that illuminate the significance of various
actions and commands are carefully observed. The purpose
of the book within which the narrative occurs is studied, as
well as the narrower context of the passages immediately preceding and following the section under examination. The state
of theological knowledge and commitment is also surveyed.

When these things have all been done, the interpreter is
then in a position to understand the significance of the narrative in its original setting. Finally, based on this understanding and using a process of deduction, the interpreter attempts
to articulate the principle(s) illustrated by the story, principles
that continue to possess relevance for the contemporary believer. We will look at two narratives to illustrate this process
of principlizing.

Example 1: The "Unholy Fire" of Nadab and Abihu (Lev. 10:1-11)

The story of Nadab and Abihu is interesting both because
of its brevity and because of the sternness and uniqueness of
the judgment on them. It raises curiosity because it is not

immediately apparent what the "strange fire" (NASB) was, nor why it brought such a quick and forceful response from God.

The Actions of the Narrative

Aaron and his sons had just been consecrated to the priest-hood (Lev. 8); after commanding that the fire be kept burning continually (6:13), God had confirmed their sacrificial offering by kindling it miraculously (9:24).

Nadab and Abihu, Aaron's two oldest sons, took "strange fire" and made an incense offering to the Lord. Immediately they were struck dead by fire from God. Moses uttered a prophecy, and then commanded Aaron's relatives to take the dead bodies of Nadab and Abihu from the camp. Aaron and his two remaining sons, who were also priests, were commanded not to show the traditional signs of mourning (letting their hair hang loose and tearing their clothes), although their relatives were allowed to do so.

God then gave Aaron three commands (Lev. 10:8-10): (1) neither he nor any of his priestly descendants were to use fermented beverages before entering their sacred duties; (2) they were to distinguish between the holy and the common, the clean and the unclean; and (3) they were to teach the people all of the Lord's statutes.

Significance or Meaning of the Actions

Historical-cultural analysis. Israel had just come out of, and continued to be surrounded by, idolatrous worship. There was an ever-present danger of syncretism, i.e., combining the worship of the true God with the practices of pagan worship.

Contextual analysis. This was the inauguration day of Aaron and his sons as initiators of the Levitical priesthood. Their actions would undoubtedly be regarded as precedents for those who followed. Similarly, God's acceptance or rejection of these actions would affect further developments of the priesthood itself and the priestly activities.

Lexical-syntactical and theological analysis. Fire was regarded as a divine symbol in almost all ancient religions, including Judaism. The unholy or "strange" fire which Nadab and Abihu offered is explained as fire which God had not commanded them to offer (v. 1). A similar expression is found in Exodus 30:9, where incense that had not been prepared according to the directions of the Lord is called "strange incense." Further analysis of the time sequence of chapters 9 and 10 suggests that Nadab and Abihu offered the incense offering between the sacrificial offering (9:24) and the sacrificial meal which was to have followed it (10:12-20), i.e., at a time other than the time designated for an incense offering. Keil and Delitzsch suggest that it is not improbable that

> Nadab and Abihu intended to accompany the shouts of the people with an incense-offering to the praise and glory of God, and presented an incense-offering not only at an improper time, but not prepared from the altar-fire, and committed such a sin by this will-worship, that they were smitten by the fire which came forth from Jehovah. . . . The fire of the holy God (Ex. 14:18), which had just sanctified the service of Aaron as well-pleasing to God, brought destruction upon his two eldest sons, because they had not sanctified Jehovah in their hearts, but had taken upon themselves a self-willed service.[2]

This interpretation is further borne out by God's prophecy through Moses to Aaron immediately after fire had consumed Nadab and Abihu. "This is what the Lord spoke of when he said: 'Among those who approach me I will show myself holy; in the sight of all the people I will be honored' " (v. 3).

Shortly after this, God spoke directly to Aaron, saying:

> "You and your sons are not to drink wine or other fermented drink whenever you go into the Tent of Meet-

---

2. C. F. Keil and F. Delitzsch, *Commentary on the Old Testament* (Grand Rapids: Eerdmans, 1973), Vol. 1, p. 351.

ing, or you will die. This is a lasting ordinance for the
generations to come. You must distinguish between the
holy and the profane, between the unclean and the clean"
(vv. 9-10).

Some commentators have inferred from these verses that Nadab and Abihu were under the influence of intoxicating beverages when they offered the strange fire. The text does not
allow us to assert that with absolute certainty, although it is
probable that God was giving commands related to the offense which had just brought the judgment of death upon
Nadab and Abihu.

The principal lesson of the three commands is clear: God
had carefully shown the way by which the Israelites might
receive atonement for their sins and maintain a right relationship with Himself. The distinctions between holy and unholy, clean and unclean, had been clearly demonstrated by
God to Aaron and his sons, who had been instructed to teach
these things to the people. Nadab and Abihu, in an act of self-
will, had substituted their own form of worship, obscuring the
distinction between the holy (God's commands), and the profane (man's self-initiated religious actions). These actions, had
they not been quickly rebuked, might easily have led to the
assimilation of all kinds of personal pagan practices in the
worship of God.

A second lesson is found in the fact that reconciliation with
God depends on the grace of God, not on man's self-willed
and self-initiated practices. The means of reconciliation and
atonement had been given by God. Nadab and Abihu attempted to add something to God's means of reconciliation.
As such they stand as an example to all people and all religions
that substitute their own actions for God's grace as a means
of reconciliation and salvation.

Application

God is the initiator of His mercy and grace in the divine-
human relationship; we are the respondents to that grace.
Believers, particularly those in positions of leadership within

the believing community, have a God-given responsibility to teach carefully that salvation comes by God's grace, not through man's works, and to distinguish between the holy and the profane (v. 10). To believe and to act as if we are the initiators rather than the respondents in our relationship with God, particularly if we are in positions where others are likely to model their behavior on ours, as in the case of Nadab and Abihu, is to invite God's displeasure on ourselves.

Example 2: An Analysis of the Temptation Process

Sometimes a narrative provides several principles or truths that continue to possess relevance, as does the narrative of the first temptation, found in Genesis 3:1-6. The actions of the narrative are found in a straightforward recounting of the text:

> Now the serpent was more crafty than any of the wild animals the Lord God had made. He said to the woman, "Did God really say, 'You must not eat from any tree in the garden'?"
> The woman said to the serpent, "We may eat fruit from the trees in the garden, but God did say, 'You must not eat fruit from the tree that is in the middle of the garden, and you must not touch it, or you will die.' "
> "You will not surely die," the serpent said to the woman. "For God knows that when you eat of it your eyes will be opened, and you will be like God, knowing good and evil."
> When the woman saw that the fruit of the tree was good for food and pleasing to the eye, and also desirable for gaining wisdom, she took some and ate it. She also gave some to her husband, who was with her, and he ate it.

Significance of the Actions

Satan's temptation of Eve can be conceptualized in six steps, steps that can be seen in Satan's temptation of believers today.

Step one is found in the first verse. The Hebrew may be paraphrased in the following way: "Now the serpent was more crafty than any wild creature that the Lord God had made. He said to the woman: 'Is it really a fact that God has prohibited you from eating of *all* the trees of the garden?'"

What is the dynamic here? Why did Satan ask this question? He obviously knew what God had said to Adam and Eve, or he would not have been able to ask what he did. Furthermore, he deliberately distorted what God had said. "Is it really a fact that God has prohibited you from eating of *all* the trees of the garden?" Satan's ploy is rather obvious: he was getting Eve to take her eyes off all the things God had given her to enjoy, and to focus on the one thing that God had forbidden. There were probably a thousand pleasurable things Eve could have done in the garden, but now all her attention was focused on the one thing she could not do. We might call this first step *maximizing the restriction*.

Eve was now prepared for Satan's next step. In response to Eve's statement that God said that eating of the fruit of the tree would result in death, Satan boldly declared: "You will not surely die." The results of such-and-such an action won't really be as bad as God has said. This might be called *minimizing the consequences* of sin. Satan minimized the consequences of sin in two ways: first, by telling Eve that the consequences of sin would not be as bad as they had been stated to be, and second, by eventually focusing her attention so completely on the tree that she forgot about the consequences entirely (v. 6).

The third step Satan took might be called *relabeling the action*. In verse 5 he says: "For God knows that when you eat of it your eyes will be opened, and you will be like God, knowing good and evil." Here Satan planted the suspicion in Eve's mind that it was not because the fruit of the tree would injure her that God had forbidden her to eat it, but because He did not wish her to be like Himself. Satan deftly tried to remove his temptation from the category of sin by relabeling it. In this particular instance, partaking of the fruit was relabeled as a way of expanding her consciousness. She would become a more complete person if she tried it once. Before this time Eve had thought of the forbidden action as disobedience: now she sees it as a necessity if she is to become a complete and mature person.

Satan then quickly added another aspect to his temptation, an aspect which might be called *mixing good and evil*. Verse 6 reads: "The woman saw that the fruit of the tree was good for food." C. S. Lewis has commented that evil is often a perversion of something good that God has created. In this instance Satan added potency to his temptation by mixing good with evil: Eve saw that the tree *was* good for food.

The fifth aspect of Eve's temptation is found in the middle part of verse 6: "She saw that the fruit of the tree was . . . pleasing to the eyes." This might be called *mixing sin with beauty*. Temptation often comes wrapped in the form of something beautiful, something that appeals to our senses and desires. It is often necessary to think twice before we recognize that a beautiful object or goal is really sin in disguise. In this incident Eve failed to discriminate between the beautiful package and the sinful contents that the package contained.

Finally Eve took a sixth step: the narrative tells us that "she saw that the fruit of the tree was . . . desirable for gaining wisdom." In essence she swallowed the devil's lie. This step might be called *misunderstanding the implications*. Although this may seem like a less significant point in the temptation process, it is perhaps the most crucial. In effect, by accepting Satan's statement, Eve was calling God a liar, even though she might not have recognized those implications of her action. She accepted Satan as the truth-teller and God as the prevaricator: by partaking of the fruit she was implicitly stating her belief that Satan was more interested in her welfare than God was. Yielding to the temptation implied that she accepted Satan's analysis of the situation instead of God's.

Application

Many of the same dynamics of Eve's temptation are often present in Satan's temptations of believer's today. With only brief introspection his tactics of maximizing the restriction, minimizing the consequences, relabeling the action, mixing good and evil, and mixing sin with beauty can frequently be found operating in our own lives.

Guidelines for Principlizing

1. Principlizing focuses on those principles implicit in a story that are applicable across times and cultures. The details may change, but the principles remain the same: e.g., Satan may continue to tempt us by maximizing a restriction, but is not likely to do so by using a fruit tree.

2. When deriving the meaning of a story as a basis for principlizing, the meaning must always be developed from a careful historical, lexical analysis: the meaning must be the author's intended one.

3. From a theological standpoint, the meaning and principles derived from a story must be consistent with all other teachings of Scripture. A deductive principle drawn from a narrative which contradicts the teaching of some other scriptural passage is invalid.

4. Principles derived by this method may be either normative or nonnormative. For example, it is valid to say that Satan sometimes uses the above methods to tempt believers today, but it would be invalid to say that he *always* uses these methods, or that he uses *only* these methods.

5. Texts have only one meaning, but may have many applications. Principlizing is a method of application. The meaning is the author's intended one, but the applications of that meaning may refer to situations which the author, in a different time and culture, never envisioned. For example, the author of Genesis intended to give us a narrative account of the

first temptation—not a psychological analysis of the temptation process. In order for our application of the text (through principlizing) to be valid, it must be firmly grounded in, and thoroughly consistent with, the author's intention. Thus if the author's intention in a narrative passage was to describe an event of temptation, it is valid to analyze that passage deductively in order to understand the sequence and process of that particular temptation and then see how it might apply to our lives. It would not be valid to generalize from that same text principles about the way temptation always takes place, since the author did not intend the text to be the basis for normative doctrine.

Translating Biblical Commands from One Culture to Another

In 1967 the United Presbyterian Church in the U.S.A. adopted a new confession of faith which contained the following statement.

> The Scriptures, given under the guidance of the Holy Spirit, are nevertheless the words of men, conditioned by the language, thought forms, and literary fashions of the places and times at which they were written. They reflect views of life, history, and the cosmos which were then current. The church, therefore, has an obligation to approach the Scriptures with literary and historical understanding. As God has spoken his word in diverse cultural situations, the church is confident that he will continue to speak through the Scriptures in a changing world and in every form of human culture.

While this statement obviously addresses some very basic cultural issues, it does not give specific guidelines for interpreting the Scriptures in "diverse cultural situations." Two important questions it does not answer are: (1) To what extent are biblical commands to be understood as culturally conditioned and thus not normative for believer's today? and (2) What kind of methodology should be applied to translate biblical commands from that culture to our own?

At one end of the spectrum are those interpreters who believe that often both the scriptural principle and the behavioral command which expresses that principle should be modified in light of historical changes. At the other end of the spectrum are those who believe that scriptural principles and their accompanying behavioral commands always should be applied literally within the church today. Many believers adopt a position somewhere between these two views.

The majority of evangelical churches have, by their actions, implicitly agreed that some biblical commands are not to be adopted wholesale into our time and culture. For example, the command to greet one another with the holy kiss is made five times in the New Testament,[3] yet very few churches observe this command today. Likewise, few Protestant churches observe the command for women to wear veils when praying (1 Cor. 11:5). Few churches continue the practice of footwashing spoken of in John 13:14, because the changing cultures and times have lessened the need and significance of the practice.

More controversially, some evangelical churches now have women who preach, although Paul stated in 1 Timothy 2:12 that he permitted no woman to teach or have authority over men. Many evangelicals, men and women alike, are wondering whether the traditional husband-wife roles delineated in Ephesians 5 and other passages are to be continued in our culture and time. Similar questions are being raised on a number of other issues as well.

In 1973 a conference was convened by the Ligonier Valley Study Center to address the question "Is Scripture culturally

3. Rom. 16:16; 1 Cor. 16:20; 2 Cor. 13:12; 1 Thess. 5:26; 1 Peter 5:14.

bound?" Speakers at this conference included some of the leading contemporary evangelical scholars. The difficulty and complexity of the issue is demonstrated by the fact that the major outcome of the conference was refinement of the question, rather than any substantive answers. Thus the question is one of immense importance, yet one that has no easy nor agreed-on answers at this time.

If we adopt, as most evangelical Christians have, the view that some scriptural commands are culturally limited while others are not, then it becomes necessary to develop some criteria for distinguishing between those commands which apply literally and those that do not. If our procedure is not to be simply an arbitrary one, where we dismiss those commands and principles with which we disagree and retain those with which we agree, we must develop criteria, (a) the logic of which can be demonstrated, (b) which can be consistently applied to a variety of issues and questions, and (c) the nature of which is either drawn from Scripture or, at least, is consistent with Scripture.

Establishing a Theoretical Framework for Analyzing Behavior and Behavioral Commands

First postulate: A single behavior usually has ambiguous significance for the observer. For example, if I look out my study window and see a man walking up the street, I do not know whether he is (a) getting some exercise by taking a walk, (b) on his way to catch a bus, or (c) leaving home after an argument with his wife.

Second postulate: Behavior takes on more meaning for the observer as he ascertains more about its context. As I observe the man in the above example more closely, I hypothesize that he is a student on his way to a class because of his age, dress, briefcase, and books. However, I also observe a woman, apparently his wife (because of similar clothing styles) following about fifteen feet behind him, walking with her head down. I immediately wonder if they have been fighting, and she is following him in an attempt to pacify him after he left the house in anger. I quickly dimiss this hypothesis when I recognize that the clothing styles indicate this couple is from a culture where it is normal and expected that the wife walk a certain distance behind her husband whenever they are together in public.

Third postulate: Behavior that has a certain meaning in one culture may have a totally different significance in another culture. In American society, for a woman to follow her husband at a distance of fifteen feet, with her head down, would usually indicate a problem in their relationship. In another culture, this same behavior may be considered normal and expected.[4]

Let us examine the implications of these three postulates.

First, the meaning of a single behavior cannot be ascertained apart from its context. Analogously, the meaning of (and principle behind) a behavioral command in Scripture cannot be ascertained apart from the context of that command.

Second, the meaning behind a given behavior can be more accurately ascertained the more one knows about the context of that behavior. Similarly, the more we know of the context of a behavioral command, other things being equal, the more we will be able to ascertain accurately the meaning of (and the principle expressed by) that command.

Third, since a given behavior in one culture may have a different meaning in another culture, it may be necessary to change the behavioral expression of a scriptural command in order to translate the principle behind that command from one culture and time to another.

4. For many other examples of behavior which has different meanings in different cultures, see Edwin Yamauchi, "Christianity and Cultural Differences," *Christianity Today*, 23 June 1972, pp. 5-8.

Two aspects of biblical command need to be differentiated: the behavior specified, and the principle expressed through the specified behavior. For example, the holy kiss greeting (behavior) expressed brotherly love (principle).

In making transcultural applications of biblical commands, three alternatives can be considered:

1. Retain both the principle and its behavioral expression.
2. Retain the principle but suggest a change in the way that principle is behaviorally expressed in our culture.
3. Change both the principle and its behavioral expression, assuming that both were culture-bound and are therefore no longer applicable.

As an example, let us look at the custom of the veiling of wives as an expression of voluntary submission to their husbands (1 Cor. 11:2-16). Three approaches have been taken by various commentators:

1. Retain both the principle of submission and its expression through the use of veils.
2. Retain the principle of submission but replace veiling with some other behavior that more meaningfully expresses submission in our culture.
3. Replace both the principle of submission and all expressions of submission with a more egalitarian philosophy, believing that the concept of hierarchy within the family is a culture-bound one.[5]

Thus the analysis of biblical commands into (a) principles, and (b) behaviors that express those principles, possesses little worth unless there are some means for differentiating between those principles and behaviors that are culture-bound and those that are transcultural.

5. See Letha Scanzoni and Nancy Hardesty, *All We're Meant to Be* (Waco: Word, 1975), pp. 40, 64-67, for a discussion of the cultural significance of veiling among various Mediterranean cultures during biblical times.

Some Preliminary Guidelines for Differentiating Culture-bound from Transcultural Principles and Commands

The following guidelines are called preliminary for two reasons: First, they are incomplete in that they do not cover every biblical command and principle, and second, they are at this point tentative, intended to initiate discussion and further exploration of the issue.

Guidelines for Discerning Whether Principles Are Transcultural or Culture-bound

First, determine the reason given for the principle. For example, we are to love one another *because* God first loved us (1 John 4:19). We are not to love the world and its values, *because* love of the world and love of God are mutually exclusive (1 John 2:15).

Second, if the reason for a principle is culture-bound, then the principle may be also. If the reason has its basis in God's unchanging nature (His grace, His love, His moral nature, or His created order), then the principle itself should probably not be changed.

Guidelines for Discerning Whether Commands (Applications of Principles) Are Transcultural or Culture-bound

First, when a transcultural principle is embodied in a form that was part of the common cultural habits of the time, the form *may* be modified, even though the principle remains unchanged. For example, Jesus demonstrated the principle that we should have an attitude of humility and willingness to serve one another (Mark 10:42-44) by washing the disciples' feet (John 13:12-16), a familiar custom of the day. We retain the principle, although it is possible that there are other ways to express that principle more meaningfully in our culture.

Again, James argued that believers should not show partiality within the church meeting by having the rich sit in chairs and the poor sit on the floor (James 2:1-9). We retain the principle of nonpartiality, but the application of the principle takes on different dimensions in our time and culture.

Second, when a practice that was an accepted part of a pagan culture was forbidden in Scripture, this is probably to be forbidden in contemporary culture as well, particularly if the command is grounded in God's moral nature. Examples of practices that were accepted parts of pagan cultures but were forbidden in Scripture include fornication, adultery, spiritism, divorce and homosexual behavior.

Third, it is important to define the intended recipients of a command, and to apply the command discriminately to other groups. If a command was given to only one church, this *may* indicate that it was meant to be only a local rather than a universal practice.

Some Suggested Steps in Translating Biblical Commands from One Culture and Time to Another

1. *Discern as accurately as possible the principle behind the given behavioral command.* For example, Christians are to judge individual sin within their local community of believers because, if unchecked, evil will have an effect upon the entire community (1 Cor. 5:1-13, especially v. 6).

2. *Discern whether the principle is timeless or time-bound (transcultural or culture-bound).* Some suggestions for doing this were offered in the last section. Since most biblical principles are rooted in God's unchanging nature, it seems to follow that a principle should be considered to be transcultural unless there is evidence to the contrary.

3. *If a principle is transcultural, study the nature of its behavioral application within our culture.* Will the behavioral application

given then be appropriate now, or will it be an anachronistic oddity?

The danger of conforming the biblical message to our cultural mold is very great. There are times when the expression of a God-given principle will cause Christians to behave in a way different from non-Christians (Rom. 12:2), but not needlessly so, not for the sake of the difference itself. The criterion for whether a behavioral command should be applied in our culture should *not* be whether or not it conforms to modern cultural practices, but whether or not it adequately and accurately expresses the God-given principle that was intended.

4. *If the behavioral expression of a principle should be changed, suggest a cultural equivalent that would adequately express the God-given principle behind the original command.* For example, J. B. Phillips suggests that "Greet one another with a hearty handshake" may be a good cultural equivalent to "Greet one another with the holy kiss."[6]

If there is no cultural equivalent, it might be worthwhile to consider *creating* a new cultural behavior that would meaningfully express the principles involved. (In a similar but not strictly analogous manner, some of the newer wedding ceremonies express the same principles as more traditional ones, but in very creative and meaningful new ways.)

5. *If after careful study the nature of the biblical principle and its attendant command remain in question, apply the biblical precept of humility.* There may be occasions when even after careful study of a given principle and its behavioral expression, we still may remain uncertain about whether it should be considered transcultural or culture-bound. If we must decide to treat the command one way or the other but have no conclusive means to make the decision, the biblical principle of humility can be helpful. After all, would it be better to treat a principle as transcultural and be guilty of being overscrupulous in our

6. See Fred Wright, *Manners and Customs in Bible Lands* (Chicago: Moody, 1953), pp. 74-75 for further discussion of this Oriental custom.

desire to obey God? Or would it be better to treat a transcultural principle as culture-bound and be guilty of breaking a transcendent requirement of God? The answer should be obvious.

If this humility principle is isolated from the other guidelines mentioned above, it could easily be misconstrued as ground for unnecessary conservatism. The principle should be applied only after we have carefully tried to determine whether a principle is transcultural or culture-bound, and despite our best efforts, the issue still is uncertain. This is a guideline of last resort and would be destructive if used as a first resort.[7]

Chapter Summary

1. Principlizing: Based on a historical-cultural, contextual, lexical-syntactical, and theological analysis of the narrative portion, ascertain by deductive study (1) the principle(s) that passage was intended to teach, or (2) the principles (descriptive truths) illustrated within the passage that remain relevant for the contemporary believer.
2. Transcultural transmission of biblical commands:
   a. Discern as accurately as possible the principle behind the command.
   b. Discern whether the principle is transcultural or culture-bound by examining the reason given for the principle.
   c. If a principle is transcultural, determine whether or not the same behavioral application in our culture will express the principle as adequately and accurately as the biblical one.
   d. If the behavioral expression of a principle should be changed, suggest a cultural equivalent that will express the God-given principle behind the original command.

7. The main ideas and some of the phraseology of these last two paragraphs were taken from R. C. Sproul, "Controversy at Culture Gap," *Eternity*, May 1976, p. 40. Sproul's discussion refers to a related but slightly different issue.

e. If, after careful study, the nature of the biblical principle and its attendant command remain in question, apply the biblical precept of humility.

Resources for Further Reading*

J. O. Buswell, Jr. *Systematic Theology*, 1:365-384.

Charles Kraft. "Interpreting in Cultural Context." *Journal of the Evangelical Theological Society* 21 (1978):357-367.

A. B. Mickelsen. *Interpreting the Bible*, pp. 159-176.

R. C. Sproul. "Controversy at Culture Gap." *Eternity*, May 1976, pp. 13-15,40.

Merrill Tenney. *New Testament Times*.

Fred Wight. *Manners and Customs of Bible Lands*.

George Ernest Wright. *The Old Testament Against its Environment*.

Edwin M. Yamauchi. "Christianity and Cultural Differences." *Christianity Today*, 23 June 1972, pp. 5-8.

Exercises

(As in other chapters, some of these exercises apply hermeneutical skills discussed in previous chapters.)

BT58: Basing his view on 1 Corinthians 6:1-8, a pastor stated that it is wrong for a Christian to sue another believer. Is this hermeneutically valid? Why or why not?

BT59: Pacifists have sometimes used Matthew 26:52 as part of their argument that Christians should not be involved in military activity. From the standpoint of valid hermeneutics, what principles and/or behavioral commands can we draw from this passage?

BT60: In Deuteronomy 19:21 God's command is "an eye for an eye, a tooth for a tooth." Jesus, claiming that he was fulfilling the law, said: "Do not resist an evil person. If someone strikes you on the right cheek, turn to him the other also" (Matt. 5:39). How do you reconcile these two statements?

*See also the references in chapter 3 on historical-cultural analysis.

BT61: In 1 Timothy 2:12 Paul says that he does not allow a woman to teach or have authority over men. Using the model presented in this chapter, discuss these questions: (1) What was the meaning of this text for Timothy? (2) What application should it have for us today? (3) What implications does your view have for (a) female Sunday school teachers, (b) female hospital chaplains, (c) female seminary teachers, (d) female pastors, and (e) female missionaries?

BT62: There are three main types of church government — the episcopalian, the presbyterian, and the congregational — and some denominations use a mixed model. Investigate how each of these types functions, then do a word study of the terms *bishop*, *elder*, and *deacon* as used in the New Testament. What are the implications of your New Testament study for the models of church government?

BT63: Some believers use Acts 4:32-35 as the basis for Christian communal living today. What hermeneutical considerations are relevant to such an application of this text?

BT64: Basing his view on Ephesians 6:1-3, a noted Christian teacher teaches that children should never go against their parents' wishes, but should allow God to direct them through their parents. Is this a valid understanding of the text as Paul originally gave it? If it is, is it as valid to apply it in the same way today in our American culture? If you answered affirmatively to both of the above questions, does this obligation ever end?

BT65: With the rising divorce rate in the twentieth century, many churches are being faced with the question of what roles, if any, divorced and remarried persons may play in the leadership/service functions of the church. How do you think the teaching of 1 Timothy 3:2,12 applies to that question?

BT66: A number of conservative denominations believe that Christians should totally abstain from the use of alcoholic beverages. Other denominations believe that the Bible teaches moderation. Study the relevant verses on the use of alcoholic beverages. Are there scriptural principles besides the passages specifically dealing with alcohol that might apply to this question?

BT67: As a preface to his exposition of a text a minister said, "I have gotten this message from no other man. I have consulted no other commentaries: it comes straight from *the Book!*" Comment on this method of expositional preparation.

BT68: A minister preached a sermon on Philippians 4:13 ("I can do all things through Christ who strengthens me"). The sermon title was "The Omnipotent Christian." However, it was readily apparent that neither he nor any other Christian was omnipotent in the way this term is usually understood. What hermeneutical principle was this sermon violating? What is a hermeneutically valid understanding of the meaning of this verse?

Epilogue:

The Task of the Minister

The task of the minister, as it relates to the content of this text, is twofold: (1) he is to be a minister of the Word of God, and (2) he must minister the Word of God accurately. I quote with approval the words of Ramm:

> The preacher is *a minister of the Word of God.* . . . His fundamental task in preaching is not to be clever or sermonic or profound but *to minister the truth of God.* The apostles were called *ministers of the word* (Luke 1:2). The apostles were ordained as *witnesses of Jesus Christ* (Acts 1:8). Their task was to preach what they heard and saw with reference to the life, death, and resurrection of Jesus Christ. The elder (pastor) is to labor *in word and doctrine* (1 Tim. 5:17). What Timothy is to hand on to others is . . . *the truth of Christianity* which he heard from many Christians (2 Tim. 2:2). Paul instructs Timothy . . . to "preach *the message*" (2 Tim. 4:2. Grk: *Kērukson ton logon*). Peter says he is an elder by virtue of having *witnessed* the sufferings of our Lord (1 Peter 5:1).

The New Testament servant of Christ was not one free
to preach as he wished, but one bound to minister the
truth of Christianity, to preach the word of God, and to
be a witness of the Gospel.[1]

The servant of Christ must do more than preach the Word.
It is possible to be earnest, eloquent, and knowledgeable in
the Scriptures, and yet preach it either inaccurately or in less
than its full truth (e.g., Apollos in Acts 18:24-28). Paul commands Timothy, "Do your best to present yourself to God as
one approved, a workman who has no need to be ashamed,
rightly handling the word of truth" (2 Tim. 2:15, RSV; emphasis
added). A workman would feel ashamed if incompetence or
shoddiness were detected in his work. Paul tells Timothy that
the way he can stand unashamed and approved before God
is by *rightly handling* the Word of truth. Thus the twofold task
of the pastor, as defined in the above Scriptures, is (1) to
preach the Word of God, and (2) to interpret it accurately.

Types of Contemporary Preaching

Most of the preaching done today can be conceptualized
on the following continuum:

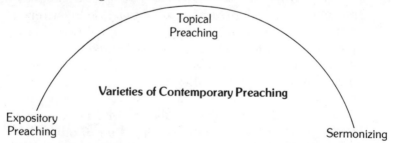

Expository preaching starts with a given passage and investi-
gates it, using the processes we have labeled historical-cultural,
contextual, lexical-syntactical, theological and literary analyses. Its primary focus is an exposition of what God intended

---

1. Bernard Ramm, *Protestant Biblical Interpretation*, 3rd rev. ed. (Grand Rapids:
Baker, 1970), pp. 195-196.

to say in that particular passage, leading to an application of that meaning in the lives of contemporary Christians.

Sermonizing begins with an idea in the mind of the preacher—a relevant social or political issue of some kind, or a theological or psychological insight—and expands this idea into a sermon outline. As part of the process, relevant Scriptures are added as they come to mind or as they are found with the aid of study helps. The primary focus of this method is the elaboration of a human idea in ways that are consistent with Scripture's general teaching in that area.

Topical preaching begins by selecting a topic related to Scripture in some way or another (e.g., biblical themes, doctrines, Bible characters). If the sermon is developed by selecting relevant Scripture passages and developing an outline based on exposition of those passages, this might be called "topical-expository" preaching. If the sermon outline is developed by ideas that come to the mind of the preacher and then validated by attaching a relevant Scripture verse, this might be called "topical-sermonizing."

The majority of sermons preached today appear to be of the topical-sermonizing or sermonizing variety. If the proportion of expository preaching to sermonizing is any indication, the majority of theological schools appear either not to be training their students in the skills needed to do expository preaching, or not to be encouraging them to use expository preaching as an alternative to sermonizing.

From the perspective of one who is primarily a "consumer" rather than a "producer" of sermons, I would like to offer some personal observations on some of the similarities and differences I see between sermonizing and expository preaching.

Sermonizing and Expository Preaching: A Comparison

The similarities of these two methods of preaching include, among other things, the fact that both are done by intelligent,

God-fearing men who are committed to feeding the flock for whom God has given them responsibility. Both methods are used by articulate, eloquent men who preach with forcefulness and dignity. And both appear to be used by God to feed His flock, if the size of congregations is in any way a valid measure.

There are some differences as well. First, there is a basic difference in procedure as mentioned above. Expository preaching begins with a passage of God's Word, expounds that text, and then applies it to the lives of contemporary believers. Sermonizing begins with an idea in the mind of the preacher which is elaborated into a sermon outline, with Scripture references sometimes appearing to reinforce a particular point. (These differences are relative rather than absolute, and vary from minister to minister, and sometimes from sermon to sermon with the same minister.)

Second, there is often a difference in the hermeneutical methods. When listening to sermonizing messages, I have had the fairly common experience of either: (a) hearing a verse or portion of a verse read as the text, followed sometimes by a message which could not be derived from that text if it had been read within its context, or (b) hearing a passage read which is not really related to the subsequent sermon. This is not to suggest that eisegesis is confined to sermonizing and exegesis to expository preaching. However, when a minister is constructing a series of messages from a particular book of the Bible, a study of the material before and after a passage presents many built-in safeguards against eisegetical interpretation. When a minister is attempting to find a passage to validate his already established ideas, there is a greater temptation to use a passage that represents a verbal parallel to that idea even if it is not a real parallel.

Third, there is a difference in the biblical authoritativeness of expository preaching and sermonizing. Biblical authoritativeness should not be confused with human persuasiveness. Human persuasiveness depends on articulateness, colorful use of illustrations, verbal inflection, use of electronic amplifying

equipment, etc., and is not related to the type of sermon—
expository preaching or sermonizing. However, sermonizing,
no matter how brilliant from the standpoint of human persuasiveness, remains at base a word from man to man. Though
it may be done by a minister highly respected by his congregation, his psychological or social or political theories must
compete with the theories of hundreds of other "authorities"
who also influence his congregation.

To speak with the authority of a "Thus saith the Lord" the
minister must expound *His* Word. The thundering authority
of Moses, Jeremiah, Amos, Peter, and Paul came from speaking forth as the Holy Spirit empowered them (2 Peter 1:21).
We will not regain that sense of divine authority by dabbling
in popular psychology and footnoting our speculations with
a verse from God's Word. The only way to regain the authority
of a "Thus saith the Lord" is to return to an exposition of His
Word.

Finally, there is no promise to be found in Scripture that
God will bless human sermonizing. God does, however, promise to bless the declaration of His Word:

> As the rain and the snow
>   come down from heaven,
> and do not return to it
>   without watering the earth
> and making it bud and flourish,
>   so that it yields seed for the sower
>   and bread for the eater,
> so is my word that goes out from my mouth:
>   It will not return to me empty,
> but will accomplish what I desire
>   and achieve the purpose for which I sent it.
>   (Isaiah 55:10-11).

Resources for Further Reading

Andrew Blackwood. *Expository Preaching for Today.*
John A. Broadus. *A Treatise on the Preparation and Delivery of Sermons.*

Phillips Brooks. *Lectures on Preaching.*

Walter C. Kaiser, Jr. *Toward an Exegetical Theology: Biblical Exegesis for Preaching and Teaching.*

Lloyd Perry. *A Manual for Biblical Preaching.*

Haddon W. Robinson. *Biblical Preaching: The Development and Delivery of Expository Messages.*

SUMMARY

The Processes Involved in Interpretation and Application of a Scriptural Text

I. Historical-Cultural and Contextual Analysis
   A. Determine the general historical and cultural milieu of the writer and his audience.
      1. Determine the general historical circumstances.
      2. Be aware of cultural circumstances and norms that add meaning to given actions.
      3. Discern the level of spiritual commitment of the audience.
   B. Determine the purpose(s) the author had in writing a book.
      1. Noting explicit statements or repeated phrases.
      2. Observing parenetical or hortatory sections.
      3. Observing issues that are omitted or focused on.
   C. Understand how the passage fits into its immediate context.
      1. Identify the major blocks of material in the book and show how they fit into a coherent whole.

2. Show how the passage under consideration fits into the flow of the author's argument.

3. Determine the perspective which the author intends to communicate—noumenological (the way things really are) or phenomenological (the way things appear).

4. Distinguish between descriptive and prescriptive truth.

5. Distinguish between incidental details and the teaching focus of a passage.

6. Identify the person or category of persons for whom the particular passage is intended.

II. Lexical-Syntactical Analysis
   A. Identify the general literary form.
   B. Trace the development of the author's theme and show how the passage under consideration fits into the context.
   C. Identify the natural divisions (paragraphs and sentences) of the text.
   D. Identify the connecting words within the paragraphs and sentences and show how they aid in understanding the author's progression of thought.
   E. Determine what the individual words mean.
      1. Identify the multiple meanings a word possessed in its time and culture.
      2. Determine the single meaning intended by the author in a given context.
   F. Analyze the syntax to show how it contributes to the understanding of a passage.
   G. Put the results of your analysis into nontechnical, easily understood words that clearly convey the author's intended meaning to the English reader.

III. Theological Analysis
   A. Determine your own view of the nature of God's relationship to man.

B. Identify the implications of this view for the passage you are studying.

C. Assess the extent of theological knowledge available to the people of that time (the "analogy of Scripture").

D. Determine the meaning the passage possessed for its original recipients in the light of their knowledge.

E. Identify the additional knowledge about this topic which is available to us now because of later revelation (the "analogy of faith").

IV. Literary Analysis

A. Look for explicit references which indicate the author's intent regarding the method he was using.

B. If the text does not explicitly identify the literary form of the passage, study the characteristics of the passage deductively to ascertain its form.

C. Apply the principles of literary devices carefully but not rigidly.

1. Simile

a. Characteristic: an expressed comparison.

b. Interpretation: usually a single point of similarity or contrast.

2. Metaphor

a. Characteristic: an unexpressed comparison.

b. Interpretation: usually a single point of similarity.

3. Proverb

a. Characteristic: comparison expressed or unexpressed.

b. Interpretation: usually a single point of similarity or contrast.

4. Parables

a. Characteristics: an extended simile—comparisons are expressed and kept separate; the story and its meaning are consciously separated.

b. Interpretation: determine the focal meaning of

the story and show how the details fit naturally into that focal teaching.

5. Allegories
   a. Characteristics: an extended metaphor—comparisons are unexpressed and intermingled; story and its meaning are carried along together.
   b. Interpretation: determine the multiple points of comparison intended by the author.
6. Types
   a. Characteristics:
      (1) There must be some notable resemblance or analogy between the type and its antitype.
      (2) There must be some evidence that the type was appointed by God to represent the thing typified.
      (3) A type must prefigure something in the future.
      (4) Classes of the type and its antitype: persons, events, institutions, offices, and actions.
   b. Interpretation:
      (1) Determine the significance within the time and culture of both the type and its antitype.
      (2) Search the text for the point(s) of correspondence between the type and its antitype as they relate to salvation history.
      (3) Note the important points of difference between the type and its antitype.
7. Prophecy
   a. Characteristics:
      (1) Be aware that the style is generally figurative and symbolic.
      (2) Watch for supernatural elements such as information conveyed by the announcement of angels, by visions, or by other supernatural means.
      (3) Notice the emphasis on the unseen world

that lies behind the action of the visible world.
    (4) Follow the action to its usual conclusion by
        a sovereign intervention of God.
  b. Interpretation:
    (1) Determine the specific historical situation
        surrounding the composition of the writing.
        Study intervening history to see whether or
        not the prophecy has been fulfilled.
    (2) Study parallel passages or other cycles within
        the same prophecy for further information.
    (3) Analyze whether this passage is part of a
        progressive prediction, is capable of
        developmental fulfillment, or includes pro-
        phetic telescoping.
V. Comparison with Others
  A. Compare your analysis with that of other interpreters.
  B. Modify, correct, or expand your interpretation as
     appropriate.
VI. Application
  A. Principlizing: Based on a historical-cultural, contex-
     tual, lexical-syntactical, and theological analysis of the
     narrative portion, ascertain by deductive study (1) the
     principle(s) that passage was intended to teach, or (2)
     the principles (descriptive truths) illustrated within
     the passage that remain relevant for the contempo-
     rary believer.
  B. Transcultural transmission of biblical commands
     1. Discern as accurately as possible the principle be-
        hind the command.
     2. Discern whether the principle is transcultural or
        culture-bound by examining the reason given for
        the principle.
     3. If a principle is transcultural, determine whether
        or not the same behavioral application in our cul-
        ture will express the principle as adequately and
        accurately as the biblical one.

4. If the behavioral expression of a principle should be changed, suggest a cultural equivalent that will express the God-given principle behind the original command.

Appendix A

A Sample Bibliography of Works Relating to Hermeneutics from Various Theological Viewpoints

Barrett, C. K. *The Interpretation of the Old Testament in the New Testament.* In *The Cambridge History of the Bible.* Vol. 1, ed. P. R. Ackroyed and C. F. Evans. Cambridge: University Press, 1970, pp. 377-411. The author believes that the New Testament authors borrowed both legitimate and illegitimate hermeneutical principles from their contemporary culture.

Bartsch, Hans. *Kerygma and Myth.* 2 vols. London: S.P.C.K., 1962-64. A discussion of Scripture from the perspective of the "New Hermeneutic."

Childs, B. S. *Biblical Theology in Crisis.* Philadelphia: Westminster, 1970. A discussion of the American neoorthodox theology movement by one of its members.

Hasel, G. *Old Testament Theology: Basic Issues in the Current Debate.* Grand Rapids: Eerdmans, 1972. Although not a book on hermeneutics explicitly, this book points out the central issues that distinguish various schools of interpretation.

Marle, Rene. *Introduction to Hermeneutics.* New York: Herder and Herder, 1967. A general text written from a liberal perspective.

Palmer, R. E. *Hermeneutics.* Evanston, Ill.: Northwestern University Press, 1969. Excellent text on the "New Hermeneutic."

Von Rad, G. Typological Interpretation of the Old Testament. In *Essays on Old Testament Hermeneutics*, ed. J. L. Mays. Richmond: Knox, 1963, pp. 17-39. An example of typological theory by one who believes that the Old Testament is a product of documentary development, a human recounting of God's actions, and that therefore it cannot be trusted as either reliable or accurate.

Appendix B

Readings on Revelation, Inspiration, and Inerrancy from a Variety of Theological Perspectives

Baillie, John. *The Idea of Revelation in Recent Thought.* New York: Columbia University Press, 1956. Neoorthodox perspective.

Beegle, Dewey M. *The Inspiration of Scripture.* Philadelphia: Westminster Press, 1963. An evangelical who denies inerrancy.

Boice, James Montgomery. *The Foundation of Biblical Authority.* Grand Rapids: Zondervan, 1978. A series of lectures prepared by contributors to the International Council on Biblical Inerrancy.

Bruce, F. F. *The New Testament Documents: Are They Reliable?* Chicago: InterVarsity, 1960. Excellent treatment of the subject by a prominent evangelical scholar.

Brunner, Emil. *Revelation and Reason.* Philadelphia: Westminster Press, 1946. A Neoorthodox approach.

Childs, B. S. *Biblical Theology in Crisis.* Philadelphia: Westminster Press, 1970. A discussion of the American neoorthodox movement by one of its members.

Dodd, C. H. *The Authority of the Bible.* New York: Harper & Brothers, 1929. A liberal perspective.

Geisler, Norman. *Inerrancy.* Grand Rapids: Zondervan, 1980.

Fuller, Daniel. "Benjamin Warfield's View of Faith and History." *Bulletin of the Evangelical Theological Society* II (1968): pp. 75-82.

Fuller, Daniel and Pinnock, Clark. "On Revelation and Biblical Authority." *Christian Scholar's Review.* A short discussion by these two well-known contemporary theologians on the issue of "limited inerrancy."

Henry, Carl F. H. *God, Revelation and Authority.* 4 vols. to date. Waco, Tex.: Word, 1976-.

Hodge, Archibald A. and Warfield, Benjamin B. *Inspiration.* 1881. Reprint. Grand Rapids: Baker, 1979.

Lindsell, Harold. *The Battle for the Bible.* Grand Rapids: Zondervan, 1976. This book traces the history of the debate between biblical errancy and inerrancy, and describes the doctrinal changes in groups that have adopted an errant Scripture position.

_____. *The Bible in the Balance.* Grand Rapids: Zondervan, 1979 or 1980.

McDonald, H. D. *Theories of Revelation: An Historical Study, 1700-1960.* Grand Rapids: Baker, 1979.

Montgomery, John W., ed. *God's Inerrant Word: An International Symposium on the Trustworthiness of Scripture.* Minneapolis: Bethany, 1974. An excellent volume from the conservative evangelical perspective. See especially the chapters by Montgomery, Pinnock, and Sproul.

Nicole, Roger R. and Michaels, J. Ramsey, eds. *Inerrancy and Common Sense.* Grand Rapids: Baker, 1980.

Packer, James I. *Fundamentalism and the Word of God.* Grand Rapids: Eerdmans, 1972.

_____. *God Has Spoken: Revelation and the Bible.* Rev. ed. London: Hodder and Stoughton, 1980 (?).

Pinnock, Clark. *Biblical Revelation.* Chicago: Moody, 1971. Excellent comparison of various perspectives on the nature of Scripture, revelation, and inspiration written from a conservative evangelical position.

Rogers, Jack B., ed. *Biblical Authority.* Waco, Tex.: Word, 1977.

_____. and Donald K. McKim. *The Authority and Interpretation of the Bible: An Historical Approach.* San Francisco: Harper & Row, 1979.

Schaeffer, Francis. *No Final Conflict.* Downers Grove: InterVarsity, 1975. Five short essays illustrating the author's thesis that Scripture is true whether it is speaking of "upper storey" or "lower storey" knowledge.

Warfield, B. B. *The Inspiration and Authority of the Bible.* Nutley, N.J.: Presbyterian and Reformed, 1970.

Wenham, John. *Christ and the Bible.* Downers Grove: InterVarsity, 1972. An excellent discussion of Jesus' view of the Bible and of objections to Jesus' views.

Appendix C

A Bibliography on Sensus Plenior*

Bergado, G. N. "The 'Sensus Plenior' as a N.T. Hermeneutical Principle." Master's thesis, Trinity Evangelical Divinity School, 1969.

Bierberg, R. "Does Sacred Scripture Have a *Sensus Plenior*?" *Catholic Biblical Quarterly* 15 (1953):141-162.

———. *The Sensus Plenior of Sacred Scriptures.* Baltimore: St. Mary's University, 1955.

———. "Pere Lagrange and the *Sensus Plenior*." *Catholic Biblical Quarterly* 18 (1956):47-53.

———. "The *Sensus Plenior* in the Last Ten Years." *Catholic Biblical Quarterly* 25 (1963):262-285.

———. "Hermeneutics." In *Jerome Biblical Commentary*, ed. R. E. Brown, J. A. Fitzmyer, and R. E. Murphy. Englewood Cliffs, N.J.: Prentice-Hall, 1968, pp. 605-623.

Coppens, J. "Levels of Meaning with the Bible." *How Does the Christian Confront the O.T.?* XXX OT *Concilium*, ed. Pierre Benoit, Roland Murphy, et. al. New York: Paulist Press, 1968, pp. 125-139.

Franzmann, M. "The Hermeneutical Dilemma: Dualism in the Interpretation of Holy Scripture." *Concordia Theological Monthly* 36 (1965):504.

---

* Taken from a bibliography prepared by Dr. Walter C. Kaiser, Trinity Evangelical Divinity School. Used by permission of the author.

Hirsch, E. D. *Validity in Interpretation*. New Haven: Yale, 1967.

Hunt, I. "Rome and the Literal Sense of Sacred Scripture." *American Benedictine Review* 9 (1958):79-103.

Krimholtz, R. H. "Instrumentality and *Sensus Plenior*." *Catholic Biblical Quarterly* 20 (1958):200-205.

Longenecker, R. "Can We Reproduce the Exegesis of the N.T.?" *Tyndale Bulletin* 21 (1970):3-38.

Nemetz, A. "Literalness and *Sensus Literalis*." *Speculum* 34 (1959):76-89.

O'Rourke, J. J. "Marginal Notes on the *Sensus Plenior*." *Catholic Biblical Quarterly* 21 (1959):64-71.

――――. "Theology and the *Sensus Plenior*." *Ecclesiastical Review* 143 (1960):301-306.

Ricoeur, P. "The Problem of the Double Sense as a Hermeneutic Problem and as a Semantic Problem." In *Festschrift* for M. Eliade, ed. J. M. Kitagawa. Chicago: University of Chicago Press, 1969, pp. 63-74.

Sutcliffe, E. F. "The Plenary Sense as a Principle of Interpretation." *Biblica* 24 (1953):333-343.

Vawter, B. "The Fuller Sense: Some Considerations." *Catholic Biblical Quarterly* 26 (1969):85-96.

General Bibliography

Adams, J. McKee. *Biblical Backgrounds.* Nashville: Broadman, 1934.

Althaus, P. *Theology of Martin Luther.* Philadelphia: Fortress, 1966.

Baly, Denis A. *Geography of the Bible.* New rev. ed. New York: Harper & Row, 1974.

Barrett, Charles K. *Luke the Historian in Recent Research.* London: Epworth Press, 1961.

Barrett, Charles K., ed. *New Testament Background: Selected Documents.* New York: Harper & Row, 1961.

Bauer, Walter. *Greek-English Lexicon of the New Testament and Other Early Christian Literature.* Trans. and ed. W. F. Arndt and F. W. Gingrich. 2nd rev. aug. ed. Chicago: U. of Chicago Press, 1979.

Berkhof, Louis, *Principles of Biblical Interpretation.* Grand Rapids: Baker, 1950.

_____. *Systematic Theology.* 4th rev. and enl. ed. Grand Rapids: Eerdmans, 1949.

Blackwood, Andrew. *Expository Preaching for Today.* Reprint. Grand Rapids: Baker, 1975.

Blass, Friedrich W. and Albert debrunner. *Greek Grammar of the New Testament and Other Early Christian Literature.* Chicago: U. of Chicago Press, 1961.

Broadus, John A. *Treatise on the Preparation and Delivery of Sermons.* Rev. ed. New York: Harper & Row, 1944.

Brooks, Phillips. *Lectures on Preaching.* London: H. R. Allenson, 1877.

Brown, Francis, S. R. Driver, and Charles A. Briggs. *Hebrew and English Lexicon.* New York: Oxford, 1952.

Bruce, F. F. *The New Testament Documents: Are They Reliable?* 5th rev. ed. Grand Rapids: Eerdmans, 1960.

Bullinger, E. W. *Critical Lexicon and Concordance to the English and Greek New Testament.* Grand Rapids: Zondervan, 1975.

————. *Figures of Speech Used in the Bible.* Grand Rapids: Baker, n.d.

Buswell, James Oliver, Jr. *Systematic Theology of the Christian Religion.* 2 vols. Grand Rapids: Zondervan, 1962-63.

Chafer, L. S. *Dispensationalism.* Rev. ed. Dallas: Dallas Seminary Press, 1951.

Clouse, Robert. *The Meaning of the Millennium: Four Views.* Downers Grove, Ill.: InterVarsity, 1977.

Costas, Orlando. *The Church and Its Mission.* New ed. Wheaton: Tyndale, 1975.

Cox, William E. *Examination of Dispensationalism.* Phillipsburg, N.J.: Presbyterian & Reformed, n.d.

DeVaux, Roland. *Ancient Israel.* 2 vols. New York: McGraw, 1965.

Douglas, J. D., ed. *New Bible Dictionary.* Grand Rapids: Eerdmans, 1962.

Edersheim, Alfred. *The Life and Times of Jesus the Messiah.* Reprint. Grand Rapids: Eerdmans, 1972.

Fairbairn, Patrick. *Typology of Scripture.* 2 vols. Grand Rapids: Zondervan, n.d.

Farrar, Frederic W. *History of Interpretation.* 1885; reprint. Grand Rapids: Baker, 1961.

France, R. T. *Jesus and the Old Testament.* Downers Grove, Ill.: InterVarsity, 1971.

Freeman, James. *Manners and Customs of the Bible.* Plainfield, N.J.: Logos, reprinted in 1972.

Fullerton, Kemper. *Notes on Hebrew Grammar.* 5th rev. ed. Cincinnati: Lane Theological Seminary, 1898.

Gesenius, Friedrich H. W. *Hebrew Grammar.* 2nd Eng. ed. Oxford: Clarendon, 1949.

Gesenius, William. *Hebrew and Chaldee Lexicon.* Grand Rapids: Eerdmans, 1949.

Girdlestone, Robert B. *Synonyms of the Old Testament.* Reprint. Grand Rapids: Eerdmans, 1948.

Grant, Robert M. *A Short History of The Interpretation of the Bible.* Rev. ed. New York: Macmillan, 1972.

Gutierrez, Gustavo. *A Theology of Liberation.* Maryknoll, N.Y.: Orbis, 1973.

Haley, J. W. *An Examination of the Alleged Discrepancies of the Bible.* Grand Rapids: Baker, 1977.

Harrison, Roland K. *A History of Old Testament Times.* Grand Rapids: Zondervan, 1957.

Heaton, E. W. *Everyday Life in Old Testament Times.* Reprint. New York: Scribner's 1977.

Jeremias, J. *Parables of Jesus.* Rev. ed. New York: Scribner's, 1971.

Kaiser, Walter, Jr. *Classical Evangelical Essays in Old Testament Interpretation.* Grand Rapids: Baker, 1972.

———. *The Old Testament in Contemporary Preaching.* Grand Rapids: Baker, 1973.

Kitchen, K. A. *Ancient Orient and the Old Testament.* Downers Grove, Ill.: InterVarsity, 1966.

Kittel, Gerhard and Gerhard Friedrich. *Theological Dictionary of the New Testament.* 10 vols. Grand Rapids: Eerdmans, 1964-76.

Kraft, Charles. "Interpreting in Cultural Context." *Journal of the Evangelical Theological Society* 21 (1978): 357-367.

Ladd, George Eldon. *Crucial Questions About the Kingdom of God.* Grand Rapids: Eerdmans, 1952.

———. *A Theology of the New Testament.* Grand Rapids: Eerdmans, 1974.

Lampe, G. and K. Woolcombe. *Essays on Typology.* Napeville: Allenson, 1957.

Lewis, Gordon R. *Testing Christianity's Truth Claims.* Chicago: Moody, 1976.

Lindsell, Harold. *The Battle for the Bible.* Grand Rapids: Zondervan, 1976.

Longenecker, Richard. *Biblical Exegesis in the Apostolic Period.* Grand Rapids: Eerdmans, 1975.

Ludwigson, R. *A Survey of Biblical Prophecy.* 2nd ed. Grand Rapids: Zondervan, 1975.

Mickelsen, A. Berkeley. *Interpreting the Bible.* Grand Rapids: Eerdmans, 1963.

Miranda, J. *Marx and the Bible.* Maryknoll, N.Y.: Orbis, 1974.

Montgomery, John W., ed. *God's Inerrant Word.* Minneapolis: Bethany, 1974.

Morris, Leon. *Apocalyptic.* Grand Rapids: Eerdmans, 1972.

Moulton, James H. and George Milligan. *Vocabulary of the Greek Testament.* Grand Rapids: Eerdmans, 1949.

Noth, Martin. *Old Testament World.* Philadelphia: Fortress Press, 1966.

Payne, J. Barton. *Encyclopedia of Biblical Prophecy.* New York: Harper & Row, 1973.

Pentecost, J. Dwight. *Things to Come.* Grand Rapids: Zondervan, 1958.

Perry, Lloyd. *Manual for Biblical Preaching.* Grand Rapids: Baker, 1965.

Pfeiffer, Charles. *Biblical World.* Grand Rapids: Baker, 1964.

Pinnock, Clark. *Biblical Revelation.* Chicago: Moody, 1971.

————. "Liberation Theology: The Gains, The Gaps." *Christianity Today,* 16 January 1976, pp. 13-15.

Pritchard, James B. *Ancient Near Eastern Texts Relating to the Old Testament.* Princeton: University Press, 1950.

————. *Ancient Near East in Pictures Relating to the Old Testament.* Princeton: University Press, 1954.

Ramm, Bernard. *Hermeneutics.* Grand Rapids: Baker, 1971.

————. *Protestant Biblical Interpretation.* 3rd rev. ed. Grand Rapids: Baker, 1970.

Robertson, A. T. *Grammar of the Greek New Testament in the Light of Historical Research.* Nashville: Broadman, 1947.

————. *Word Pictures in the New Testament.* 6 vols. Nashville: Broadman, 1943.

Ryrie, C. C. *Dispensationalism Today.* Chicago: Moody, 1973.

Schultz, Samuel J. and Morris A. Inch, eds. *Interpreting the Word of God.* Chicago: Moody, 1976.

Scofield, C. I. *Rightly Dividing the Word of Truth.* Reprint. Grand Rapids: Zondervan, 1974.

Sproul, R. C. "Controversy at Culture Gap." *Eternity* (May 1976), pp. 13-15,40.

Strong, James. *Exhaustive Concordance.* Nashville: Abingdon, 1890.

Surburg, Raymond. *How Dependable Is the Bible?* Philadelphia: Lippincott, 1972.

Tenney, Merrill. *Interpreting Revelation.* Grand Rapids: Eerdmans, 1957.

————. *New Testament Times.* Grand Rapids: Eerdmans, 1965.

Terry, Milton S. *Biblical Hermeneutics.* Reprint. Grand Rapids: Zondervan, 1974.

Thayer, Joseph H. *Greek-English Lexicon of the New Testament.* Reprint. Grand Rapids: Zondervan, 1956.

Thiele, Edwin. *The Mysterious Numbers of the Hebrew Kings.* Rev. ed. Grand Rapids: Eerdmans, 1965.

Thompson, John Arthur. *Bible and Archeology.* Grand Rapids: Eerdmans, 1962.

Thomson, William. *The Land and the Book.* 2 vols. New York: Harper, 1858.

Trench, Richard C. *Notes on the Parables of Our Lord.* Grand Rapids: Baker, 1948.

Trench, Robert C. *Synonyms of the New Testament.* Grand Rapids: Eerdmans, 1950.

Tyndale New Testament Commentaries. 20 vols. Grand Rapids: Eerdmans, 1957-1974.

Vine, William E. *Expository Dictionary of New Testament Words.* Old Tappan, N.J.: Revell, 1940.

Walther, C. F. W. *The Proper Distinction Between Law and Gospel.* St. Louis: Concordia, 1929.

Weingreen, Jacob. *Practical Grammar for Classical Hebrew.* 2nd ed. New York: Oxford, 1959.

Wenham, John. *Christ and the Bible.* Downers Grove: InterVarsity, 1972.

Wight, Fred. *Manners and Customs of Bible Lands.* Chicago: Moody, 1953.

Wigram, George V. *Englishman's Greek Concordance.* Rev. ed. Grand Rapids: Baker, 1979.

_____. *Englishman's Hebrew and Chaldee Concordance.* Reprint. Grand Rapids: Zondervan, 1978.

Wright, George. *The Old Testament Against its Environment.* London: SCM Press, 1957.

Yamauchi, Edwin. "Christianity and Cultural Differences." *Christianity Today*, 23 June 1972, pp. 5-8.

_____. *The Stones and the Scriptures.* Philadelphia: Holman, 1977.